THE GALLOPING GHOST

THE
GALLOPING
GHOST

RED GRANGE

AN AMERICAN FOOTBALL LEGEND

Gary Andrew Poole

HOUGHTON MIFFLIN COMPANY

BOSTON • NEW YORK

2008

Library of Congress Cataloging-in-Publication Data
Poole, Gary Andrew.
The Galloping Ghost : Red Grange, an American
football legend / Gary Andrew Poole.
p. cm.
Includes bibliographical references and index.
ISBN 978-0-618-69163-0
1. Grange, Red, 1903–1991. 2. Football players —
United States — Biography. I. Title.
GV939.G7P66 2008
796.332092 — dc22
[B]   2008014751

Book design by Melissa Lotfy

Illustrations by Michael Prendergast

Printed in the United States of America

DOC 10 9 8 7 6 5 4 3 2 1

This book is for
Leslie, Rose, and Joe

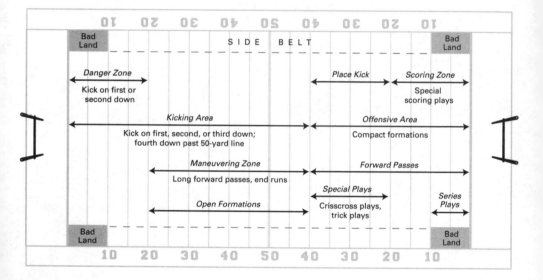

CONTENTS

AUTHOR'S NOTE

RED GRANGE PLAYED way before my time, but his ghost always hovered above the American sporting landscape. "Now *there* was a great player," the geriatric fans would remind us. Most of those old-timers never saw him play, but to them he was, and is, the football version of Babe Ruth. Every ten years since 1924 American football fans would celebrate the anniversary of the game that made Grange famous, and Red would repeat, verbatim, the clichés. With his side-mouthed delivery, Red told the tales with a slight grin, not exposing his two false front teeth — in his day, lips were the only mouthpieces. The sportswriters would visit his house from time to time, and Red would walk outside and greet them in the driveway ("Park next to the Buick!") and then invite them into his living room for a chat and some of Muggs's burned-nearly-to-a-crisp roast. The writers would nod respectfully at this grandfatherly man (who was supposedly childless), transcribe his words, and keep the legend alive: *the greatest college player ever . . . the man who popularized professional football . . .* They had never met a human, athlete or no, with such humility. "They built me up way too much," he would say, referring to the writers and public who idolized him. That was Grange's greatest legacy. He never believed in his own greatness. He lived the ideals of football: sacrifice for the team.

Later in life Grange didn't get out much because he loathed traveling, but he was coaxed away from his Florida tract home and beloved dachshunds to toss the coin at Super Bowl XII. Always a snappy dresser, he wore a burgundy coat and a wide tie as he walked briskly, Miss America on his right arm, to midfield. This was a few years before the Parkinson's really hit, before he started getting really tremorish. It was on January 15, 1978, in New Orleans, and Pat Summerall had the call. "Ladies and gentlemen, we direct your at-

tention to the center of the field where one of professional football's immortals . . . Red Grange of the Chicago Bears, will toss the
coin . . ." The invisible crowd, lost in the Superdome's dark vacuum
of artificiality, nodded and clapped politely. The Broncos' and Cow-
boys' captains recognized him; Grange, used to being a player, just
looked confused, not knowing where to stand. ("It's tough to toss
the coin when Miss America is looking at you," he quipped.)

The thing about Grange was that only a handful of Americans
had seen his electrifying runs or any real evidence of his greatness.
And if they had seen it, it was in film footage that was so rare and
damaged by nitrocellulose decomposition that it proved nothing.
But the legend persisted through the century. Mention Red Grange
to just about anyone with an interest in football, meaning just about
everyone, and the reply would be reverent: *the Galloping Ghost* . . .
It was a pitch-perfect nickname, conjuring an image that fit the
man, on and off the field. When Red went into the Lake Wales Hospital Extended Care Facility in 1991, the columnists started the buz-
zard circle and the old yarns were repeated — and repeated — some
more, like a last bit of CPR. Dempsey and Jones were dead. Ruth
was long gone. They had all been friends, and back in the twenties
their names had been splashed alongside each other's on the sports
pages. Grange was the last star of the Golden Age of Sports, and its
most mysterious.

But the fading war stories never satisfied, never answered the
question of how Red Grange came to forever popularize football, and
define manhood, for a generation and beyond. To understand the
man and the game he played, I have searched America for Grange's
ghost. Regrettably, I never met Red Grange, but — through newspapers, letters, oral histories, interviews, radio broadcasts, court documents . . . the forensics of biography — I have reconstructed his days
of fame. I did not experience Grange's athletic brilliance firsthand,
but I visited and retraced his steps in the stadiums where he ran so
elegantly, and I traveled to Wheaton, Chicago, New York, Los Angeles, Florida, and to Forksville, Pennsylvania, in dead winter.

Gary Andrew Poole, 2008

All-American

RED GRANGE

EVERY AUTUMN WEEKEND tens of millions of Americans watch college and pro football, making the game our national communion. For the players, the energy of the crowds and the thrill of making decisions on the fly, of testing one's mettle, and of living by the code of football are things that don't exist anywhere else in life. Teddy Roosevelt loved the game, believing the "rough, manly" sport created a better nation, but forewarned that the game should not degenerate into the "sole end of one's existence." That is difficult to avoid. There is nothing like being on the field, but there is something more to it, even spiritual, about the camaraderie of being around teammates, of working together to produce greatness and beauty.

If you were to draw a line through the mud of American history and find one man who could be considered the founding father of our football culture, it would be Red Grange. The football nation owes a debt to the man known as the Galloping Ghost, whose brilliance, courage, and humility created, and gave meaning to, the game loved today.

Grange was something untouchable, a gliding, effortless machine, desperate men falling beneath him, trampled by his wooden-cleated boots, nose cartilage broken by his jabbing straight-arms. One felt drawn to his muscled strength, which was not readily visible underneath because of his dark blue football sweater, but it was obvious as he trotted on the field that his five-foot-eleven, 175-pound frame could manhandle a coal shovel or a block of ice. Then he was handed the football and his legs flowed into their gliding stride . . . His physical brilliance was so breathtaking that they were writing poems in the newspapers to capture it. But there was more to it, something invisible inside of him that let him inflict pain, and absorb it.

In the heart of the "Roaring 1920s," which stands in quotes because it was a poetic lie cooked up by newspaper writers, Harold "Red" Grange became an American obsession, the first national star of the gridiron. From 1924 to 1927 there was no one bigger. Even though his hair color was a deep auburn, not red, they called him Red. Harold was an effete intellectual's name, unfitting for a football player turned god. And God, Grange ran beautifully with his long strides. Grange's genius came from running in the open field and running away. His abilities would make him into a national hero, and he is still acknowledged as the best college football player in history. In the 1920s he would become one of four athletes who defined American sports: Babe Ruth, Jack Dempsey, Bobby Jones, and Red Grange. They were the country's first athletic pantheon, its Mount Rushmore, and to this day they remain immortal. And for a few brief years, Grange outshone them all.

In an era of fewer total plays (110 plays per game during the 1920s versus 150 today), a tendency to run between the tackles, and a tighter field without hash marks, making the game look a lot like rugby, Grange would regularly run for 200 yards, triple what most halfbacks were gaining. (Notre Dame great George Gipp averaged 177 yards of offense on much better teams.) On top of his run totals, Grange would commonly pass for 100 yards per game using a ball so thick it was almost impossible to grip; and he played defense, too, specializing in intercepting the ball, often making two or three interceptions per game. And, boy, he could drop-kick. But legends are much more than statistics: they seize moments, they possess beauty, they provide drama. People always asked Bob Zuppke, Red's University of Illinois coach, about Grange's style, but he never felt he adequately captured it in words until one day, visiting the Grand Canyon, he saw a deer run onto the grass plains of the north rim and he yelled, "There goes Red Grange." The freedom of movement was so similar. "Red had that indefinable something that the hunted wild animal has — uncanny timing and the big brown eyes of a royal buck," said Zup.

Grange might be likened to a fleet, lithe animal, but that was only a third of it. With his swiveling hips, sexuality permeated his running style. His handsome coppered face, deep-set eyes, and muscular body were reproduced in every newspaper, resulting in a few movie roles and an avid female fan base. But he was no pretty boy. Grange was all testosterone, a man's man, tough as holy hell, regularly playing hurt, with bruises, concussions, bites, strangulation, broken nose, and cuts, blood running down his face, without a hint of complaint. His blind stoicism would play a part in his legacy, as well as in his undoing. He lived the football code and passed it down to subsequent generations.

Football is a violent game. Those are just words. The real-life results of our lust for aggression are not as easy to come to terms with. They are men who cannot walk and who do not know their own names. Their bodies have been broken: amputated feet, replaced hips, chronic arthritis. Their brains have been smashed, resulting in constant dizziness and the onslaught of Parkinson's. *Take it for the team, son, take it for the team.* That's the football code. "The code" is not written down, but it is known by everyone who has ever put on a football uniform. Men play the game, and they remember their high school playing days with a weepy fondness. The price — well, the price is what it is, and most ex-players would do it again. It is the gifted college boys and the professionals who endure more than anyone because the collisions pile up like repeated car wrecks. Too many unlucky football veterans live their remaining days in pain and the fog of lost memories, but it's more than worth it, and it's not even the freebie college education or the big money in the pros. For their sacrifice, producing clutch plays and exposing their God-given ability, they are promised something bigger: a place in America, the chance to be a winner.

Grange sacrificed himself for the code, and he was thought of as the biggest winner of all. And although he had the personality of a quiet warrior, Red eventually overcame his profound shyness and became an unlikely rebel, taking on the sporting establishment, hobbling the college football machine, and bringing credibility to the professional game. With a master plan from his unscrupulous — yet wickedly brilliant — manager, Red's very being became part of the national psyche. In sandlots, alleys, and, mostly, open fields, kids would fight for the right to make-believe they were Grange. His exploits brought him fame, every breath rendered by writers like Grantland Rice, Westbrook Pegler, John O'Hara, and Damon Runyon. The game evolved from him, and yet he carried his fame quietly and with monumental humility. The *New York Times* called

Grange "the most famous, the most talked of, and written about, the most photographed and most picturesque football player the game has ever produced." Damon Runyon, smoking one of his chain of forty daily cigarettes and banging on his typewriter, described him as "three or four men and a horse rolled into one for football purposes. He is Jack Dempsey, Babe Ruth, Al Jolson, Paavo Nurmi and Man o' War. Put them together they spell Grange."

PART I

1

A Boy

WHEATON, ILLINOIS, 1910

RED! RED!

Red Grange made his way to the podium as the photographers' magnesium powder flashed. The Grange worshipers rose and sang "Illinois" while Red stood, head bowed. There was the dreaded bustle of humanity at these sorts of dinners and Red — neck hot with sweat — was the center of it all. On the field he was a perfectly balanced shape running through attackers, but in public he was uncoordinated. It didn't matter. In the Midwest, and particularly in his hometown of Wheaton, Illinois, Red Grange was gaining a degree of fame for his football talents, and now Wheaton wanted to make him its own. Looking out at the room — the Frisky Five Orchestra, orange and blue ribbons, kids' crayon drawings of his likeness, the high school boys wearing their football togs as they waited the tables, and the twelve football-shaped balloons bouncing into the ceiling, which represented his twelve TDs for the 1923 campaign — Grange began his speech. He recounted the previous season's national championship campaign. Stammering and stuttering in his midwestern accent — he sounded as if he was grinding his molars — Red was a painful orator, but the boosters loved hearing about the bloody collegiate battles as they schemed how they could turn the boy into their own commodity. Red was just a big kid, twenty years old, not really comprehending the attention from the men's groups, the congressmen, and the newspapermen. The All-American honors and the poetry dedicated to him ("With the speed and strength of ten / Like a lion from his den"; "Of antlered speed / And lion breed / And red fox craft and cunning, / Fearless in fight, And in his flight / The swiftest stag out-running!") were all fine, if not a little peculiar, but football banquets provided him with something more tangible: a free meal of turkey and peas.

. . .

Families rise and fall in America, and the Granges seemed on the ascent. Red had come a long way. He had been born in the lumbering town of Forksville, Pennsylvania, in the Endless Mountains. After his mother died — in dead winter, she had a tooth pulled, it hemorrhaged, and she bled to death before she could make her way through the snow to a proper doctor — Red had moved to Wheaton, where his father had family. Red's Pa was named Lyle, a man known for his bare-knuckle fistfights, and he brought Red, Red's little brother, Garland, and his two daughters west to Illinois. Lyle had no use for the girls (they would come for a short while and then return on the eastbound train), but his boys, Harold and Garland, remained. Unlike the Endless Mountains, the horizon in Wheaton was flat and lifeless. "It didn't have the beautiful, mountainous terrain," Red lamented.

Pa worked odd jobs while his sons — anyone will tell you — raised themselves. Red did most of the household chores, cooking and watching his kid brother. When the school year came around, Harold would toil at a farm, milking five cows in the mornings, take the milk to the creamery, and then walk two miles to school, after which he would return to work for the afternoon grind. School broke up the day's monotony, sort of — "Hated it just like any other kid" — so his real joy came from running and hitting. When he found the time, he would sneak out and play football, as if it was an addiction. On a field overlooking a marsh, set within an orchard, convex in shape, with 50 yards on one side of a rise and 50 yards on the other, Grange would play football, on the sly because for Grange's father, who had once beaten a man to the brink of death, football was just too dangerous. On the nation's country fields and in city tenements, kids could not resist playing the game, which had become wildly popular, especially in the heartland. But kids did not have any organization or protective equipment, and they were just running into each other at full force, maiming and too often killing each other. Newspapers would recount college games in all of their glory, but bored newspaper editors would write headlines, in agate type, yawning as they described "another football death" on some back lot. But try watching your own boy turn a yellowish hue as he bled to death or hearing his neck being snapped.

Grange would take kickoffs, which sailed up and over the top of the rise, tuck the ball into the crook of his arm, and run. The boys had no uniforms, just their oldest trousers with the pant legs cut off. The opposition would suddenly swarm over the top like the Charge of the Light Brigade, and the boys would ram into each other at full speed, cracking bones, sustaining concussions, and worse. Like so many before them, angry, gleeful ruffians finding pleasure in inflicting and receiving war wounds. Learning to "take a knock and give one," Red would say. "To get kicked around a little bit and not get mad about it, and you learn to go out and give out just as you receive."

One night Red came home from the orchard. Two vertebrae at the base of his spine had been knocked out of place. Red could not sit down to dinner; standing, he waited for his father's wrath. Lyle, who was now a cop, noticed how his son weathered the pain, the hereditary toughness, the ability to take it. It moved him. When his wife died he had vowed to raise his boys and educate them as much as he could afford. He decided not to beat Red. "If you're so set on playing football," he said with uncharacteristic softness, "I'm going to be your best fan." The old man would hope for the best.

No one is simple; no one can be explained away easily, except from a distance. Lyle, who had been born John Nelson Grange, maybe in 1867 or 1868, in the shadows of the Civil War, was never ashamed. "I never had the chance for much schooling when I was a lad. In the lumber camps, it was necessary for a fellow to be a regular he-man if he wanted to get along." Lyle was the only policeman in town, working all the time, patrolling on his coughing Harley-Davidson. He once came upon a sixteen-year-old who was hiding a whiskey bottle in his back pocket. Lyle grabbed his billy club, took dead aim, and with a home run swing smacked the kid in the leg, the bottle breaking, the whiskey pouring down the boy's leg. "I'm sure you're a good guy and everything, but you'll be careful from now on, won't ya?" Red stayed up nights worrying about what might happen to his old man. And before high school started, he told Pa that he wanted to drop out.

"How do you mean that?" asked Lyle.

"I think I ought to go out and earn my own keep," answered Red.

"What's the matter? Don't you like the way I keep you?"

"You know I don't mean that," replied Red. "We're getting along all right, Dad."

"And we're going to keep on getting along all right. There'll be better times coming, Harold. It's tough, it may get tougher, but I don't quit. I don't quit easy."

Football was an escape, for both of them. On the orchard field Red would play with his friends. Lyle would sneak up and watch them, struggling to understand his boy's gift.

Red was now in college and a burgeoning star, but the Granges were still three men living in an apartment where the noise of a train rattling by broke the silence of the day, their clothes were worn down to the patches, and loans needed to be repaid. Because of his football acumen, Red was being offered jobs well above his abilities, but football was never about easy money. Football was an escape from the solitude. It was the same reason small-town boys go to war: a need to break through the prison of low expectations.

Of course, none of this was expressed at tonight's dinner in honor of Red Grange. Red thanked the townspeople for their support. Now that he was a football idol, the town elders listened intently to whatever he said, no matter how banal. At the end of his little speech the men clapped a bit too wildly and waited for the variety show featuring highlights from the life of their native son.

Puffing after-dinner cigars, the Wheaton townsfolk cheered the skit about the University of Illinois's 1923 football season. The lead character, as "Red Grange," yelled, "I've already killed six guys like you!" and then plowed over the other actors. The men — tongues orange and blue from ice cream — cackled and clapped. Then the local reverend, who wore a football pin labeled "Grange 1923," pleaded with the people of Wheaton to help get "the world playing together." He turned to the guest of honor, handed him a silver loving cup, and said, "We care, and love you, Harold Grange." They all chanted for him.

Red! Red!

Football told the narrative of autumns near and far, and the recently completed Illini season had been a spectacular success, Grange the maestro of 1923. Everyone in the room could recite Grange's season:

The Nebraska Cornhuskers had ended the 1922 campaign with a win over Rockne's Notre Dame, in a brutal fray filled with fans jeering religious-tinged taunts, ominously reminiscent of the streets of Belfast. So bettors had the 1923 Nebraska-Illinois game at even money, but Coach Zuppke had a "mysterious optimism," according to the *Chicago American*. The reporters couldn't figure out his excitement because Earl Britton, the Illini's buffalo-haired blocking back and the team's kicker, had spent the week in the hospital with plaster of Paris on his bum knee. Before the game Zuppke offered a prediction, wagging his finger at the newspapermen and booming in his gravelly German accent, "Watch this fellow Grange!" Ten thousand people had entered the intricate iron front gates of old Illinois Field to watch all the men, but Grange thought they were all staring at him. The blazing sun soaked his sweater; he could feel the orange 77 on his back. He fumbled a kickoff and the crowd sang an *Ahhhh,* and then on his first carry he was bored square in the chest so hard he thought his back was broken. Playing for the next ten minutes Grange felt as if "the shattered ends of my ribs [were] chafing my lungs." It was the last time he ever played nervous. He came out of it, catching a pass for a TD ("a beautiful jump and running catch," said Walter Eckersall, the University of Chicago great and referee of the game). Grange went on a sweep, Britton leading on pure adrenaline, through Nebraska's scarlet-clad players for another TD. Then he returned a punt for a 65-yard dash — shooting down the sideline, straight-arming and sidestepping six Nebraska men — to the end zone. In thirty-nine minutes, 208 yards and three touchdowns. Illinois won 24–7. The papers called Grange "a hero," and he became a marked man. It didn't matter . . .

Against Butler — Illinois's annual patsy game — the Illini battled in a driving rain. The college season lasted only seven games, maybe eight, but the players played on offense and defense so Coach Zuppke intended to rest Grange for the conference opener the following week. But Zup's hand was forced when the game was tied going into the final quarter. He put Grange into the lineup and Red ended up with 142 yards and scored two quick touchdowns to win the contest, 21–7. Gawkers started coming to watch the Illini's practices, grueling affairs under klieg lights that went late into the cold autumn nights . . .

Illinois played Iowa, a team they hadn't bested in three years, the next week. Iowa's scouts called Grange "the fastest man we have ever seen on the gridiron," and the *Iowa City Press-Citizen* did the whole homer routine: "Grange? Iowa will camp on him like Nick

Carter on the trail of a criminal." Game time was cold as hell — the crowd wore heavy overcoats as the chilling wind swept across the field. During the game Red was getting his leather-encased head beaten in. Usually Grange would be hit, his head slamming on the turf, and he would rise and say, "Swell tackle, kid. That's the way to hit 'em!" But in the early stages of the contest, he was "knocked off his base," according to one gleeful Iowa player, and at halftime the trainers packed Red's skull in ice. With five minutes left in the contest, it was Iowa 6, Illinois 3. The Illini had the ball on their own 19-yard line. The plays went to Grange, and finally he plastered through three Iowa linemen and the mud for a score. In sixty minutes Grange had run for 175 yards. Illinois 9, Iowa 6. Back in Champaign, four thousand die-hards had watched the matchup on the Gridgraph — a large board representing a football field. A special telegraph wire had been set up for the play-by-play and a light operator would create the scene on the faux field. The operator would draw out the tension by showing that Grange had the ball, then shut off the light and turn it on again far down the field. "Grange scores!" The students jumped up and down screaming for seven minutes . . . A couple of weeks later thirty-five thousand people, enduring a drizzling rain, attended the next contest against Northwestern at Chicago's Cubs Park because the Fighting Methodists' home field, Dyche Stadium, in a leafy Evanston neighborhood, could not hold the crowd for a Grange game. Red played for nineteen minutes, ran for 251 yards, and scored three touchdowns. One of the TDs came about from an interception. The Chicago Bears, who had trained at Cubs Park earlier that day, stuck around after practice to watch the game. "The first thing you know he intercepts a pass," said Ed Healey, the Chicago Bear and Professional Football Hall of Famer who watched the contest. "Well, gee, he goes off to the left and a guy's coming toward him, but he feints and sidesteps and goes to the right. Another guy takes a cut at him. Jesus! He stiff-arms the guy and marches up the center and cuts toward the sideline, and away he goes, ninety yards for a touchdown. I'm telling you, I had never witnessed any such performance in my lifetime." "GRANGE AND ILLINI TROUNCE PURPLE, 29, 0," headlined the (Chicago) *Sunday Herald-Examiner*, giving the team and the sophomore equal billing . . .

With three games remaining, the University of Illinois was in reach of a conference title and a national championship, but they had to play three tough, emotional battles. Chicago came first. On November 3, sixty-four thousand fans witnessed the Maroons versus the Illini in Champaign's not-yet-completed Memorial Stadium, many there to witness the man the papers were now calling football's Babe Ruth. Alonzo Stagg, Chicago's coach who had once been a Yale Divinity School student, spent the week preparing to stop Red, trying to find two ends who wouldn't allow Grange to find the open field. It rained the night before the Chicago tilt, creating a field of sticky, plastery gunk. Outside the half-built Memorial Stadium the mud was like quicksand, and hundreds of people lost their shoes as they tried to make their way to their seats. The Maroons "knocked Grange silly" by one account, but taking yourself out of a game showed weakness and it was also strategically damaging. The rules of that time stated, "A player who has come out of the game during the first half may not go in again until the second half and a player who has come out of the game during the second half may not return to the game." Grange scored in the third quarter — "an army unto himself," one reporter called him, responding to one play in which five Maroons seemed to have him stalled when Grange thrust them aside with amazing ease. Illinois won the contest, 7–0. Afterward Red returned to his frat house, where two hundred Wheaton residents came to see him. For an hour he stood on the cinder driveway, the mist and drizzle dropping on his bare head as he shook hands . . .

Wisconsin came on November 10. For years both schools had been bickering about professionalism — Illinois Athletic Director George Huff was barely on speaking terms with his counterpart — and the matchups were always filled with sucker punches in the piles, ear pulling, and biting. Just a few days before the contest, a Wisconsin player was barred for "professionalism" because he had taught a boys' swimming class at a YMCA. Wisconsin students were legitimately upset about the absurdity and they blamed Illinois for being behind it. It was an open secret that football players were given jobs in which they merely had to show up on payday. So Wisconsin boosters started even more rumors that Grange was a pro. He responded with a statement: "The story that I played professional football at Rock Island, Green Bay or any other place

in the world is an absolute lie. I have never played football anywhere except in high school and at Illinois. If anyone thinks differently I welcome an investigation." It was a mutual pummeling. In
the second period a hard tackle nailed Red, but he plugged along
until he was socked in the stomach during a pileup and taken out
of the contest. It was the Wisconsin rooters, who had traveled to see
him and who were won over by his resplendent running, who clamored for his return, one sloshed fan yelling, "Where does Grange
play Sunday? I want to see him." Despite being half-killed, Grange
ran for 140 yards and scored one touchdown on a 30-yard run for a
10–0 win. The papers called him the "Illini Flash" and the "Wheaton Flash," two nicknames that were too flaccid to endure the test of
time . . .

Coming into the season's last game against Ohio State, it was obvious that if a team could stop Grange, it would stop Illinois. Once
again the field was sopping wet. For three periods Ohio State —
and their field's sandy mud — stuffed Red. The championship rode
in the balance. It was the final quarter of the season, and Illinois
had a slim 3-point lead. Red took the ball directly from center,
tucking it next to the six vertical brown leather stripes on the front
of his sweater, and started through right tackle. Coach Zuppke
grimaced. The play was over. Grange was about to be tackled, and
the ball would be turned over to Ohio; but Red reversed himself,
straddling the line, hands clutching toward him. It was one of those
plays that just don't work from the very beginning. But suddenly
Grange shot — he was already at full speed — through the left tackle,
streaking past Ohio's secondary for a 34-yard score. "When Red ran
a play," said Zuppke, an awed football scholar, "his imagination pic-
tured the part and duties of every one of his teammates." He finished with 184 yards. Illinois won 9–0.

The perfect season. Along with his twelve touchdowns, Red
had gained 1,260 yards in the six games he played. Walter Camp,
the "Father of Modern Football," named Grange an All-American,
which was like George Washington saying you were a good American. In the local newspapers midwesterners would read about his
speed and elusiveness (*Could it be true?*) and hope that they could
see him one day. Thousands had watched him play, but the majority of the people relied on newspaper accounts, or friends, or the oc-

casional radio broadcast. Most folks would never see him in action, but they had no trouble imagining him.

Despite all the accolades, throughout Wheaton's honorary dinner for him and afterward, into the spring and summer, something would gnaw at Red Grange. Even if Grange, and his Illini team, would forever be considered one of the best, something was missing. Grange's legs were becoming a Midwest sensation, but they were not yet a literary one. Grange and Illinois had not been tested by their archrival, the University of Michigan. The Wolverines had also experienced a stellar 1923 campaign, going undefeated in the conference, getting a player named to the All-American team (Jack Blott, center), and they were also named national champions. Both squads should have been satisfied but they hadn't really proved themselves, so the upcoming 1924 Michigan-Illinois game would be a winner-take-all coronation. Fielding Yost, the Wolverines' coach, all blood 'n' guts, considered Illinois coach Bob Zuppke's squads gimmicky cowards. He scoffed at the Illini and their bow-tied shrimp of a coach, but in the press he targeted Grange, trying to throw him off his game and needling him with a barb: "All he can do is run."

Red would spend the off-season focused on conditioning his body for the next football campaign, and particularly the Michigan game. The Granges lived down the street from the ice warehouse, where in the summers Red made his money and built his rugged frame. Illinois Coach Bob Zuppke, who spent hours studying papers from the fledgling science of psychology, would work on his brain. In letters sent from Zup's summer place in Muskegon, Michigan, Coach told Red — and the rest of the team — about Michigan headman Fielding Yost's American speaking tour in which he defamed the Illinois boys and Red Grange. The players, Grange especially, brooded all summer.

A Galloping Ghost

RED GRANGE RUNNING AROUND END

A VELVETY BARITONE voice broke the morning air. It belonged to Earl Britton, Red's loyal football buddy, his Falstaff.

"*Grandy!*"

Outside Red Grange's fraternity house, astride a motorcycle, sat Britton. With a touch of irony, Britt had nicknamed his friend Grandy, as in grandiose. Rushing out of his simply appointed room in the Zeta Psi house, which was located on the University of Illinois campus, Red ignored the boxes of candy, cookies, nuts, and cake and the piles of letters mailed to him from admirers and hopped on the back of the black bike, clutching his friend's form-fitting leather jacket. Taking the university's star attraction out on a joy ride a couple of days before the big game drove quite a few people to distraction. After all, just the previous spring Britt had crashed his motorcycle and ended up in a hospital. But that was just Britt — or "Tiny" as some sardonically called him — six foot two and 210 pounds of good times and easy laughs. The men would zoom through Champaign-Urbana and then get some ham and eggs, visit the haberdashery, and, if it struck their fancy, go to class. They were still young kids, not totally understanding the game's importance to the adults around them, or to themselves.

Red and Britt could see that the whole world was about ready to bear down on this Midwest college town of thirty thousand set within the Illinois cornfields, one hundred miles from anywhere. Champaign-Urbana's streets reflected the nation's love of college football. Bright orange and blue banners were dangling from the brick buildings of Main Street, the businesses and hoteliers were putting up photographs of the Illini football team and headshots of Grange, all in preparation for the onslaught of Homecoming

Week 1924, the most spectacular the cow town had ever seen. Soon enough the forty extra trains would roll in, carrying the Chicago reporters (the New York ink-stained wretches would be at the Notre Dame–Army matchup in the Polo Grounds) and the WGN radio crew lugging their equipment; the Michigan jerks bragging about their team's twenty-game win streak and taunting the hometown folks, predicting an ass-kicking; fat old alums getting drunk and gazing longingly at the college dames. Everyone had been counting down the eleven months till the Michigan-Illinois showdown. Red would be shielded from much of the mob scene because he was expected at football practice and chalk talks. But he knew the world was watching. It was never easy for Red to handle the attention. He had been brought up in a provincial household with few friends or visitors. Some Michigan Zeta Psi brothers would be coming this week and he would meet and greet them, politely introducing himself ("Hiya, my name is Grange"), as if he needed an introduction. Grange spoke simply, inaudibly, avoiding attention. His careful bearing hid the speed and power within him.

His hands told much of his story. Even the nicest suit donated by a booster could not cover the calluses of a common laborer. *He can grasp a football as easily as an ordinary person can pick up a cucumber!* And it was those hands — that body built in toil — that endeared him to the masses. To the coeds who couldn't help their lustful stares he would give a gothic smile, shuffle his feet, and extend his hand, muttering — "Name's Grange" — and they would know he was one of them. But he wasn't, really. He was there to run. How fortunate that the world was prosperous and universities were opening their doors to men like him, who could not read a line of Latin, whose philosophy came from newspaper sports columnists, not Cicero. He would be targeted by American intellectuals who would ridicule and satirize his intelligence. He was an obvious, and easy, target, but the snobs missed the bigger story. In the language of America, Red Grange represented upward mobility and satisfied an innate need for violence and pageantry. Red was full of insecurity so the attention could be overwhelming. He slunk between classes, hiding in the peace and shadows of the campus. He spent time with those he mistrusted the least. But his reticence couldn't keep fans from watching him. Fellow students would see him on campus; maybe he was in their English History class, but more likely they would gawk as he walked his 110 steps across the Illinois quad, amid the Georgian pillars and the rumblings of new construction. Students would notice how he stared, squinted, shut his eyes, and then reopened them. He seemed to argue with himself, and then he would reveal a dumb smile. Odd behavior. Perhaps he had been hit in the head one too many times and had the brain fever. In reality it was a visual exercise that Red had concocted: he worked all of the time on memorizing his world, "getting everything in proportion and leaving out nothing," he said. His "photographic eyes" helped him on the field, he believed, because he carried a "mental picture of the field and the position of all the men in the game." When he had flunked Transportation the previous year and made up the test, the professor commented that his work looked like he had copied it straight from the textbook.

Coming into this game, Red wanted to prove himself to Fielding Yost, Michigan's mythic leader, and to his coach, Bob Zuppke, who acted as his surrogate father, and to his daunting real father. Despite his positive press clippings and stellar 1923 season, Grange hadn't played very well this season. He nursed aches and pains. It was a football player's lot in life. He was used to it and young enough that his body could fully recover in just a couple of days after most contests. The Michigan game would be the third of the 1924 season. Illinois had gone to Nebraska for its opener on October 4 and beat the Cornhuskers, 9–6. Grange had not scored — worrying Illinois fans — but Red had also done something different in the game: he passed the ball. In another one of Coach Zuppke's creatively deceptive schemes, the Illini's headman had been working with Red on tossing the oval. Although hardly a common or popular strategy, passing was nothing new to Bob Zuppke. When he was coaching high school ball, his teams specialized in forward passes, laterals, and reverses. When someone told Zup that Knute Rockne brought on the era of the forward pass in 1913 when Notre Dame defeated Army, Zup replied, "That is perfectly true — except that 70,000 forward passes had already been completed by that time."

Grange was not a natural quarterback, but his enormous hands were able to grip the pigskin, which was twenty-three inches around the middle (a modern ball is an inch slimmer), therefore nicknamed the "cantaloupe" by many players. Throwing was a skill many players could not master for physiologic reasons, meaning the ball would be shot-put in ugly end-over-end passes. On several plays Grange faked a throw and ran, as he did once for 37 yards. It was difficult to defend, and Michigan's athletic director, Fielding Yost, who was in Lincoln scouting the game, took note of it. Then the week before, the annual breather game against Butler actually played true to character (and so did Grange, with two touchdowns), the Illini shutting them out, 33–0. The Michigan scrap—the papers described the games, accurately likening them to brawls—was easily the matchup of the year, Knute Rockne, Notre Dame's popular headman, saying, "The eyes of the Middle West turn to Urbana Saturday for the Illinois-Michigan game. The Illini seem to have the edge right now, but the game is sure to be nip and tuck . . . Yost will build a special defense for Grange and will stop him most of the afternoon. This lad is resourceful, though, and may pull one at any time." The question on everyone's mind: how would Michigan's Fielding Yost stop Illinois's star, and how would Bob Zuppke set him free?

Coach Zuppke was elfish with cowlicked hair, darty eyes, and German-inflected English. He looked over the practice field and hitched up his wrinkled khaki pants, studying the violence. He liked to say, "Men do their best if they know they are being observed." But, at the

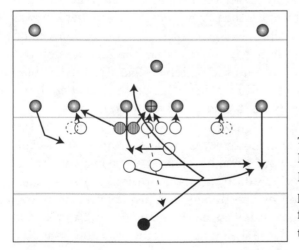

THE CUTBACK PLAY. In the Michigan game, Bob Zuppke designed plays that had Grange faking a sweep and then cutting back.

moment, his players were not reaching his expectations. He went over to a 190-pound blond farm kid and the diminutive Zup, giving up 50 pounds, put the boy on his butt, screaming into his ear, "That's the way we do it at Illinois!" Coach Zuppke was a football obsessive. He planned everything, from what he said and how he said it, to pregame meals and the psychological impact of different uniform colors. Taking on Michigan's headman Fielding Yost, his most hated rival, was always the highlight of Zuppke's season, and Zup's competitive fire was not always easy to keep in check. Yost was the most famous coach of the early part of the century. In 1901 his team outscored eleven opponents 555–0, and Yost had three national championships. Zuppke, forty-five, had three national championships, too, but the press didn't always take him as seriously. Zup relied on trick plays — like the "screen pass" — and couldn't always squeeze consistent performances from his typically undersized charges. For Yost and Zuppke, this game represented a test of wits, wills, and football philosophies. (Grange noted, "Zuppke and Yost were great pals but they detested each other.") Zuppke planned to jolt big, slick Michigan with a lively offense led by Grange. Most teams wanted to simply pin down and wear out their opponents with defense. It would undoubtedly be the strategy of Fielding Yost. Zup had disassembled and put together Michigan's team a thousand times, and in practice he was emphasizing sweeping runs accentuated with cuts into the middle and quick blocking. Because they were hardly practicing defensive alignments, the traditional blueprint for victory, the players were worried that Zup was putting all his eggs into the Grange basket. How many times could they practice pushing Grange to the outside while Zuppke stomped over to remind Red to cut into the middle? What was Coach's plan for defending Michigan's intimidating offense, which tended to roll straight over you, ate up the clock, and exhausted opponents?

The humid air was jam-packed with questions. Zuppke looked out on the practice field, and his eyes targeted Grange. It was this boy on whom he would put down his chips. And he knew if Grange didn't perform, and Illinois didn't win, the previous season's championship would forever be questioned. Red just kept his head lowered, not daring to look at his coach. Psychologically, Zuppke had Grange pegged from the first day he met him: realizing that Red was hard enough on himself ("a lone wolf," Zup called him), he promised himself never to yell at the boy. Zuppke seemed to come from a different world from any other men Grange had encountered. Zup was tough as hell, but he was also an avid painter and he read Kant for fun (a "perpetual contradiction," Grange called Zuppke). Red had never been to a museum and only cracked open the sports pages. Bob Zuppke was an everyman's intellectual, the opposite of Grange's father, and intellect always intimidated Red more than brawn. Despite their different personalities and interests, Zuppke and Grange shared a common passion: a love affair with football.

As a kid Red cheered for Bob Zuppke's Illini teams and so when the two met the first time, Red was meeting his hero. It happened a few years back, when Red was in high school. Unlike many of the football powers, Zuppke refused to recruit players because he felt that it should be an honor to play collegiate football. "The honor of playing for Illinois is payment enough," went his mantra. During his twenty-nine-year tenure, he never strayed from that belief. For Zuppke, glad-handing a seventeen-year-old punk was beneath him. He had recruited Red Grange in the most mild-mannered way possible. After the 1918 influenza pandemic hit, many high schools canceled athletics, but they resumed in 1919, Grange's first high school semester. In his high school career Grange collected sixteen letters in four sports — baseball, basketball, track, and football — but people started taking notice in his junior year in football when he tallied at least three touchdowns in every game. His slashing speed and manly strength overpowered high school boys, and in his senior year he sprinted for six TDs against the favored and undefeated Downers Grove team, Wheaton winning 63–13. He ended his high school career with seventy-five touchdowns, and in his prep career he lost only one game. In an era when placekicking was a prized skill, Red made thirty consecutive kicks after touchdowns. During track season Grange went to Champaign for a meet. Zuppke strolled over from his office to watch. Track meets were the testing grounds for potential recruits and Grange could run a 440-yarder in under 50 seconds and the 100-yard dash in 9.8 seconds (the world record in that era was 9.6). With his talkative charm ("I have frequently seen dawn breaking as he was in the midst of one of his famous ora-

tions or addresses," said Grantland Rice, the sportswriter) and winning records, Zuppke was a darling of the increasingly thirsty sports
pages and the men and boys who devoured them. Grange won his
event and Zup loped over to him. "Your name Grainche?"

"Yes."

"Where are you going to college?"

"I don't know." Michigan had asked about him, but no one else
had even considered the boy.

Zuppke put his arm around Grange's shoulders. "I hope here.
You may have a chance to make the team here."

They walked a block near Green Street and Zuppke regaled the
boy with football stories as freshmen sporting little green beanies hurried by. Grange called the conversation the biggest thrill of
his life, and that was the extent of the courtship. At Illinois Grange
would be close to home; at $400 in total yearly expenses, it was
relatively inexpensive; and, if he did play football, he would follow in the cleats of his childhood heroes, All-Americans Bart Ma-
comber and Potsy Clark, both Illinois stars and national champs in
1914. Living expenses could be arranged because Grange's Wheaton
neighbor, George Dawson, was a member of the football team and
a fraternity, and frats were encouraged to rush, and even financially
supplement, a potential star.

Grange enrolled. The next September, Red, a timid and gangly
freshman, went for a tryout. Through the gymnasium's window he
wide-eyed the three hundred other hopefuls. Frightened by the size
and speed of the men, he returned to his fraternity house, but his
Greek brothers paddled him for cowardice. When he returned to
the tryout a coach asked him who he was and where he was from.
"I never heard of Grange and I don't know where Wheaton is,"
scoffed the man. The slight hurt the sensitive Grange, who set upon
proving himself, winning wind sprint after wind sprint and working his way up from the seventh team. Zuppke pit the freshmen
against the varsity squads, expecting the frosh team to become dog
meat. At the first contest Grange caught a punt, and then — *bam* —
he whizzed by everyone 60 yards for a touchdown. He also scored
another TD on a shorter run. The smaller and inexperienced freshmen nearly upset the varsity. Put Grange on an athletic field and his
central nervous system fed information to his muscles at a faster

clip than in anyone alive. Within his body was what physiologists call "differentiation and control over the active dynamics of the distal limbs accompanied by an economy of force." Red Grange was scorching fast. But Zuppke told his coaches to bench him. "Put in a man who can give the varsity some practice," Zuppke cracked, but with the little he had already seen of Grange he knew that Illinois's football future looked promising. In fact, he had never seen such an incredible freshman team: Grange, Earl Britton, Moon Baker, and Frank Wickhorst (the latter two men would transfer the next season and become All-Americans for different schools). Zup knew that when Grange played on the varsity squad, Illinois would have a great chance at winning titles.

But Saturday would be their biggest test yet.

Zuppke broke up his squad into two teams for a scrimmage. Each team had the ball eleven times, and Zup recorded the yardage for each side with the winner having the most yards. At 4:20 p.m. the freshman team, equipped with Michigan uniforms, went against the first team. Finally the Illini would get a smidgen of defensive work. They were finally — a little too late, perhaps? — learning Michigan's offense. Coach Zuppke had the freshmen use nearly every play that the Wolverines had used since 1903, including the "83," the most famous of the day. The Wolverines would line up overbalanced to the right, and the quarterback would take the ball and hide it while his teammates blocked for the fullback, who ran toward the right. When the play seemed to end, the quarterback passed to a halfback, and the halfback ran around the pile. It took patience, speed, and powerful linemen to execute, and it could be difficult to defend. Zuppke also wanted his team to get their timing down. Illinois was using replacements for players who were injured or ineligible to play. Injuries and poor grades were really killing this team, which was a definite underdog. Of the role players, Wally McIlwain had flunked five hours the previous year but managed to make them up. He would play, but he was a little sick and on the verge of puking. Walter Crawford, the backbone of the left side of the line, had gone to summer school to make up his classes, but he had been found ineligible. Bernie Shiveley, number 78, an agile, athletic guard, was hurt. Louis Slimmer, a replacement guard, was out there trying to keep up, but he was not very heavy or fast. Frank

"Rock" Rokusek, the broad-shouldered, chiseled captain and a left end, had not played the last game against Butler because of a hurt leg. But the core of the team was ready: Grange, Earl Britton, and Jim McMillen, a muscular guard who was also a champion heavy-weight wrestler.

Zuppke insisted on precision. Grange wasn't always precise to the play, but watching Grange, seeing him as no one else did, excited Zup. He hoped the pressure of expectations and the significance of Illinois's new stadium, and Michigan's twenty-game winning streak (they had surrendered only four touchdowns the previous *two* sea-sons), wouldn't intimidate the rest of the squad. The Michigan way had always been to give the other team the ball and hit them, dispirit them. Would Michigan's Coach Little dare to deviate from Yost's style? Unlikely. But Yost might try something radical, maybe even try to control the game on offense. That was Zuppke's fear, that Yost would change his team's style and not let Grange touch the ball. That was a strategy that could actually work.

Zuppke carried a funny little secret as he crisscrossed the prac-tice field. For months leading up to today's game, he had sent let-ters to his players describing Fielding Yost's supposed scurrilous words about Illinois. *The players were still mad!* But Yost had really spent a quiet summer in Europe visiting ancient battlegrounds. Zup loved the hatred his ploy had engendered in his charges. But would his team carry the intensity into the game? Darkness approached. Bob Zuppke knew there was an onslaught of special trains entering Urbana and Champaign, filling the towns with even more alumni, party seekers, scalpers, and scam artists, so after practice he took his team away from the chaos, to the Champaign Country Club. Maple trees were shedding their leaves, but it was warm, an In-dian summer evening. It had been months of Michigan this, Michi-gan that. Now it was up to Grange and his blockers. The team knew the drill. Zup wanted the routine to be the same before every game. There was a weigh-in, a bath, and each player had to drink a small glass of orange juice ("this not only serves as an appetizer but aids to quench the thirst for water"), then the players settled in for a rare meat dinner, and sleep.

Fielding Yost — barrel-chested with a confident chin and eyes that never showed doubt — felt fairly confident about Saturday's big game. Yost and the Michigan football team were on a train headed to Champaign-Urbana. They had been sent off from Ann Arbor on the overnight express by hundreds of Wolverines fans. The Michigan supporters wore fedoras and golf caps, colorful suits, black dog fur coats, and some of the women sported knickers, although most had Shaker sweaters and slim-fitting skirts (clasped corsets underneath to create boyish hips). They sang songs and cheered the team on to certain greatness. Their optimism still echoed in the cars.

Yost was actually not the coach of the Michigan team — he had been booted upstairs to athletic director the previous year — but he controlled the team with his very domineering presence. Everyone called the man "Hurry Up" Yost because of the way he prodded himself and the people around him. It was said that when Yost went into coaching, the nation lost a great general. During the Great War he would hang large-scale maps of the front line — red markers for French troops, white for British, blue for American, and black for German — and play soldier, lecturing his men about military strategy for twenty minutes before practice. To people who doubted the importance of football, Yost sneered in a distinct West Virginia drawl: "Objections to football have been heard in certain quarters on account of its alleged brutality and the violence of the exercise demanded in its play. It is certainly not a game for weaklings or improperly trained boys, but statistics show that accidents of a serious nature are no more frequent in football than in horseback riding, hunting, yachting and many other kindred sports."

The Michigan men, Yost's men, in the Pullman looked unbeatable. Thirty-four players ready for battle. They would outweigh their smaller opponents by a good twenty pounds, they were Michigan-trained, and quirky Bob Zuppke could be out-coached. But Illinois did have Red Grange, an All-American wild card. Yost had never seen anyone as fast as Grange, and Yost had been around football forever. Hurry Up grew up in a log cabin, and in his teens he worked as a deputy sheriff in a mining town where he could fistfight with the best of them, but his innate cleverness took him to Ohio Normal College in 1890. At the school he played impromptu "rugby football," before any real rules had been set; they were hundred-man-a-side wars. Yost joked that each man brought his own bottle of witch hazel for a postgame rubdown. They played within a fenced-in hedge, swarming the ball in a massive brawl, and Yost specialized in preying on the weaker men, stealing the ball from the ones who carried it "like a farmer carrying a pumpkin." When he started coaching Michigan they played the local high school team, on a sandlot, all the players sporting uniforms that looked like baseball togs. His team had been filmed by a Thomas Edison Company man with a kinetograph. The footage showed players colliding in rugbylike scrums and the curious crowd, in black-clothed stiffness, looking on. But the game had evolved from its disorderly, preindustrial roots into a postindustrial form of violence. Everyone knew Fielding Yost, a man whose name was all over the football record books. At the end of Yost's first season the Pasadena Tournament of Roses Association invited Michigan to play Stanford, where he had coached the year earlier. Although he was successful, Stanford decided that they wanted only alumni coaching their teams. So on a hot New Year's Day, 1902, in Pasadena's Tournament Park, he would get his revenge in the first Rose Bowl, murdering Stanford, 49–0, the game being stopped after Stanford begged for mercy. Yost's Wolverines, who became known as the "point-a-minute" teams, went through another 11–0 season in 1902 and remained undefeated until 1905, when they lost a heartbreaker to the Walter Eckersall–led University of Chicago, 2–0, a game that Yost would ruefully remember in song:

> *Eckersall, Eckersall*
> *Eckie, Eckie, break your neckie*
> *Eckersall!*

Yost's coaching triumphs had continued into the 1920s. At age fifty-three he was still the tough, domineering son of a bitch he had always been. It could not have been easy for George Little, the Wolverines' rookie coach. The players felt it and they even wrote a parody of the situation and sang it to Yost on the Champaign-bound train:

> *Oh Mister Little, Oh Mister Little*
> *We congratulate you on your football team.*
> *Many folks have traveled here, from places far and near,*
> *And you certainly will show them some machine.*
> *Oh Mister Yost, Oh Mister Yost*

It's very good of you 'bout me to boast
But really, can't you guess, what makes Michigan a success
It's YOUR fine work, Mister Little, — No, it's YOUR
Work, Mister Yost!

Yost just turned his head, the chiseled face of an ex-athlete, and walked away from the overly cheeky boys. Yost's detractors, and there was a growing contingent, believed Hurry Up was too con-servative, a man stuck in the good old days. Had the game passed him by? Some teams were even passing the ball on a regular ba-sis, a strategy Yost was not ready to embrace despite having Benny Friedman, a sophomore who hurled the football as if it was meant to spiral. Perhaps football was changing, but Yost was not going to bend to fads. He knew how to stop speedsters like Grange. In fact, it was quite simple. The porter yanked up the blinds to let the morn-ing light into the southwest-bound Pullman. Fielding Yost sat on the green velvet cushions pondering game strategy. How do you stop speed? You take down the man who possesses it. Yost knew the teams that had done well against Grange had beaten him down. He had seen how the Nebraska men had roughed him. Perhaps Grange was not so fast after he was really hit. Maybe Yost would embolden the Michigan players by letting Grange have the ball and then instruct them to hit him hard. Yost refused to play scared and that would be a shock in itself. Yost's idol was Stonewall Jackson, a general who knew how to surprise an opponent. There was some-thing cunning, brave, and noble about not backing down, especially against someone as worthy as Grange.

Later that morning Yost got up to stretch the legs on his lumber-ing frame. People would describe him as a bear pacing in a small cage. A short stogy moved back and forth across his lips. The pre-vious year the team was undefeated. Edliff Slaughter, guard, would be an All-American before the year was up. And any Michigan player, it seemed, could be considered for postseason honors: Har-old Steele, right guard; Tom Edwards, tackle; Bob Brown, center; Charlie Grube and Dutch Marion, ends; and in the backfield, Herb Steger — a triple-threat man — Jim Miller, and Ferdinand Rockwell. Benny Friedman, whom many people would later consider the best quarterback of the era, was a third-stringer. But the Wolverines also had their share of injuries to some experienced players. Would the young replacements have enough courage, or what Yost called "sand," on such a grand stage? Were any of his players chronic bed wetters? Yost had spent the summer studying Zuppke's book, *Football: Technique and Tactics.* One of his assistants had even gone through it, making little notes on Zuppke's numerous and creative play diagrams: *forward pass to weak side on crisscross . . . a double pass swinging end run . . . a triple pass end run . . . a forward pass after a triple pass . . .* But Yost wasn't going to deviate from his own philosophy. "We let the other fellow rush the ball and waste his energy in his own territory. Football games aren't won — they're lost." George Little, Michigan's figurehead coach, embraced this philosophy to the extreme. But he could not have found it easy to be the field general with the legendary Yost traveling with the team, sticking his hand in everything, pulling all the strings.

By the time the Wolverines had eaten breakfast, gathered their belongings, arrived in Champaign, and stepped off the train at 9:00 a.m., it was already a madhouse. The reporters were there, licking their pencils and swarming on Yost (not Coach Little).

"Coach Yost. What about Grange?" the reporters asked.

"I know Grange is a great runner," said Yost coolly, "but we've got eleven good men who are going to stop him."

"How are you going to stop him?"

Yost took a puff on his cigar and smiled. "There are eleven good tacklers on this Michigan squad and those eleven good tacklers are going to be after Mr. Grange all afternoon. Anything else you want to know, gentlemen?"

Grange was donning his uniform, putting on his shoulder pads, heavy pants, and woolen socks. He was intimidating: because he did so much manual labor, his muscles were better defined than those of his teammates, but he also had a presence; he moved more gracefully, more animal-like, than anyone else in the room. He put his blue sweater over his neck. His teammates did the same. The morning played to Zup's pregame script: breakfast — fresh orange juice, cornflakes and cream, two poached eggs on toast (no extra toast!) — followed by a brisk ten-minute walk among the Champaign Country Club's foliage. Then they practiced ball handling, got taped up, and had a light lunch — a small steak or lamb chop, half a baked potato, one piece of buttered toast, and a cup of weak tea. The boys had been restless. Red came over to Britt and started wrestling with him. Just goofing around. Then Rock came over to help Red. Britt was on top of them in no time when suddenly there was a hush. Zup stood over the boys, glowering. "What in the hell are you trying to do" — he screamed at Britt — "kill the best half-back I ever had?" The wrestling agitated Zuppke, but the grace with which Grange wore his fame — *just one of the boys* — made him a natural leader. They were at the stadium by one. Now they were in the sanctuary of Memorial Stadium, lost in their thoughts, when Zuppke stomped in and started yelling.

Zup loved psychology. His brilliant oratorical skills could convince the smallest players to give up their bodies and skulls for the glory of Illinois. During Red's freshman year his coach talked about Socrates and threw out dates like 1923 BC and 1924 BC. Red was enthralled. Zuppke could make anything relevant to football and to a man's man like Grange. "Football is at its best when it's played under a *man*, and that is my definition of Zup," said Grange. Zuppke was more than a simple motivational speaker, however. Once, before an important tilt against an all-powerful Minnesota team, he gave a pregame speech that consisted of one line: "I am Louis XV; after me, the deluge!" Filled with wonder about what Zuppke meant, the Illinois players forgot the other team's power and skill and pulled an upset. Zuppke had another nutty ploy planned for today. For anyone who has never sat in a pregame locker room, it might reek of inconsequence, the kind of yarn told by elderly and sentimental jocks. But for the men in that room that day it held great import.

"Is there anything in the rule book that says you have to wear stockings?" Zuppke tested his men on the rule book ad nauseam. Nothing, was the reply.

"Take your stockings off!"

It was common for men to bite each other in the piles so the men replied, "Coach! The teeth marks! They'll scratch us! They'll cut us up!"

"Take your stockings off!"

He knew his sockless Illini would psych out the Wolverines because every player from time immemorial had worn thick socks as protection. Zup also knew that anything deviating from normal would get under Yost's conservative hide and throw off the status quo–conscious Wolverines. After they removed their stockings, the men waited for one of Zuppke's pregame speeches. It was quiet, just the muffled sounds of outside. Five minutes before they took the field of play, Zuppke leaned down on the carpet and picked up a penny as everyone studied him. "Here's that unlucky penny," he explained. "Two years ago, we played at Ann Arbor and Michigan beat us. I picked a penny off the floor and put it in my pocket and that is what licked us." He was serious. Then he walked over to the window, opened it, and sailed the penny outside. Zuppke said, "That'll have no effect on us today." The united Illinois team stormed onto the field and Grange felt as if the crowd was on top of him. The fans chanted, "Seventy-seven! Seventy-seven!" — Grange's number. He wore those numerals, more apt for a lineman, because when they were handing out uniforms, he said, "The fella in front of me got number seventy-six."

Grange! Grange!

Fielding Yost had entered the stadium and gazed at the field, looking to see if the Illini had a mascot yet. Yost was obsessed with mascots, and he had been trying to get a live wolverine to bring to games. He had sent former players and alumni searching the state for one, and he was eventually sent ten live wolverines from Alaska, but they grew so vicious that Yost had to give them away to various zoos. The Illini didn't have a mascot yet, but something else caught his eye. The Illini were not wearing any damn socks. He called over J. C. Masker, the referee, who was dressed in the regulation all-white outfit. Yost complained about his sockless opponents. Coach Little whined at Zup: "Zuppke, you're going to grease those boys' legs." The Michigan players felt the Illinois players' legs, but they were not slick. Zup's plan had worked surprisingly well. Yost was upset, muttering about "Zuppke's tricks." The Wolverines were obviously distracted.

A furious Yost told his team: "Kick off to Grange. Let him know he hasn't got us worried. Hit him and hit him hard. See that he stays hit."

Michigan was falling into Zuppke's trap. Now it was up to Grange.

He looked to the stands. Wheaton, most of Wheaton, was there. His hometown had about nine thousand residents, and as Grange looked to the stands, he swore seventy-five hundred of them were watching, including his father, just as he had when Red played at Wheaton's orchard field. The whistle blew. The pigskin flew through the air. Grange wore neither mouthpiece nor facemask. "I've got it, Wally," Red said as he stepped in front of his teammate and caught the ball.

It was the suddenness of the speed that astonished everyone.

"I was standing on the five-yard line," said Grange. He started to the left, then he cut to the right, and then again to the left. "I was the most surprised person in the ballpark. Things just seemed to open up. I got down to the forty-yard line and went straight . . . Every guy did what those Xs and circles say you're going to do on the chart." It was spectacular: the perfect blocking, the grass like an enlarging meadow, his feet, one after another, galloping like a just mature colt, the loudness of the crowd which he no longer heard. Grange's legs glided inside his football pants, made of tan-colored moleskins with a heavy wool liner. Grange was like a sliver, audaciously invisible, and the Michigan players had failed to catch him. "It was my greatest thrill," said his friend Earl Britton. "Wally McIlwain took out one fella and I took out another one and Red went between us and then I got up and the pleasure was getting up and watching him run. I liked to block for him because I liked to watch him run." To make a 95-yard kickoff return for a touchdown, Grange had one man to beat. "That was Rockwell, their quarterback," said Red. "He was playing safety man . . . After the ten guys got me this far, I thought wouldn't it be awful if this one fella tackled me here about the five-yard line?" Then he was touching the ball down in the dirt and grass, curling around the pigskin as if he was sliding with a baby in his arms, the blunt hands of his mates who had allowed him to run so beautifully patting him on his leather shoulder pads.

Grange had run past the best team in the nation.

Yost was in shock. One of Yost's sayings, or what he called "Hurry Ups," was "Hurry up and score in the first few minutes of the game, before your opponents realize what is going on." A minute had not yet passed, and Illinois had hurried up and scored. In the 1920s teams could choose if they wanted to kick off or not. Fielding Yost, through his conduit, Coach George Little, could have saved his team, but pride and stale thinking got in his way. They decided to kick to the Illini again. This time Grange was thrashed at his own 20-yard line. Perhaps the kickoff return for a touchdown had been a fluke. Perhaps Yost's strategy would now work. "At Meechigan, we believe that position is more important than possession," said Yost. Yost was demeaning Zuppke's penchant for a more open style. The newspapermen were talking among themselves, predicting that, as in the Nebraska game a few weeks earlier, Illinois would go to short passes to try to stretch out the bigger Michigan men. Zuppke had instructed his men to run the ball. *Why was Zuppke going head-to-head with Yost? Why on earth would he try and out-muscle Michigan?* It was all a ruse. The runs into the line were a setup.

Then after a screen pass to stretch out Michigan, Illinois was ready to strike again. About Grange, Zuppke said, "He thought in terms of long runs. He was not as effective from compact formations. You had to give him room and freedom of movement back of the scrimmage line." Toward the end of the previous day's practice, Zuppke had told his coaches to gather the team. "Bring those little fellers over here but don't let them get hurt on the way over," he said. Behind him was an enormous chalkboard and he diagrammed plays. "We make it a fetish to insist that the back run hard, and harder, and still harder! We have noticed that the instant we let down on this the entire backfield goes in a slump. The back should learn to run so fast and hard that everything in front of him appears to be in a blur . . . Each back must be taught to run both in angles and curves. The back must learn to avoid being tackled near the sidelines." Zuppke drew a big *S* on the board, snaking through the Michigan team. Grange represented the *S*. It was clearly up to him. Zuppke had been working with him throughout the previous year and in the off-season to fine-tune his running style. But it is difficult to change your style after you have been doing something else for probably ten or fourteen years. Zuppke drew on the blackboard to show the simple fact that cutting in was the smart way to run, not running down the sidelines. Zuppke told the team that Michigan had scouted Illinois, they knew Grange's proclivity, and they would crowd the sidelines. If Grange didn't do as he was coached, Fielding Yost's boys were going to pound him into Memorial Stadium's sod.

The Illini were ahead because of Grange's long touchdown run, but the game had just started. Michigan was stopping the Illini's interior attacks, and they were gaining a little confidence. Zuppke knew it was time to unleash Grange on an *S* run. Red was given the ball. It looked like he would go to the outside, but he didn't. It had been only moments since Grange's figure — blue sweater and yellow helmet — had galloped the length of the field, atop the brittling grass, and now he held the oval and circled — cutting back as the team had practiced — and then he dodged players, Britt, a descendant of sharecroppers, and the other Illini farm boys scything Wolverines. Grange skirted the end 67 yards for another touchdown. "It was so easy it was pitiful," wrote Ralph Cannon of the *Chicago Journal.*

The fans were not used to such long runs and final scores rarely added up to more than 10 points. Grange had already pulled off the unthinkable. One hundred yards of running against Michigan would be considered a feat in itself. No one ever scored against Michigan. He abhorred overconfidence, and yet he would say, "On October 18, 1924, I don't believe any college team in the United States could have licked the University of Illinois." The fans could see it, too. They knew that they would see his image once and never again. To brains schooled in Emerson, Whitman, Keats, and Dickinson, Grange's athleticism was filtered through the mind's poetic regime, bringing forth favorite heroic couplets. They had all passed underneath Memorial's relief of an ancient Olympian victor. And before them Grange strode atop the grassy plain of what would be known as "Zuppke Field" — years later chiseled in the limestone just outside the north end zone. The crowd watched Grange's teammates give him "ferocious blocking" — the plangent sound of thin leather shoulder pads striking each other — as he pranced. As Grange slid, touching the ball in the end zone, his teammates gathered around him again in panting congratulations. The stands creaked and the people, all standing and stomping, created a seismic quaver — it felt like being in a boat next to a dock, rocking back and forth. Britton made the extra point. 14–0.

Go, Illini, Go!
Go, Illini, Go!
Oskee-wow-wow! Illinois
GO!!
Yea-a-a, Grange!
Um-m-m BOY!

Yost's stubbornness bordered on hubris, or suicide.

With their leaders' instructions, Michigan decided to kick off yet again, but luckily for the downtrodden Wolverines the game fell into a momentary back-and-forth battle for field position. Michigan seemed to catch its breath, for a split second. Yost's "punt, pass, and pray" strategy might have worked if his own team could have rolled over the Illinois boys, but the Illini were playing tough defense, too. The Wolverines turned the ball over again. Soon enough Grange was handed the football; his knees reached high, his hips twisted like a snake; it looked like he was flowing rather than running. *It couldn't happen!* The reporter Harold Johnson called it "the greatest exhibition of broken field running ever witnessed on a Big Ten gridiron." The first *S* run had confused the Wolverines and so now they overcompensated by plugging up the middle, so Grange went around the end 56 yards for another TD. Red was a football illusionist. No one could understand how he did it. The noise was deafening now, Grange hearing it like a din, a continual clap of thunder, the fedoras and boaters joyfully bobbing up and down within the hazy outline of the stands. 20–0.

Grange was treating the game like a schoolyard pickup game. He held the ball on field goals. He joshed with Britt about their last high school basketball game, in which they had played against each other. With time ticking down, Britton had thrown the basketball the length of the court to beat Grange's team by a point. "I am not going to make you look good again," said Grange, grinning to his pal. Britton laughed, his concentration gone; he missed the extra point, and the score remained 20–0. During most games the crowd would have groaned at the missed try, but they were so excited chatting among themselves that they forgot about it. The great Wolverines looked completely flummoxed.

•   •   •

Zuppke relaxed on the sideline, and his team sat in chairs strewn about. Despite the hot day, they were sporting overcoats presented to them by some boosters. Zup was positively gleeful. Zup, at the height of his coaching powers, was now making the princely sum of $8,000 a year, plus the money he made on speaking tours. But Bob Zuppke wasn't about money. He really wasn't. Zup liked cars and nice hotels but his belongings didn't define him. He lived in a small apartment downtown. He was married but he didn't have any kids. The importance of his life, what made him, emanated from Memorial Stadium. He loved this brand-new red fortress and he never wanted to leave it. He had been through so much to get here, to this moment. The son of a jewelry designer, Zup grew up in the south side of Milwaukee in a German neighborhood. At Zuppke's first game at West Division High in Milwaukee, he broke his collarbone. After the game the principal banned football because of all the injuries the team suffered. Zup started his own team. Eventually he went to the University of Wisconsin; he was too small to play varsity football, but he never missed a game. He had a hunger to be a part of the sport, but he had a competing interest. He wanted to create, to be an artist.

After college he traveled to New York, where he pursued his love of painting and found work as a sign painter. Only semitalented, he was fired from job after job, spending many of his days walking through the tenement alleys where inside the cramped rooms children did piecework, and wide-eyed, whiskered men, the skeletal masses, stared through him, like a stream of vomited humanity from Bowling Green to the Bronx. He studied the hazy outlines of the buildings, visiting galleries and forming prayer groups, sermonizing in his German accent. He was literally a starving artist, knowing the hunger and stench of the poor. Many football players would have considered him a bum, another of the dirty-faced shadow dwellers, and it seemed that Robert C. Zuppke, circa 1906, would be lost to anonymity.

His artistic failure freed him. He had always had a passion for football. His knowledge of the game (throughout high school he tended to talk about it constantly) was unparalleled. Someone told him about a $1,000-a-year high school coaching job in Muskegon, Michigan. It turned out to be a natural fit. As a player he had been undersized, so he had studied the sport with an objective eye and a hunger for the success that had eluded him as an athlete. Under his tutelage his high school boys would play and beat college squads, and his reputation grew in the Midwest, where sports were gaining in popularity. Zuppke, being small himself, was an expert on teaching leverage blocking and how best to use speed over power, brains over brawn. Zuppke had ambition, so he eventually moved to the higher-profile Oak Park High School, in Oak Park, Illinois, a Protestant, upper-middle-class Chicago suburb. The Hemingways lived there. Ernest called it a town of "wide lawns and narrow minds," and during Zuppke's tenure Hemingway played on the line. As a junior the clumsy boy — six feet tall, 150 pounds, with feet so big they could barely find cleats for him — played on the lightweight squad, and as a senior he was a second-string guard on the varsity. Papa wrote a football-themed short story in high school and later said, "Scrimmaging against Zup's first team was tougher than shooting lions in Africa," and in "In Another Country" he mulled over the game, football as metaphor for manliness. But as a football player, Papa was a useless oaf.

After three straight seasons without a loss and a 1912 National High School Championship to his credit, Zuppke entertained offers from Purdue, Northwestern, and Illinois. He took the Illinois job for $2,700 a year and immediately started putting his own style in place. In its raw days football was ripe for invention, and Zuppke, the frustrated painter, liked to create more than anything. His innovations displayed deception and humor (he invented the screen pass and various trick plays, including the flea-flicker and the onside kick), as well as efficiency and esprit de corps (the offensive huddle, about which opposing teams would hum "Ring-around-the-Rosy" to the Illinois men because they thought the huddle was unmanly and slowed down the hitting). Each coach of this era — Bob Zuppke, Fielding Yost, Knute Rockne . . . — made an imprint on his school. In 1920 only 17 percent of Americans graduated from high school, yet university sports teams had millions of supporters, and athletic departments made money based on gate receipts, so winning teams brought funds to school coffers and power to successful coaches, who were rivaling baseball managers as America's sports spokesmen. For many years some colleges would not hire a coach unless he had graduated from the school. It was as much about professors

disliking the attention given to outside — some would say merce-
nary — coaches, as about fear of change, of altering the school's very
identity; to understand a place, the headman had to be brought up
in its mores. Many coaches — some alumni, some not — were hired
during this time and they did more than conform to the school;
they gave the institutions their very identities.

Sports told the tale of a culture, and William Randolph Hearst
gave it a forum. After he bought the *New York Journal* in 1895, he
expanded the sports pages to four times his rivals' coverage; the
other papers eventually followed suit. Within coaches' proclama-
tions, dutifully reported in the papers, were philosophies of how
boys should become men, of how society would become stronger through the tests of athletics. Supporting Illinois was as much
about supporting Zuppke's vision, just as Michigan boosters followed Fielding H. Yost's. For Robert Zuppke, who had laid out today's game plan, it was the culmination of all that he had hoped
football could be. Red Grange's performance bordered on the spiritual. Football, some say, is an orchestra of violence. A play starts
like sheet music, on a chalkboard with Xs and Os and arrows. It's
really not so simple. Two forces are working against each other,
so perhaps a guard slips and pushes the defender the wrong way,
or a quick defensive end fights his way into the backfield, disrupt-
ing a play. The coach hopes for an orchestra, but the Xs and Os
are more like jazz — constant improvisation. Zup would say, *Just
as paintings are made up of dabs and swabs of different pigments,
so football compositions are an orderly conglomeration of different
types of men in motion.* Coaching from the sideline was against the
rules in 1924, a rule that would be loosened through the years, finally leaving the college rule book in 1967. Zuppke, and the other
football coaches of the world, put their teams on the field as men
who would decide their own fate through physical strength and
speed, and test their ingenuity by calling their own plays. But they
also followed the philosophy of their head coach. Zup had helped
Red become a better player, but what Grange possessed went beyond coaching. Zuppke, as if in a dream state, had sat back on
his wooden chair, smoking a cigar, and watched his Xs and Os
move, and it would be the closest ever to perfect harmony, to a work
of art.

• • •

The game was far from over.

Tempting fate for the third time and seeming to ignore the reality of what was happening on the field, Michigan kicked off to Illinois, but the kicker hit it good and true and the ball went over
the line for a touchback. After a few plays Illinois punted. Michigan
fumbled the punt, giving Illinois the ball. There was a groan from
the Michigan fans because Illinois had it on Michigan's 44-yard
line, and they feared the inevitable. Grange was handed the ball; he
circled the end, got loose, and ran. Many listeners to Quin Ryan on

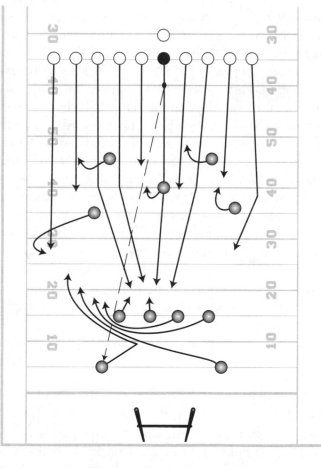

THE KICKOFF RETURN PLAY.
With his speed and ability to avoid tackles, Grange
always threatened to score on kickoff returns.

WGN thought it was a hoax. The newspapermen, who had lugged their typewriters to the press box, were tip-tapping their keys. It would be a story with which they would regale their colleagues over highballs and one that they would carry to their deathbeds. Grange went the distance for another score and the people just stood and kept standing . . .

Red! Red!

Only twelve minutes had ticked by and Grange had posted four touchdowns. When the Michigan players had lowered themselves to knock him down, Grange had run toward them with increasing speed, but at the last moment, like a swerving train, he avoided them. There was deception to his running but it started with a manly toughness. He could take any hit and tacklers knew it. Or, as Zuppke observed, "Red dodged on the fly and doubled his speed at the moment of possible contact." To Yost's comment that "all Grange can do is run," Zuppke replied, "And all Galli-Curci* can do is sing." The year 1923 had been an All-American season but it was nothing compared to what he was creating this day, October 18, 1924. Red Grange was creating a fable on the field. *Four touchdowns in twelve minutes . . .*

> *Oskee-wow-wow!*
> *Skin-nee-wow-wow!*
> *Illinois, Illinois*
> *Y-e-a!*
> *Yea team! Yea team!*
> *Fight 'em, Fight 'em, Fight 'em*
> *Chee-hee, Chee-ha*
> *Chee-ha-ha-ha!*
> *Illinois, Illinois, Illinois!*

Michigan decided to kick again. Steger smartly booted it away from Grange to another Illinois player, who returned it to the 25-yard line. Grange was low on coal. Like all of his teammates, Grange played on offense and defense, and when the trainer came onto the field with water he was exhausted.

"Tired, Red?"

"Zup better get me out before I fall down."

---

* Amelita Galli-Curci was one of the best operatic sopranos of the era.

At the end of the first quarter Grange trotted toward the side-line. As if at the end of a particularly moving aria at La Scala, the crowd gave him an ovation for five minutes. The players — on both teams — paused, breathless. "The greatest spontaneous ovation ever given an athlete," admitted Michigan's Herb Steger. Zuppke, the lit-tle Napoleon, greeted Grange with a sparkle in his eyes. "Grainche, if you had any brains you should have had five touchdowns," he barked ironically, adding with a laugh, "You didn't cut right on that one play." As the crowd and the players gathered themselves, Grange sat out the entire second quarter. "The second quarter was just football because Mr. Grange wasn't there," noted the *Chicago Tribune.* "Michigan, however, perked up after the wild Illinois man was out."

Trying to summon a comeback, Michigan's Steger went for 2 yards, then he took it off the Illinois right tackle and ran 15 yards for a touchdown, and the extra point was good. 27–7. The rest of the quarter was a back-and-forth game with Michigan trying its tra-ditional shift plays in which blockers would, as Yost said, "veil" the runner. Against Illinois on this day they didn't produce anything ex-cept pathetically short gains. Meanwhile, Grange caught his breath on the sideline while his father and the crowd watched him slump-ing in his chair, leather helmet still strapped onto his head. Grange squinted at the Wolverines running their tiresome plays as the half came to its closing seconds.

CHEE-HEE, CHEE-HA, CHEE-HA-HA-HA
ILLINOIS, ILLINOIS, ILLINOIS!

During the break the crowd paced excitedly through the cramped walkways, the underbelly of the red brick and mortar, and they would make their way to the colonnade, where even with the peo-ple joyfully buzzing about Grange it was impossible not to succumb to melancholia. Memorial Stadium had been officially dedicated the day before. Memorial, a stately structure of rust-colored bricks and white columns, looked like a midwestern interpretation of the ancient Greek stadia. Through the success of his teams (scores of conference championships and mythical national championships), fund-raising efforts, and Grange's popularity, Robert Zuppke could take much of the credit for building the $2 million fortress. Building football stadiums had become a popular trend on college campuses, and it seemed as if every school was asking its alums, many flush with cash in the booming economy, to contribute. Illinois wanted to keep up with Yale and the University of Chicago. The stadium had taken three years to build. On each side of the structure, about halfway up, were two long corridors, each with a double row of columns, each column bearing the name of one individual, student or graduate, who had lost his life in the Great War. The people were wandering in it now, a part of its pain and glory. Lives lost. A football stadium built. *Read the name on the column,* people would whisper. Carved into the Bedford limestone were the names of the dead, and then people would turn, north or south, looking through the column rows, and it felt like they went to haunting infinity.

Inside the locker room the Michigan players got an earful. Yost was known for his rants. "God intended ye to be a football player. He made ye big. He made yer muscles strong. He gave ye good health and endowed ye with all the attributes of Hercules. But ye're a-playin' out there like a wooden Indian in front of a cigar store! Are ye goin' t' get me naow? I'm goin' to ding ye in the slats — I'm goin' t' nail ye to the cross! I'm goin' t' hootcha-ma-cootchy down the field for a touchdown, y' know! Listen to Yost, y' know, and ye'll be a man!"

But it didn't matter how Yost or Little arranged his men; it was Grange whom the people now admired. With his breakaway speed and infinite moves, he was making game strategy a moot point and erasing the existing legacy of plodding, scrumlike football. The game was only half over and the great Fielding Yost was already making plans to succeed Coach Little and redeem his beloved Michigan's reputation.

After taking their seats, the fans began their applause as the men emerged from the brick-lined locker rooms for the second half. To frantic cheering Grange ambled onto the field. E. A. Batchelor, a syndicate reporter whose story would be carried in the *New York Herald Tribune* among other publications, would write what everyone was thinking: "The only way to stop him is to use shotguns, lassoes and hand grenades, and then forfeit the game."

After a first down on some short running plays it was Grange's turn to get the ball again, and again he was loose, darting 35 yards, and to Zuppke's delight, he cut back. Illinois drove to the Michigan 28-yard line. After Grange had a pass grounded (much like a punt) in the end zone, Michigan punted, and after a couple of plays Red took the ball and jogged for 11 yards and an easy score. The crowd screamed, knowing that they were witnessing a moment of immortal beauty. Illinois 33, Michigan 7.

In the press box the typewriters were getting a workout. L. H. Northard of the *Detroit Free Press*: "When histories are written on the feats of redheaded warriors, Grange must be given his place with those old heroes, Richard the Lionhearted, Frederick Barbarossa, and Eric the Red."

At the end of the third quarter, Illinois had the ball again and Grange was flicking short passes. As the quarter ended, the Illini had the ball, Grange making a 20-yard strike to M. R. Leonard, who wriggled in for a TD. The score was now 39–7; soon Michigan added 7 points in a futile comeback, the game ticking down its remaining seconds.

Grange finished with 402 yards — 212 rushing, 64 passing, and 126 on kickoff returns. He had intercepted two passes. He had run for five touchdowns and thrown a sixth. *Six touchdowns! Against Michigan?*

The crowd, the coaches, the press had witnessed the greatest ever performance in college sports because of the setting, the opponent, and mostly the way Grange ran. "It reads like a fairy tale," wrote F. H. Young of the *Bloomington (IL) Pantagraph*. The happily-ever-after part was yet to be determined.

After the game the Wolverines gathered themselves. They had not lost a game since 1921. Little later revealed that at first he thought to himself, "'There goes our season.' But, strangely, my kids didn't let down." Proving Grange's excellence, Michigan went on to beat Wisconsin, 21–0; Minnesota, 13–0; Northwestern, 27–0; and Ohio State, 16–6. During the 1924 season they would become known as the "Comeback Team," but Little would not remain with the team for long. When the Wolverines sank into their train seats after the Illinois game, Yost prattled on about the disaster and couldn't help but see Little with sadness and contempt. Little shrunk within him-

self, repeating, "When we win, it's Yost's team; when we lose, it's Little's." Three years later, Grange's rhythmic tromp through Michigan
still haunted Little. He wrote to Yost, "I wish you would tell your
publicity man not to connect my name only with having improperly
set the team against Grange and Illinois."

Despite the headlines, which screamed "GRANGE RUNS WILD;
GRANGE THRILLS CROWD," the humble Grange deflected the accolades. He would rather talk about his blockers. "Blocking is the
toughest job on a football field, and you get . . . absolutely no pats on
the back, no headlines." Grange believed that men who thought too
highly of themselves were punished. He liked to tell a story about a
high school player who wanted the glory, who wanted to score every touchdown, and whose teammates taught him a lesson by not
blocking so the other team could beat the shit out of the boy. Within
the chaos and the brutality there was a code of selflessness, and it
was a culture that Red Grange didn't like to cross, but the writers
didn't pay attention to that selfless bunk. The reporters were filing
their stories, many of which would be replayed in the thousands of
other papers across the country, and trying to figure out an angle
on this kid. For the writers who had seen the game, he was for real
and they were describing him in the most florid language imagin-
able, but Damon Runyon and the rest of the elite New York scribes
weren't so sure. Walter Camp, who was in ill health, was making
train reservations to witness Grange against Chicago three Satur-
days away. Grantland Rice, the premier sports columnist of his day,
had been covering the Army–Notre Dame game for the *New York
Herald Tribune*. It would become an enduring fiction that Rice saw
Grange's performance and gave him the Galloping Ghost nickname
(that would come soon enough), but Grannie had an alibi; he was in
the process of writing the most famous sports lead ever: "Outlined
against a blue-gray October sky, the four horsemen rode again. In
dramatic lore they were known as famine, pestilence, destruction,
and death. These are only aliases. Their real names are Stuhldreher, Miller, Crowley, and Layden." Maybe Grannie, looking at the
wire reports, wearing his omnipresent gray fedora, had picked the
wrong game to cover. He would need to venture to the Middle West
and meet Red Grange.

History has moments of collision. Ideas, economics, and behavior fight with each other. After the bloodshed the people go in a different direction. As the people left Memorial Stadium that October day, no one realized that Red Grange had just initiated one of these collisions. Inside, Red felt redemption. He had proved to everyone that he could compete with and excel against the greatest dynasty in the country. He was still too young to comprehend what the game meant to American sports fans and what his increasing fame would do to him. His naiveté was endearing but also dangerous. A group of old-time Illini boosters burst into the locker room searching for him. Grange stood in the corner, his back to the mob, getting dressed, then quietly escaped to Champaign's Virginia Theatre for a postgame movie. With this one performance, Red Grange had created a lasting mystique for himself and secured Robert Zuppke's coaching legacy. After the papers were published the next day his name would be on the lips of America. But as great as Grange and the Michigan game turned out to be, it was only the first baby step in creating something more profound. It was at the Virginia Theatre where Red would meet an unusual man of extraordinary abilities who would use Red Grange's talent to change American sports forever.

3

||||||||||||||||||||||||

C. C. Pyle

CHARLES C. PYLE

THE VIRGINIA THEATRE was Red's place of escape. Out there — off the field; away from Zup's Sunday chalk talks, the needy reporters, and the farm-girl coeds — was something bigger and less understandable, something visible but unexplained. Boys on city streets were strung out on paregoric. Rural bandits were sticking up motorists and crushing their skulls with baseball bats; Negroes were to blame, according to the papers, but Red Grange knew just enough to be suspicious of the crap the newspapermen came up with. He used to play with the black kids on Wheaton's east side. "There'd be about twenty guys, and I'd be the only white kid. They took me in."

Somehow, sitting in the Virginia Theatre and looking straight into Marion Davies's eyes took Red away from the exhaustion of his own celebrity, the flurry of need that seemed to follow him everywhere. The Virginia was a movie palace completed in 1921 and designed by the "Picture Palace Gothic" master C. Howard Crane. Red had a piddling $55 a month on which to live, but he needed only 30¢ to enter the luxurious escape of the Virginia Theatre. Through the front door he passed by the stained-glass exit signs, the granite fireplaces, the maize columns, the green trim, the fresh-cut flowers, and an organist humped over the glossy white Wurlitzer, along with the Virginia Orchestra tuning their instruments. As it turned out, admission to the Virginia was gratis for Red. All of the football players were comped by some nice — but rather mysterious — fella named Charles C. Pyle, the theater's manager. Red would nod to him whenever he saw him; Charlie, eyes twinkling, would smile back. Charles C. Pyle, the manager of the Virginia Theatre, was loquacious, debonair, and clever. His brain was like a lightning storm of ideas, most of them illegal. He was about nine months, a year tops, from being thrown out of Champaign, Illinois, for yet another scam. He was looking for his next one. When Red Grange came into the Virginia Theatre, Charlie — an old vaudeville man — sized him up immediately. Grange was the sort of athletic idol who was relentlessly likable, shy, and malleable. Charlie was already devising a way to approach the boy. Pyle, a football fan and a voracious newspaper reader, could tell Grange was an obedient fella. Charlie, who had a genius for looking into the future, already had a scheme cooking in his brain. Red didn't seem so hot in the smarts department so Charlie would need to lay out something nice and simple for this kid.

Charlie was the sort of guy who pushed his smile on you, one of those smiles that is hard to believe in and makes you feel guilty that you can't quite grasp why you don't believe in it, but it still makes you feel good. He had the appearance of success. Rumor had it that Charlie had built, lost, and was building another fortune, but the reality was much more complicated. This was, after all, the era of another famous Charles, Charles Ponzi. Of course, most people didn't know Pyle's darker side. Sure, Charlie Pyle stood out in Champaign, a college town with tweedy professors and students with clothes mail-ordered from Sears. Charlie, an oak of a man, had canary-colored hair, which was barbered almost every day, and a small mustache that would be made unpopular by Hitler in about ten years. Although he was in his late thirties when he arrived in Champaign, he carried a walking cane and wore spats. His hand-tailored clothes, in which he resembled a Rockefeller, were often bought on layaway. Charlie believed that if you strolled around the world as if you owned it, pretty soon you probably would. It had already worked for the theater. Although his ownership of the Virginia was in serious dispute and causing him scandalous concern, he was still controlling the place from the Virginia's main office, the one painted maroon with low-slung wooden beams looking out to West Park Street and the theater's garish grand sign, VIRGINIA THEATRE, blaring in candy red.

Building the theater had been Charlie's crowning achievement to date and the perfect testament to his dubious ways. Charlie's education was substandard, his qualifications well suited for a barkeep or a Bible salesman. He favored women, performers usually, whom most men would find too dangerous to touch. His first wife was a vaudevillian. (He deserted her and his daughter after going broke.) His second wife, Martha Russell, was also an actress. He made films with her (even shooting in Mexico, where he was put in jail by Pancho Villa), but in typical fashion he brought in investors, and crashed again, and the couple split. Pyle quickly found someone else, a twenty-seven-year-old looker named Effie, a woman who had two kids and had been abandoned by her husband. Their union would last a long time, but Charlie was hardly ever around. Champaign was not far (but far enough) from Charlie's Chicago apartment on East End Avenue, where he lived with long-suffering Effie and her teenage kids, near the Jackson Park Golf Course, amid second-generation German, Irish, English, and Danish immigrants. Chicago's South Shore was a former truck farm that had been subdivided for apartments, all crammed close enough together that Charlie could hear his working-stiff neighbors — teachers, salesmen, janitors, and managers, or more accurately assistant managers. Charlie gorged on the carnal pleasures of the city, and yet he spent most of his working time in smaller burgs, like Kokomo, Indiana, and Decatur and Champaign, Illinois.

After Charlie Pyle's 135-mile train ride to Champaign, he would unpack his suitcase at the Inman Hotel, a new six-story place on the corner of University Avenue and Walnut Street, where the sportswriters laid their heads. He would spend some of his working hours at the Rialto Theatre, which he managed, booking movies and vaudeville acts. Around town it was easy to spot Charlie, but what made anyone trust him was that he was a regular fellow, not some high hat, but a guy with Madame Nicotine dangling from his lips and a ready grin, someone you could trust not to blab some indiscretion to the wife. He was a daily fixture in the barbershop where his hair (short on the sides, slicked back) and mustache were given the royal treatment. From the barber's chair he would listen to the laborious chitchat.

Didja hear about the cow over at the university?

World record holder for milk production. Announced it yesterday.

You don't say! How much?

Eighteen thousand eight hundred and forty-seven and four-tenths pounds of milk.

You don't say!

Charlie would listen and hold court, too, clamoring to some town official or banker about a show at one of his theaters:

What a Wife Learned . . . *About a woman who went seeking more than marriage could give. It's a terrific show! Terrific!* he would say, using his favorite word. *Bring the lovely wife, or the girlfriend. Here are two free passes, my friend.*

Champaign was gripped with optimism, and in some ways Charlie was emblematic of it. The Athens of rural Illinois! With the influx of residents and the frenzy of construction, Champaign gurgled with an optimistic spirit. With eased admission standards, money pouring in from state coffers, and the illusion of endless prosperity, university towns throughout the Midwest were experiencing similar excitement. A person like Charlie Pyle, an out-of-towner, did not engender suspicion as much as reinforce the feeling that Champaign was an extraordinary place with fresh air *and* sophistication. Charlie also bragged about his "large experience" in the sale and marketing of bonds, chatting up his company at 20 North LaSalle Street in Chicago. Besides his supposed financial experience, he also talked up his work as an "experienced real estate broker" and his knowledge of the entertainment industry, including his love of musical instruments. (He sold counterfeit Bartola organs.) Charlie would drop some names, which was not difficult because his first wife was the funny and chubby actress Dorothy Fischer, sister to stage and film star Margarita Fischer ("a lovely brunette of a Spanish type" was how the papers described her; she was usually cast as an "ethnic": a Gypsy, a Mexican, an Italian, a Chinawoman, a Negress). Charlie's daughter, Kathrine, had bit parts in some silent movies and he would brag about her, too, but Charlie left out the part about being a deadbeat father: his former sister-in-law, Margarita, supported his ex-wife and child. He also didn't mention the string of theater people who had threatened to literally tar and feather him for one thing or another.

The picture shows were the rage, and whole towns — except for the religious fanatics — would show up to watch a movie. The old and generally small vaudeville houses could not accommodate the demand, so there was a hot market in building enormous movie theaters — palaces, they called them — sometimes with two thousand seats. Between 1914 and 1922 at least four thousand new the-

aters opened in the United States, most of them palaces. It was a
pretty good bet that in a town of ten thousand the palace could hold
a quarter of the population — and the whole town would visit the
theater once a week. The Virginia had 1,525 plush seats. For Champaign's citizens, the Virginia was already a landmark. Whatever you
might say about Charlie Pyle, he had an amazing imagination. From
the outside the Virginia Theatre looked like a Jewish temple with
a squat dome made from midwestern bricks, dredged from prairie
rivers; inside, its mishmash of styles was influenced by Renaissance
Italy and Spain. Pyle bragged: "Two nations of Southern Europe
have been drawn upon by Architect Crane. The theatre's exterior is
of Italian design; the interior is Spanish." And Pyle just couldn't resist. "As handsome as money can make, in the words of the architect," he said. Charlie must have had a good laugh with H. E. Mc-
Nevin, his banker friend, over that one because Charlie had reneged
on paying Mr. Crane. Charlie didn't always feel it was necessary to
settle his bills.

Sucking on vanilla and bitter sweets or malted-milk chocolates,
the ticket buyers would stare at the intricate plasterwork, featuring shields and heraldic symbols; the busts of the Spanish adven-
turers Cortés, Hernandez, and Alvarado; and the Christian arms of
Ferdinand and Isabella; their sticky fingers would touch the marble walls as they stared up toward the ceiling dome, which was finished in silver leaf. The style was also a business calculation, not
just a stylistic dream state. Many theaters were fitting into a cor-
porate aesthetic — thus the Spanish Colonial Revival Fox Theatre
in Los Angeles and its litter of copycats — and there was a decent
chance Charlie was looking to sell the theater to a studio chain and
pocket some quick and easy cash. On opening night sixteen hundred people paid 30¢ to walk across the red-tiled floors and watch
the premieres of *Tol'able David*, starring Richard Barthelmess, and
a Buster Keaton short, *The Boat*. The Virginia Symphony Orchestra
played along with the movies. And it would become more exciting
every week: Charlie booked lots of acts — the Marx Brothers, Buster
Keaton, Red Skelton, and W. C. Fields, with whom Pyle was often
compared.

But Charlie was in the midst of a legal battle over the Virginia,
having been accused of being a con man. Charlie had always been

quick on his feet. Why, C. C. Pyle (born March 26, 1882) could recount the time in Boise City when he was dead broke and he convinced someone — all because of the confident way he carried himself — to give him some lumber, and then he persuaded a local
carpenter (again on his good name) to build a movie house. A town
resident scrutinizing all of the action decided to take a half share
for $2,500. The theater opened with all debts paid. Pyle peddled
his remaining interest for another $2,500. Charlie, clever Charlie,
had not put down a penny. Charlie liked big cities, especially the
numerous lovelies inhabiting them, but the confidence game would
always take him to small-town America, a place he knew well. By
pure good fortune he landed in Champaign, Illinois, home of the
University of Illinois, its legendary football program, and rising national star, Red Grange.

Terrific!

So many men — too many — have grand ambitions. Most never live
up to their big ideas because circumstances get in the way. Sometimes there is no natural talent, their flaws do not fit their dreams, or
they have bad luck. Failure can even, and often, result from geography: small-town men with big ideas do not — usually do not — make
their mark on a national stage. Throughout his life Pyle, a small-
town boy himself, would carry an understanding of rural values and
how to exploit them. Pyle grew up in a clapboard house, cater-cor-
nered from Episcopalian and Presbyterian churches, which was not
so unusual in Delaware, Ohio, a town of churches. From the Catholic church down by the Olentangy River to Ohio Wesleyan's chapel
on the hill, young Charlie was raised among steeples, and underneath them all was a community with a serious love for liquor. But
now where could he go from Champaign? He could start another
theater in another town, live in some little hotel room and do his
unique brand of labor, but it was all so tiresome in the end. He was
now in his early forties, still young and energetic and ready for his
own personal grand stage.

Pyle would see Red Grange in the Virginia Theatre. The boy
was there to find some peace, but there was no escaping the buzz
he created. With his new suit (someone had set him up with a hab-
erdasher) and Vaselined locks parted down the middle, Red looked

like Joe College sitting there: the steady murmur of voices as people milled around the ticket booth, the damp college broads, all dolled up and looking like the nuts, giggling underneath Cortés, too shy to sit next to the football star and Red too solemn to revel in the harassment. Charlie sucked on his cigarette, standing in the dimly lit balcony, the magenta paint making it even darker.

Charlie loved that Red was in his den. Bless his luck! It was a sign from the Promised Land. He needed to take Red under his well-tailored wing. It would be easy: no complex pitch or promises of percentages or other economic gobbledygook. Just like the vaudeville troupes he used to manage, Charlie would create an entertainer out of the kid. Football would be just a sort of tool to make Red even more popular. Red Grange would be bigger than college football! Charlie planned to make promises of fast money because that is what a kid from the sticks would want, but Pyle had a much grander plan in the back of his mind. Charlie closed his eyes and thought it through, considering the best time to strike. It would have to be soon. Maybe his dear old daddy, the preacher, long dead, was up there looking out for him after all.

4

||||||||||||||||||||||||||

Is He Dead?

RED GRANGE CARRYING THE BALL AGAINST
THE UNIVERSITY OF CHICAGO

O N A COLD AND WINDY DAY on Chicago's South Side, Red Grange and his Illini teammates stepped through two immense black wooden doors, which looked as if they had been pillaged from a medieval castle, and entered the University of Chicago's Stagg Field. A stream of black soot shot into the sky from a nearby smokestack. The crowd was hostile. The players just squinted at the four immense turrets at each corner of the thirty-three-thousand-seat stadium, smack in the middle of the gray Gothic campus, and prepared themselves for battle. The University of Chicago, nestled in leafy Hyde Park, was a center of college athletics because of its iconic coach, Amos Alonzo Stagg. Thousands of people were milling about on the outside, trying to get inside Stagg Field; scalpers were earning $20 a ticket. Some students balanced on a wall with megaphones, recounting what was happening inside.

As the Illini warmed up, they faced the intimidating Stagg — cotton-haired, the son of a cobbler — who stood, erect as a fence post, on the field named in his honor. "We're not out there to stop Grange. We will attack! Then attack some more!" Stagg told his team. Of all the football minds in the nation, Stagg felt he had a plan to stop Red Grange, a player he regarded as the best he had ever seen. A. A. Stagg was a legendary tactician. Along with Fielding Yost, Knute Rockne, and Robert Zuppke, Stagg was one of the country's most influential football coaches. Grange was a riddle that the Chicago coach was anxious to solve. Stagg, muscularly solid despite his old age, was a former Yale Divinity School student who had come to Chicago in 1890 and promptly married a pretty coed. (She was known to sit in the stands and diagram plays and scout tendencies for her husband.) A supremely confident yet supremely self-critical man, he had left a religious calling because he felt that he was an uninspiring orator, a notion with which his players would disagree. Standing in the autumn wind without a hat or coat, he had what the *New York Times* described as "Spartan ruggedness," a description he undoubtedly loved since as a boy he had soaked up the classics while his Orange, New Jersey, neighbors drank themselves to death on beer. At practices Stagg, sixty-two, who had been named to the country's first All-American team, would put on a uniform and let the players tackle him, while he pointed out their mistakes.

Stagg knew that his defensive alignments could create problems for Red Grange. But while Grange coupled a natural ability with a fierce hunger on the field, Stagg's offensive strategy was riding on a smashing, yet underachieving, fullback named Austin McCarty, a sandy-haired, 176-pound block of a kid who had learned the game on a vacant lot with some local toughs. It was said that McCarty loved nightclubs almost as much as disfiguring his opponents, and to his coach's dismay, music and girls seemed more on his mind than crashing the line. Stagg had complained to five hundred alumni at a football dinner a couple of nights earlier that his gruff fullback was "an enigma. I cannot understand his spirit. He had not even the loyalty to be here tonight." The previous season the Maroons had been in a tough game with Purdue when a frustrated McCarty yelled, "Gimme that football," punctuated with a couple of cuss words. On the next play he ran 20 yards and led the team to a touchdown, but after Stagg heard about the profanity, he benched the boy for the rest of the season. On Friday morning before the Illinois game a delegation of desperate Chicago alumni went to McCarty's home. McCarty explained to them that he hadn't bothered with the dinner because Stagg had upbraided him the previous year for not showing enough "pep." The alumni pleaded with McCarty to meet with Stagg, and Mac conceded and ambled over to the Stagg residence, where he met with the Old Man for an hour. No one knows what they said, but the thirty-three thousand people today could tell McCarty was wearing his game face.

Having taken note of the Michigan-Illinois game three weeks earlier, Stagg would take a less bold, but smarter, strategy into this game. The Old Man had been hammering his boys all week about Grange, who was averaging 10 yards a carry. "Did you ever see

Grange score without the ball?" he would say cunningly, expressing the exact opposite strategy of Fielding Yost and the Wolverines. As the Chicago team surveyed the scene, they knew this was an important game. Not only was Illinois their archrival, but they could also see a bunch of former Maroons football players behind their bench. These were the men of the Order of the C, and their capes, which were one-inch-thick woolen blankets, were decorated with a large letter *C*; anyone could tell the football players because their capes were decorated with white stars. They belonged to a society of men who had, wrote Stagg, "shown sacrifice, and devotion to the athletic honor for the University," and they had all gone through a ceremony in Reynolds Hall at which they received their blankets; escorted by other "C" men, they then marched into Mandel Hall, formed a semicircle, and sang "The Song of the C," as their fellow students clapped for them and — Stagg declaimed — they "passed out from our midst." The school's Gothic architecture had been chosen because the founders wanted the school to look and feel like Cambridge University, and Stagg was under orders to carry that feeling into athletics. It would be a place of ancient rites and rituals. Hearing of Grange's brilliance, the C Men had returned to watch him and to see how the Old Man would keep the boy in his place, how he would put iron in the Maroons.

For Stagg, the Illinois-Chicago game had broader implications than a Big Ten gold football. Although Stagg had a national reputation because he coached the Olympic track team and was able to put powerful Ivy League schools on his schedule, his small private school was of late losing its edge. While Zuppke refused to recruit — or, as coaches called it, "ivory hunt" — for players, with Illinois's relaxed admissions policies he had the luxury of thousands of students from which to choose. Stagg, at the smaller University of Chicago, had pioneered football's rise in the Midwest, changing the sport's landscape; as Knute Rockne said, "Western supremacy in football is a triumph of the middle class over the rich." Chicago's glory days weren't completely gone, and Stagg was using some semishady dealings to stay competitive — the C Men were promising jobs to high schoolers, and there was the regular boondoggle trip to Japan with the baseball team. Stagg might have been drowning in the rough waters of recruiting, but he could still coach, and he had never been afraid to innovate. In 1906, the first year the forward pass was legal, Stagg created sixty-four pass plays, and he dumbfounded the eastern press when his slick passing game embarrassed the once-mighty Princeton. But it was defense for which people said he had the most creative mind of any college coach. For this reason the reporters were referring to today's game as Red versus the Old Man.

For a coach who had so recently downed the mighty Michigan, Robert C. Zuppke seemed lost. Zuppke, always a little showy, had been lamenting about his team all week. Chicago outweighed his line by fifteen pounds a man. Zup had always liked small men who were swift so they could go outside and angle-block on his array of swing passes and trick plays. But that kind of game is all about timing, and practice had not been going well. After the Michigan game the Illini had beaten DePauw 45–0 and Iowa 36–0. Grange was rested against DePauw. Against the Hawkeyes Grange had carried the ball thirty-seven times, scoring twice and racking up 186 yards. *What was not to love?* Zuppke thought success was making his men chesty. When he tried to inspire them to tackle harder at practice after sluggish practice, they laughed under their breath. Champaign had become a circus — reporters and hangers-on invading the town — and his men were reacting poorly; they were going to movies and preening for the cameramen from the East. Lady writers were interviewing Grange, and one of them had affectionately put a pin on Zup's coat to give him good luck. *Curses!* Zup was superstitious. He wore several rings on his right hand during the season and he would move them from finger to finger, looking for the "right combination." So would it be bad luck to keep the pin or take it off? *Drat!* It was petrifying to play with luck! He kept it on.

From the opening play of the Chicago game, the Maroon blockers cleaved their way through the Illini as McCarty pounded through the Illinois line after them, usually carrying his clinging opponents for extra yards. McCarty, whom some described as a steamroller, would narrow his gray eyes and speed up at contact. Zuppke could appreciate what was happening. Most fans thought Stagg's offense was just a mass of people, but he angled his players at the point of attack. So that he wouldn't get banged up, Grange played in the secondary, but Chicago was tearing through the Il-

linois line. It didn't help that the Illini were missing Wally McIlwain, their excellent open-field blocker and tackler, who had suffered a broken right hand and cracked ribs. McCarty did his dirty
work right down to the Illini 4-yard line — "the shadows of their
goalposts creeping up their back," wrote Walter Camp, who, deathly
sickness or no, had come to Chicago to see Grange. The Illinois fans
were silent, but then McCarty fumbled just before scoring. They
cheered. But pinned back, Illinois decided to kick. Again McCarty
hammered them, eventually driving for a score. In the second quarter the Maroons scored on the first play, seemingly spelling doom
for Zuppke's troops. It was almost a reverse of the Michigan game
with McCarty now taking the role of Red Grange, except of course
Red ran with flair and McCarty resembled a bull. An upset was in
the works.

When Illinois had the ball, they were listless, confused, a step too
slow. Stagg had told Joe Pondelik, his star defender, to call defensive signals. The Maroons were doing the unusual: shifting, adjust-
ing their defense before the ball was snapped. Every time Grange
ran with the ball, he was stopped and pummeled. *Don't hit him too
high or too low,* they were coached. *Lower your shoulders, hit him
right below the belt line.* "What, you again?" Grange would say to
Pondelik, who even with a gimpy knee was giving Red some good
pops.

In the stands the fans were whirring. "I don't believe I have ever
seen rooters so delirious with joy as were the Chicago supporters at
the surprising elevation of power in their team," said the game's referee. "The stands were in tumult all the time." The crowd packed
every inch of Stagg Field. Red knew he had to will himself to a
higher plane. The fans watched as Red lifted himself in a conscious
effort to carry his underperforming team, and they watched as he
ran a little harder, hit with a little more vengeance. The sounds of
bodies and groans were reverberating toward them.

Illinois had the ball. Grange went for 5. Grange again. Grange
around the end for a touchdown as the small section of Illini fans
cheered. Thanks to Red they were coming back. Chicago, forgoing
its ball-control strategy, decided to kick off. Grange was handed the
ball almost every play because Zup always figured if Red got the
ball thirty times the Illini would win. But the Maroons' defense,

which was specially created for him, stifled the man because, despite Grange's effort, he was not always given a chance to start. The defenders were quicker off the ball and they were pruning the Illini plays. But there was more to it. The offensive line was told to smack the Illinois line, exhaust and debilitate them, break them down so they couldn't block for Grange. Chicago possessed the ball again and the Maroons scored, making it 21 to Illinois's 7, forcing the Illini faithful to bury their faces in their frigid hands. It had to be over. But it wasn't.

After the Chicago kickoff, Grange went around end for 25 yards, running with more determination than Zup had ever seen. Grange's brown boots, which looked like work boots and were as heavy, churned another 25 yards from a Britton pass. On the next play Grange faked a pass and went for 6 yards. It was time for some razzle-dazzle. Britton acted as if he was going to kick, and Grange squatted down, pretending to be the holder, but instead received the ball and shuffled it to Britton, who threw it to Chuck Kassell, who made a lateral pass to Grange, who strode 30 yards to the 4-yard line, making it a quadruple pass. It was Zuppke's ingenuity in action.

"Ever seen anything like that?" the reporters shouted.

No one had. They would have to get the newspaper artist to draw that up for the readers the next day.

Feeling his luck changing, Zuppke ripped off the good-luck charm from the lady writer and threw it away, and indeed his luck changed because on the next play Grange lashed his way for a touchdown, bringing Illinois to within 7. Red was doing it all by himself.

At halftime Walter Camp, sixty-five, the narrow-faced football dean who had helped author the rules for the game and who was responsible for handing out All-American honors, slumped in a chair at the edge of the Maroons' side of the field, near the pot fires burning on the sidelines to keep the VIPs warm. He said he had never seen so much offense crowded into a single half, calling Mc-Carty a "solid India rubber ball" and Grange "that streak of concentrated lightning [who] seemed to bear a charmed jacket and a pair of winged shoes." Westerners accused Camp of an East Coast bias in his All-American selections (Ring Lardner said Camp believed the United States was bounded on the west by Pennsylvania); today he was witnessing the dynamism of the Midwest style of play and the unquenchable thirst of the proletariat. It would be one of the last games he would see; Camp would be dead within four months.

Inside the locker rooms the trainers mended the players. Health would be sacrificed, but it would not be discussed. Injuries were a part of the game and the greatest players were always tough enough to play through them. Grange suffered concussion after concussion, sometimes several in one game, and yet he just weathered it. Red didn't think to complain. If he had a blackout he figured it was part of football. It was a game of toughness. The weak bowed out. The young men were told to refocus themselves from the brain trauma. The side effects were not known and winning the game was of prevailing importance. The trainers handed out strychnine and caffeine like candy. Cocaine would be injected into bleeding limbs, slowing the blood flow just long enough for the players to perform. If someone had a broken beak, Zup would laugh and tell him that a big nose interferes with peripheral vision.

In the Illinois locker room as the players were treated during halftime, Zuppke boiled. He thought his team was being outmuscled. He charged at Britton: "You're playing the Maroons like a piano — with your finger tips." Zup could be ridiculous and demeaning that way, but Britt could take it for the team. Strategy-wise Zup instructed his blue-clad boys that they would play a backfield box to contain McCarty. Zuppke hoped to God that Grange could pull them out of this mess, and that the team could go on to win the conference and repeat as national champions.

After the break the game went back and forth with punts and no gainers, the excitement building to a fever pitch. Early in the third quarter the Maroons did a quick kick, resulting in the Illini getting the ball on the 20-yard line. The Maroons were again destroying the left side of the Illini line. But Grange was able to take the ball through the Chicago right tackle, went out again, doubled back, and then, taking the course of the letter *S*, flew down the field for his third touchdown, a breathtaking 80-yard gallop. Herbert Reed of the Universal Service syndicate wrote, "Grange had started, had run, had completed his play, before the spectators could get their breath. Run after run he made, the exact duplicates of which, in method, I have never seen . . . the Maroon tacklers, visualizing now and then this ghost in gold and blue, mistook the shadow for substance, and again and again failed even so much as to lay a hand on him."

Sure, Red had gotten away for an amazing run, but most of the game was played in the head-knocking trenches where there was much groaning and crying out, spittle flying, bodies bruised. Franklin Gowdy, the Maroons' captain who would become an All-American at guard, was particularly effective in the increasingly bitter scrums. (With Stagg's support Gowdy had toyed with eligibility rules by sitting out a semester so he could play during the 1924 season.) Stagg sent player after player into the game: a Chicago player had a knee dislocated; in return, the Maroons would chop Grange's knees on one play, then they would go after his shoulder on another. They were hitting him at all angles. He stayed calm, not even showing his teeth; one in front had been broken in practice the week before. The Maroons went for his head, and they hit his Rawlings Can't-Come-Off head guard hard enough that his brain sloshed around, veins stretching, cells spewing chemicals, black dots splotching his vision. Concussions were epidemic — of 374 college football players surveyed in 1917, 44 percent had suffered at least one brain trauma; many had been knocked silly several times. Red had experienced repetitive concussions; back in high school he had been kicked in the head and was unconscious for forty-eight hours, not regaining his speech for ten days. Grange would never recall the fourth quarter of the Chicago game. Red wouldn't remember having the ball on his own 15-yard line, going for a wide-end run. Or when Britton went back, apparently to kick, but threw a pass to Grange instead, and Red, waiting out on the 35-yard line, nearly snagged the ball. He had a clear field, but the ball just rolled off his cold fingertips. With a couple of minutes to play, Britt called for a pass. Ray Gallivan shook his head and told him that Zup would never let them play again. "I'll take the blame," sighed Britt, who no matter the situation liked to treat a game as if he was playing with his friends in an Elgin sandlot. A Chicago end, rushing in to block the expected kick, spoiled the pass, almost intercepted it. Zuppke was steaming. Fortunately for Britton, on the next play he threw to Ray for a 15-yard gain. Then Britton, to Zuppke's relief, kicked out of danger.

In the final minute of play, Illinois got the ball back deep in its own territory. Grange made a long, beautiful run and he was going to score the winning TD. Red had carried his team and now he was going in for the winning score. Red had done it all with a severe concussion. The Illini faithful were happily astonished once again. But wait. A whistle tooted. Offensive holding. Ray Gallivan had blocked someone and fallen on the back of his legs. The Illinois players were hot at the chickenshit call and Britton was forced to punt away.

With seconds to the end of the contest, the teams lined up, Grange in his safety position, when he suddenly fell facedown. *Was 77 dead?* The six o'clock sun was fading, the bells of Mitchell Tower now tolling. When his teammates noticed their friend, gray and still, they carried him off the field, slapping him on the way. He had passed out from exhaustion and brain trauma; the manly thirst to sacrifice body and soul had been satisfied. Soon enough, the final gunshot indicated the end of the fury.

"I did not look for a soft game," said Red, his senses barely gathered, "and it wasn't a soft game. It was the toughest game of my life."

Red had gained a total of 300 yards and scored all three of Illinois's touchdowns. Once again Red had played what many would consider the game of a lifetime. But it was the Old Man who received many of the hosannas. "Mighty Harold 'Red' Grange, the phantom of Urbana, is in temporary eclipse and the age-old wizardry of A. A. Stagg is in the ascendancy," wrote the *Trib*. Red was already the victim of unrealistic expectations.

The tussle made McCarty — the driving, plunging, smashing 176 pounds of Irish humanity — into a Chicago sports legend as the writers christened him "Five Yards" McCarty in the papers, a moniker that would give him a lifetime of drinks in any Chicago bar.

Before leaving the field, Zup vented his frustration at Earl Britton. He confronted Britt about the risky late-game pass plays that could have cost (or won) the game. Britt and Zup had an uneasy relationship, mostly a lot of bluster. The psychology professor who profiled Zup's athletes told Coach never to praise him and always bear down on Britt because he could take it. During Britt's sophomore year Zup had told him that he could transfer to Michigan or another school and be a big star. Britt was the best kicker and full-back Zup had ever seen, but he would never be an All-American with Grange getting all the ink. Zup knew that Earl's grandparents had been sharecroppers and that his father was in and out of jobs, barely scraping by, so maybe going to another school would help his family in some way. "What would happen to Illinois?" Britt answered. "It would ruin the best team I have ever coached," Zup replied. Britt accepted his background role, but he was impish and was his own man. Sometimes when Zup was frustrated with the team, he regrettably would take it out on Britt. Mad about the loss to Chicago, he confronted Britt with one of the biggest insults he could muster: "Who in the hell do you think you are, a pro?"

Now, standing in the locker room after the contest, which many were describing as the most vicious the country had ever seen, Zuppke was despondent. An undisputed conference championship was gone. "It was a case of a frantic team against a complacent one," he complained. "Now you know why I sound gloomy; that stuff the papers call 'gloom' is plain sense. The Illinois line was not used to meeting a fast charging line; that big Chicago team got the jump on them at the start." Zuppke couldn't resist a gibe at the Old Man, adding, "On offense it was the old style game against the new." Stagg, gracious and relieved, came to Zuppke in the locker room.

"That's a fine team you have there."

"And yours is a fine one." Zuppke offered his hand and a back-handed compliment. "I suppose I ought to congratulate you; this seems to be regarded as a victory for you."

Stagg had wanted to meet Grange, but no one introduced him and Red was pretty out of it. Stagg told a reporter on his way out, "My, he certainly played a splendid game." In his autobiography, *Touchdown,* published in 1927, Stagg would write: "Taken all in all — the expected one-sided victory, the over-shadowing reputation of Grange, the irresistible sweep of Chicago from the kick-off, the tremendous upset in the first quarter, the seesaw in the second quarter, Grange's magnificent response in which he brought the Illinois score from 0 to 21 virtually single-handed, the breathless dead-lock in the final quarter, with both teams narrowly denied the winning touchdown, made it one of the greatest football dramas played on any field."

Zuppke explained it this way: "In the Michigan and Iowa games everything was too easy. We looked for a tough game, but we anticipated nothing like we encountered at Chicago."

On the train back home, Zuppke gathered the troops and to lighten the mood said, "If nothing else, you have added years to the life of the Old Man." Privately, he told his coaches that the Illini needed to recruit bigger boys.

Back in New York, Damon Runyon, the chain-smoking sportswriter, read the accounts coming over the wires. He realized Grange's significance, his ability to carry his team against perennially well-coached and nails-tough Chicago. Like the rest of his eastern colleagues, he wanted to bear witness on this man. "Grange must be a wonderful player," he said. "He must be all that his record indicates. It is to be regretted that the East will have no opportunity of seeing him in action." On that one Runyon would be proved wrong.

Some writers said it was Grange's finest performance because he had to carry his team. "There are many football players who can play havoc when the going is good," said the *Herald-Examiner's* Warren W. Brown. "When you find one who can do this when everything, everyone else has failed, then you have made a discovery."

Grantland Rice, helping to create Red's permanent Galloping Ghost nickname, would come up with some of his poetry:

> *A streak of fire, a breath of flame,*
> *Eluding all who reach and clutch;*
> *A gray ghost thrown into the game*
> *That rival hands may never touch;*
> *A rubber bounding, blasting soul,*
> *Whose destination is the goal —*
> *Red Grange of Illinois.*

Chicago had ravaged the Illini. No yard was easy, and yet Grange scored three touchdowns, carrying the Illini to a tie on his muscular shoulders. Banged and bruised, back-weary and leg-tired, Grange could barely practice that week with Minnesota looming on Saturday. The whole team was in a world of hurt, but Zup felt the squad needed to be driven so it wouldn't lose its focus. Bob Zuppke was creative but to his detriment, he often saw his players as just colors on the end of his brush. He was driving them hard, too hard, for a game against a weak team like Minnesota. Just three days after the Chicago game, Zuppke had them scrimmage rather than the usual rest. Then the next day it was another stiff drill — second squad pitted against the regulars. The Minnesota contest was an important game in the conference battle: if Illinois didn't win, Chicago would take the conference championship, and after the battle they had just gone through Zuppke didn't want to give the ultimate bragging rights to A. A. Stagg. Short of taking a razor strop to his charges, Zup tried to get them motivated by calling them "double-jackasses," but they didn't seem to have it in their eyes. The wind flapped his trousers, and his old wrinkled cap fell over his eyes, hiding his despair. "I know there have been occasions when, during the heat and stress of preparing for an important game, some of my boys have been almost mad enough at me to swing at my chin. If anyone ever did that, he'd be busy for a while," thought Zuppke, who had lost his team somehow; even Grange, his favorite pupil, seemed worn down. The disappointment of not beating Chicago, of not winning another championship, was a grand letdown.

Five days after the Chicago game, Coach Zuppke; several assistant coaches; Matt Bullock, the trainer — a quiet man whom Zuppke had promoted from assistant janitor, paying for his massage and medical training — and thirty University of Illinois football players left for Minneapolis, but they stopped in Chicago for yet another workout, leaving at dusk for Minneapolis. In Minneapolis the hometown Gophers were hungering for an upset as they read in the papers: "Grange, the incomparable, one of the greatest halfbacks of all time, is to football what Babe Ruth is to baseball and Jack Dempsey is to boxing — in a class by himself . . . Minnesota's football followers have conceded victory to Illinois, but that is merely incidental. They desire to see Grange do his stuff."

Zuppke had never been defeated in Minneapolis, and he was the bane of Gophers fans' existence. They had some history. The season of 1916 saw Zup beat Minnesota's so-called wonder team, and the Gophers were *still* reeling. They had been so confident of success back in '16 that they had designed a throne — decorated with stars and stripes — from which Walter Camp watched the game.

Ring Lardner had predicted that Illinois would earn a moral victory if it held the Gophers to fewer than 49 points, but Zuppke gave his wacky but inspirational "I am Louis XIV; after me, the deluge!" speech, which had taken the players' minds off the supposedly impossible task at hand. The Illini scored an upset, 14–9, ruining Minnesota's championship bid. Still, in the buildup profiles for this game the ever so accommodating Minnesota scribes described Zup with begrudging respect. "This, for the most part, has been the work of a gnarled, little man who never played football in college. He went to Wisconsin and sat in the stands with the rest of the undergraduates, lending his voice to the cheers when told to, but watching and studying at all times . . . He knows football; it is his life. Several years ago he was sounded out on a proposition to coach Columbia University. 'How would you feel about suggestions made by some of the alumni who might want to attend practice several times a week?' he was asked. 'I'd have them thrown off the field,' was Zup's reply. He didn't get the job, but he remained Bob Zuppke." And this year, of course, he had Grange, the superman of the gridiron and the leading scorer of the conference with 72 points. "I'm making no predictions on the game," Zuppke declared at a Minneapolis restaurant. When asked if Grange would be able to accept any speaking engagements in the Twin Cities, Coach Zuppke replied: "We will be unable to talk. Grange is up here to play football, not to talk." Two hundred Illinois rooters were cheering in the background; Zuppke would describe the atmosphere as a "co-ed carnival." Waiters were flipping coins for the right to see who would serve Red.

Said Grange: "I'm only a second stringer when it comes to public speaking. Anyway, I think the public prefers to see me play football rather than to hear me talk. Reckon I make a better impression on the gridiron. You know, I've got to keep up with my classroom duties, although a lot of people seem to think that it is all football and little education with me."

Red was always unsure of the tone in which he should reply to reporters' questions. He worried about missteps in grammar and pronunciation.

By all rights the Minnesota Gophers didn't have a chance. They were a middling team — they had won their first two games, tied Wisconsin and Iowa State, and lost to Iowa and Michigan — led by Coach Bill Spaulding, whose only claim to fame was having attended Bob Zuppke's coaching school. Minnesota's best player, Clarence Schutte, had a thick layer of tape around his torso to protect, and lend some kind of support for, his balky back.

They would play the foregone conclusion (the Illini were favored by three touchdowns) in a new $700,000 gridiron amphitheater, the gift of students, faculty, alumni, and "friends of the institution" to the University of Minnesota, which had built it in eight months. It would be formally presented to the Gophers' school Saturday, when the huge horseshoe would be dedicated to the "Sons of Minnesota" who had fallen in the service of their country. The ceremony would be broadcast using a powerful "loud speaking apparatus," but dedicating the stadium was merely a side issue for the lucky mob of forty thousand who were on hand to see Grange. The pregame atmosphere was light and gay. Ten minutes before kickoff, sorority girls were going nuts as the cross-country boys came running into the stadium. The runners were representing each sorority, and the girls were cheering because if their runner won they would get a silver trophy for their house. These were not grand, poetic gestures on a par with those of the real football schools.

The Orange and Blue were fluid on their first possession. They flawlessly passed and ran down the field for 58 yards and a touchdown, but on every down Minnesota was making the Illini pay. McIlwain, who was wearing so many braces and bandages his teammates were calling him Sir Lancelot, hobbled out of the game with an injured knee, and Dick Hall, the team's rich kid, was helped to the sideline with an injured collarbone. When Grange carried the ball, the *Herald-Examiner*'s Warren W. Brown couldn't help but notice the punishment he was enduring. "When they hit Red, they HIT him, and the word 'hit' is used for all its meaning," he wrote. And when Minnesota had the ball, Grange's sore body was being forced into the fray. There had been talk this season that Red wasn't a complete player, but he was showing the critics that he could play excellent defense. "Grange, Saturday, was as great on defense as Clarence Darrow ever was," wrote Brown.

They were rototilling Grange late the whole game, even toothing his skin with bites. Grange could feel the increasingly brutal shots and he weathered them, but he was beginning to understand that his abilities might be fleeting. In the end he might just end where he started: a poor kid from Wheaton with some newspaper clips about his athletic glory. In the third period he intercepted a pass; on the runback somebody grabbed him and threw him out of bounds, and then another Gopher came and finished him. The team was penalized for piling on. It took a few minutes for Red to get up. They had half-killed him, the home crowd cheering, the Illini fans in shock. He hobbled into the game and threw an 11-yarder, everyone thinking he was OK, but he was performing on pure guts. He tried another pass but his shoulder had such a sharp pain that he couldn't throw the ball, preferring to be driven into the turf for a 9-yard loss. Just like that a football career can end. That is football's cost and the reason it draws people to it. Red was starting to realize his susceptibility and that the forces around him, the men in charge of his life, controlled his fate. Red wondered if they always had his best interests in mind. Grand ideals are well and good but Red Grange was still the son of a cop from Wheaton, Illinois. Zup finally yanked him, Red's arm hanging limp; his shoulder blade had been torn loose. The forty thousand people in the stadium rose and cheered the All-American. In the six conference games Grange had played, he had scored thirteen touchdowns, and he would end the season leading the Big Ten in scoring for the second straight year.

For four periods of rough-and-tumble football, man after man of the Illini limped off the field, until Zuppke was forced to trudge slowly and sadly across the field to shake hands with Coach Spaulding, whose nose seemed to go in a 45-degree angle. "You knocked Grange into the drums," Zuppke muttered, bitterly. Had Zup's lack of game strategy and reluctance to recruit big players destroyed Red Grange?

The final score was 20–7.

The *Minneapolis Daily Star* headlined: "HISTORY-MAKING GAME STUNS FOOTBALL WORLD."

Privately, Grange wept bitterly over the downfall of his team, but publicly Red would not put up with any bellyaching about the sons of bitches who had cheap-shotted him. The reporters and fans never understood anything. They watch the game but don't see it, how a play breaks down because of a missed block. The reporters were starting to badger him, but he wouldn't complain about his tiring line or make any other excuses. Charles Johnson, the *Minneapolis Daily Star* columnist, reflexively, parochially, snapped: "Minnesota football players and fans can get ready to hear all kinds of wails from Illinois rooters about the rough treatment they gave 'Red' Grange Saturday afternoon. The highly touted star, who was stopped on almost every attempt to carry the ball, is lost for the season to his team because two Gophers near the end of the third quarter hit him hard. Already outsiders are saying that the Gophers ruined Grange."

Although the other boys were expressing dissatisfaction, Grange understood football and he knew Zup's tactics were not at fault. Zup's problems came from his lack of willingness to recruit the best players, especially the bigger men they needed in the pit. Red's body was peppered with bruises the color of soot. He told the newspapermen, "I am unaware of any dirty playing on the part of any Minnesota player. It's all in the game and should be looked on in that light."

Counting their three nonconference games, the Illini finished with a very respectable record of six wins, one loss, and one tie. But after the undefeated 1923 season, the triumph of this campaign's Michigan game, the other wins against great opponents — well, the players were feeling like failures. They weren't gassing among themselves, and they were barely talking with Zup. Early in the season Coach said, "They are going good, but some day a team will get wise to the weakness of that line." It didn't sit well, Zup being harsh with them to the reporters, giving opponents a free scouting report. Their friends and family read that stuff.

Grange remained loyal. Bob Zuppke was the greatest coach in the world, and a man who would have him for dinner and talk about football and what it meant to be a football player. "The boy who wants to stand out and succeeds in doing so reverses the order of Nature," Zup would tell him. "Nature is perpetually engaged in leveling itself." Zuppke didn't have children so his football players were his kids. If he could have chosen a son, he would have chosen Grange. It wasn't Grange's ability as much as his humility. After the Michigan game Grange didn't want to talk about his stellar performance; he had asked Zuppke about the *next* opponent. He was so humble in his greatness, and Zuppke saw it up close and knew that it was no act.

Despite Red's support, the newspapermen sensed that the team was not unified in its support of the coach. George Huff, the lovable Illini athletic director, had to intervene, calm down the agitation of negative voices, and tell the press that all was "harmonious." Robert Zuppke, whose very essence was tied up in the University of Illinois, was being criticized. His flashes of coaching brilliance, coupled with bouts of inconsistency, continued to haunt him. He wanted to stay. Everyone knew Princeton and Columbia had wanted to recruit Zup, but Huff, who lived only a few blocks away from his good friend, on the other side of University Park, convinced Zup to remain. To leave now would mean abandoning a player, and a boy, who came only once in a career.

Bob Zuppke had seen a lot in life. Born in Germany but raised in the States by German-speaking parents, he had never shed his German accent. He had been to big cities and small hamlets, lived meagerly, and stayed in the country's finest hotels. He was never cynical but he was a born skeptic. (When Grange had arrived as a freshman and shown his speed and ability in practice, the freshman coach had enthusiastically said, "I know we've got something." "Maybe," Zuppke responded. "Pull him away from the sidelines. Work him on the pivot. Get him going on the cutback. He can do with a little learning.") But Grange had changed him as no other player had; he became obsessed with rendering Red's natural abilities into immortality. Red was more than a son: an equal, an artist. Red Grange, Robert Zuppke believed, had only one more season of football left in his life; Red would be a senior and the boy would never consider playing professional football, an activity filled with demonic qualities. More than anything in his life, Zup wanted to make 1925 the most unforgettable season yet, to show the rest of America Grange's astonishing skills. The end of a player's senior year created a final chapter full of drama and sentimentality, and Zuppke intended to create another Grange masterpiece, even more profound than the Michigan game. So there was greater urgency, practically a state of panic, within Robert Zuppke. After the next season the world would never see the beauty of Red Grange's talent again. Zuppke's gambling psyche was already taking shape. He was going to put it all — his reputation, Grange's final season — on one game.

5

|||||||||||||||||||||||||||

Iceman

THE WHEATON ICEMAN

ICE WATER DRIPPED through his khaki shirt as Red lugged fifty-pound ice blocks up flights and flights of stairs. It was back-busting work but his mind was rarely on the cold weight on his shoulder. It cleared his mind so he could dream about the University of Pennsylvania tilt, four months away. It was the summer of 1925, a couple of months before the start of his senior year. Red was still in the world of his childhood, but he was starting to make decisions on his own. This would be a summer of secrets. Red would arrive at L. C. Thompson's Wheaton icehouse at five in the morning. Mr. Thompson gave him about forty customers and Red went to houses and businesses every day 'cept Sunday. Pa's jail was his first stop, but the majority of the customers were housewives who coddled him: "Harold, you'll die of arthritis if you live to be thirty-five," they said as he lugged their ice blocks. Many of the ladies were dressing in their finest to impress the strapping boy. Wheaton, quiet Wheaton, with his neighbors and friends, was the one place he had found relative peace in the past two years, but even that was deteriorating. The newspapers wouldn't leave him alone, and women — a different breed of woman, all bra straps and flesh — were showing up in town, too. Showgirls and wannabe showgirls knew they could suck some first-class publicity off of him. That wasn't all bad. A leggy actress appeared one June day and Red, working the ice truck, picked her up in his arms as the cameras clicked; the next thing you know, across the country newspapers showed a photo of the couple with the cheeky — and sexually infused — caption "How Would You Like to Be the Ice Man?" Red never stuck with the women who made the papers, but the actresses were something special — trouble, sure, but not like the Illinois sorority broads or the Wheaton girls who had known him as a kid who would walk around town with a piece of tape on his nose, making believe he was a football player.

But even the Wheaton folks were starting to gawk and pester him more than was comfortable. Now more than ever, he could have traded on his 1923 and 1924 seasons for some cushy desk job, or an easy summer score in the moving picture racket. After the spring semester Red had visited a movie studio up in Milwaukee. His new acquaintance Charlie Pyle had set the whole thing up, but of course he stood in the background so as not to raise any suspicion. Smartly, Charlie asked nothing of the boy. The movie producers offered Red $25,000 to sign a contract. As a preview of coming attractions, they had the enticing Virginia Valli — the brown-haired, dewy blue-eyed "outdoor girl of films" — come within centimeters of him, her dainty gloved fingers putting greasepaint on the young bruiser's flesh. Tempting, but Red (and Charlie) believed the silver screen could wait one more term. The Western Union telegrams were delivered every day, too, offering him bond salesman work in Chicago and positions in Florida real estate. Probably crooks, the lot of them, but they promised him good wages, and his day would have been taken up mostly with eighteen holes. Trading on his name, he could have had a good start in the business world and he would have made more in the college off-season than his old man received in a year. As for Red's income, he was earning a paltry $37.50 a week on the ice route. Probably should have taken the easy money. Here was the college boy's chance to learn a real business, and yet he had returned to a laborer's job. What were they teaching the boys down at Illinois? For many it simply affirmed the paucity of the public university system, and particularly football's growing role within it.

As a publicity stunt, however, which it wasn't, Grange couldn't have scripted it better. Comparing Grange to a sports figure from a later era, Ed Fitzgerald of *Sport* magazine would write, "It was as though Joe DiMaggio suddenly started delivering mail in a suburb of New York." But carrying post cards didn't build muscles. Red needed the ice route. It was the grind of Rhetoric & Composition, European History, and Trigonometry that exhausted him. The papers all said he was a good student, making mostly As and Bs, but that was a nice little fiction. His only As came from Calisthenics & Mass Games, Gymnasium, and Infantry Drill. He had nine Bs,

thirteen Cs (one in Hygiene), six Ds, and three Es, which were the
equivalent of a modern F. He spent his summers lifting blocks of ice.
Two-hundred-pound blocks would come on a rail car from Wisconsin, and Red and a helper would cut them up, lift them onto a Ford
Formatruck, and go on their route. The helper ran to see the customers' ice cards indicating how many pounds they wanted — 25,
50, 75, 100 — and Red would cart them on his back, then chip them
to fit into the icebox. The job wasn't without its hazards. One summer working the route Red had jumped on the truck's running
board, slipped, and fell under the vehicle. The truck, loaded with
two and a half tons of ice, ran over his left leg. Doc said if it had
been two inches lower, Red's leg would have been amputated. Red
was laid up for a month, had to have his leg up in a sling for about
two weeks, and couldn't move the damn thing. The first time he
took it out of the sling, he fainted. But he shrugged his shoulders.
"I played football that fall, about a month later. Somebody upstairs
was looking out for me." Still, the nerves in the back of his left leg,
about three inches up on his hamstring, were shot.

On his way back home, at about 5:00 p.m., he would walk
along Front Street, toward his apartment at number 113. As the
New Yorker described it: "Two story brick houses sheltering the
First National Bank, and an agency for the Cable Piano Company.
A small restaurant with the sign, 'EATS,' hung outside. An agency
for Mr. Walter P. Chrysler's latest mechanical marvel. A garage or
two — perfectly equipped. A gas station; an island surrounded by
a sea of electric lights, with almost the only garden in town situ-
ated in front of the pump. An agency down the street for Mr. Ford's
devices for farm. Beyond, a few clusters of wooden houses, then as
far as the eye can see — cornfields. A dull, stolid countryside. That
is Wheaton, Illinois. Socially and intellectually speaking, the Des-
ert of the Sahara." Wheaton was based on militant humility; Red
was now its torch carrier. Wheaton kids would see him and dare to
shake his hand. They would gaze at him, chat him up about the upcoming season and especially the Penn game. It was like Wheaton's
versus big-city values. Downstairs from his apartment, Millie and
Charlie Vallette, who owned the Wheaton News Agency in Hiatt's
Drug Store, would remind him that they would come to Philadelphia that fall to watch him perform. Ever since the postseason foot-

ball banquet, where Grange was elected captain for the 1925 squad, it had been all about the University of Pennsylvania Quakers. After the dinner Jack Bell, a reporter, had given him a ride home and he had told Mr. Bell: "I don't suppose it's possible that I'll ever get away as I did against Michigan, but if I ever do I hope it's against Pennsylvania over there next fall. It will be our first chance in the East and we'll show 'em that Zuppke and Illinois can stand up with the best of them."

If it was Tuesday or Thursday, Red's back was in a world of hurt because he packed ice into the meat market, which meant he had to squat down all day. "For days you couldn't stand up straight, ya know? If anything would ever get you in shape, packing those meat markets would. It would either do that or kill ya." No matter the day, he had to make dinner for Pa. Over the dinner table, he could see that his dad was hiding the worry of bills due. Red would solve the family problems, relieve his father's worry. *Soon, Pa, soon.* At night Red would read a book; Sinclair Lewis had just come out with *Arrowsmith*, which was syndicated and all the rage with a certain class, but Red preferred something real like the Ty Cobb autobiography, *Memories of Twenty Years in Baseball*, which told a nice little story about a poor kid becoming a sports star, but left out the juicy parts about the booze and whorehouses. Red also loved listening to afternoon games on the radio. (Grange played center field for the Illini, and he was good enough that Connie Mack would offer him a contract to play for the Philadelphia Athletics.) The languid heat, and Red's early morning job, sent him to bed at around eight o'clock. He lived in a dream state, a summer of suspended disbelief that can exist only in someone coming of age.

The writers took this all in, making his workaday existence into a grand metaphor. Red Grange was no cake-eater dusted with talcum powder. He was no mope, just a regular working fellow working himself into 170 pounds of muscle. He was *the Wheaton Iceman.*

Red Grange was busy working out, but he also had a secret, one that had the possibility of ruining his eligibility, destroying his future job prospects, and forever damaging his reputation. He had taken the trip to the Milwaukee studios, which was part of local gossip. But he had taken a quieter trip to Marysville, Michi-

gan, where Grange had family. He had made no deal with Charles
C. Pyle, but Charlie accompanied him on part of the trip. While in
Michigan Red contracted mumps, and as a publicity stunt, a local
blowhard named Square Deal Miller presented him with a live red
fox named "Mumps." Another opportunist, an auto dealer, had been
using Grange's name to advertise a car, calling it the "Red Grange
of traffic." With Red in tow, Pyle asked the president of the company to make it "square" by giving Red and Pyle each an automobile. For someone of his stature who wanted to stay in school, it was
a careless act of greed. Grange was starting to feel untouchable, and
Charlie's attitude was starting to rub off. The men were becoming
good friends. "I'm better known than Babe Ruth," said Grange, according to the dealer. "We, Grange and I, do not desire to be unrea-
sonable," added Pyle. "We would be quite content to compromise
this matter if your company will give us two cars — one for Grange,
and one for me, his manager." The cash value of the two machines
was $9,000. "It would be a fine advertisement for your machine if
it became known that Grange preferred it." Mr. Harold Wills, the
president, saw the value in giving Grange a car, but Pyle's demand
for two autos felt like extortion. Two cars or a lawsuit, Charlie had
said. Mr. Wills asked Red and Charlie to look over the show room,
and after they left he called Leo M. Butzel, one of the best-known
attorneys in Detroit, who told his client to boot the men out. Pyle,
of course, threatened a legal action, but the matter was dropped, at
least until some twerp reporter heard about it a few months later.

Red was worried that his growing relationship with Pyle would
be found out, but thanks praise to Jesus everything was kept hush-
hush. He had everything at stake. If his actions were unearthed, his
popularity and future earning potential could die off. The world
he was starting to enjoy, yet was not a part of, would end. Charlie
would see the boy's distress and decided that they should lie low.
He decided not to pressure Red. He decided the best way to Grange
was to keep it light. Red enjoyed being entertained. He was too shy
to lead the conversation. Charlie guided him by the nose, told him
stories about showgirls, and he had this trick with an orange where
he would make a quarter disappear into one. Red liked watching it
even after Charlie told him that he'd planted the quarter in the orange all along. Red was like a showman's apprentice.

· · ·

Charlie Pyle was a preacher's son. Pyle preferred entertainment to Jesus so he didn't go into the family business. After all, there was more money, and if breaking commandments is a measuring stick more fun, in the entertainment biz. His father had died young of tuberculosis, so his mother, Sidney, had raised him on North Washington Street in Delaware, Ohio, a town sprouting church steeples on every corner. He lived there with her, his brother, Ira, and sister, Anna. Ira had gone to Ohio Wesleyan, the local university, but he never graduated, becoming a manager with the Western Union Telegraph. (Charlie would often claim to have attended Wesleyan and Ohio State but, not surprisingly, neither university has any records of his enrollment.) Anna was a telephone operator with the Citizens Telephone Company.

There were two significant points in Charlie's young life. While working as a grocery clerk at age sixteen, he decided to make some extra money by promoting his first event (a bike race; net profit $7). Number two: At age eighteen, Charlie was working as a telegraph operator and was living at home with his mother, his brother and sister, and a lodger from Tennessee when Charlie contracted a case of pleurisy, a swelling and painful irritation of the membrane surrounding the lungs. Patients stricken with the disease have severe chest pains that create a sensation of being stabbed. His physician recommended a different climate, so Charlie got a job selling Western Union time-service clocks and a chance for bigger things. Western Union provided him with a free train pass, which was usable on twenty different railroads, and Charlie headed to the Wild West. Each clock sold would give Charlie $2, but Pyle found the clocks next to impossible to peddle, so he gave up and simply scalped his train passes through his own "tourism" company. The railroads were losing hundreds of thousands of dollars on train pass fraud and employed their own detectives to try to bust crooks like Charlie Pyle. Eventually, Charlie found himself dead broke in a small town in the Sierra Nevada.

It happened to be the Fourth of July and a mining town was holding a series of contests, including a rock-drilling race. One man would wield the sledge while his teammate held the drill and poured water. Charlie was watching the contest when suddenly the sledge slipped out of the hands of the burly miner who held it and crushed his partner's thumb to jelly. Charlie, twenty, suggested they have a boxing match to benefit the injured man; the man would get half the proceeds and Charlie and his opponent, a rather elderly 118-pound miner, would share the balance. "Charity," Charlie told his opponent as they took off their shirts, "can go too far. Let's do this: if I hit you too hard, smile and I'll lay off a bit; and if you hit too hard, I'll do the same." The crowd was enthusiastic for the first few rounds but the action slowed and they started to jeer. Charlie started to hit the little man a little harder and faster and the miner just kept smiling in a crazy way; Charlie suddenly remembered their agreement and let off. The crowd roared its disapproval and Charlie started in again, the old man grinning. In the end, Charlie was declared the winner. The pot totaled $210. The man with the destroyed thumb received $105 and Charlie and the old miner each received $52.50.

Pyle was a frontman with an accountant's ability to cut costs, bragging that he could put on *The Three Musketeers* with only one musketeer, and yet his overly ambitious schemes never kept him capitalized. After becoming a semisuccessful vaudeville man, Charlie decided to go back home and show off, but his mother did not approve of vaudeville, so he pretended that he had made a fortune in the lumber business. To impress Mom, he spent a small fortune on nice suits, watches, luggage, and hats, leaving so little money that he could only reach Great Falls, Montana. Within a couple of days he created his own newspaper, sold ads, and left with $60 in his pocket.

And now his quick-hit schemes were again collapsing; he was in litigation with his partner in the theater business. School would be starting soon. Red was in Champaign for preseason camp. Charlie was in his Virginia Theatre office, and Red Grange was in the place, watching *The Freshman*, the Harold Lloyd football flick. Charlie had already created a budding trust with the boy, but it was time to make the big play.

The Freshman could have been written for Red Grange. The movie started with this line: "Do you remember those boyhood days when going to College was greater than going to Congress — and you'd rather be Right Tackle than President?"

Lloyd wore those funny round dark spectacles, and he played

Harold Lamb, a pathetically skinny wannabe football player, who read *How to Play Football* and idolized the "college's football captain of 1925."

The next line: "The opening of the Fall term at Tate University — a large football stadium with a college attached."

Lloyd was funny and this picture was a hit. Red found it particularly hilarious with its send-up of the dean of the college, "so dignified he never married for fear his wife would call him by his first name"; the object of affection "the kind of girl your mother must have been"; and the coach "so tough he shaves with a blowtorch" — Zup to a T. When he addressed the team he said, "You dubs are dead from your dandruff down!"

Of course, Harold Lamb tries out for the team — "I'd like to play on your football team if you don't mind."

The coach needs a tackling dummy so he uses Lamb, and the men viciously hit him.

The coach yells, "This is no petting party! That's not half hard enough!"

They eventually make him the water boy, and after the rest of the team gets hurt, the coach is forced to put him in the "game against Union State":

The day of days!

When every heart in Tate stood still — and all the world watched football history in the making.

Harold yells at the rest of the team: "Come on, you old women! Are you afraid of mussing your hair? Don't you know how to fight?"

In a series of pratfalls he is knocked out, his head is stepped on, he is woozy, seeing double, and he refuses to give the ball to the referee. With seconds ticking down, Lamb blocks a kick and runs down the field, dragging men into the end zone, scoring. The coach dances with the ref.

Tate 6, other team 3.

He gets the girl.

There was a tap on Red Grange's shoulder.

"Mr. Pyle would like to see you in his office."

"Did I do something?"

"Come, please."

Grange had come to know Charlie Pyle and, of course, considered him more than an acquaintance, but he had no idea why he was being called to his office. Pyle had been planning this moment for a while, realizing he was competing against other promoters, managers, and shysters. It was important for him to be straight and authoritarian. He had gained the kid's trust by not asking him for anything, but he couldn't wait on the sideline any longer. Before Grange knew it he had been steered upstairs through a dim, hazy corridor to Pyle's office.

Charlie was there. He wore his best suit and presented his most genuine smile.

Pyle didn't just give Red Grange a pep talk — Red, he figured, had heard enough of those — but got right down to business. Red was at a crossroads. He was just coming into his athletic prime, but the end of his senior season would mean his stage would be taken away. He could take the road most traveled by college stars and put his name on a newspaper column, become a ref or a coach. None of those pursuits suited him, and they hardly seemed worthy of a man of Grange's enormous fame. Or, Grange could take a radical departure: trade on his name and go into professional football. Pro ball carried the most risk and bordered on the ridiculous. If he sullied his name in the pros, it would be difficult to ever get a newspaper job, ref, or coach.

Red would always claim this was the first time the men had ever met, but that hogwash was an obvious stretch, and the truth was altered for fear of eligibility violations, or shame. The two men hadn't only met; they had worked together on the proposed movie deal and negotiated with the car dealer. Reality distortion was part of the fame game.

"How would you like to make a hundred thousand dollars?" asked Charlie. The conversation seemed like it was taking place on another planet, or hell.

"Who wouldn't?" he replied.

"Well, I've got an idea. Sit down. I thought I could go to Chicago and talk with George Halas and Dutch Sternaman," who owned the Bears. As Pyle pitched Grange, Red listened intently. "With a man like you in the pro game, pro football will become as big a game as professional baseball. Bigger." Pyle was quite the personality. A showman, a dynamo. Charlie scared Red a little but he liked that feeling. There had been hundreds of well-groomed gentlemen who wanted a piece of Red. Charlie's words trickled into Grange like some sort of delicate French wine, which Red of course had never tasted. Everything about Pyle was everything Grange had missed out on and would never see if he continued on his path. There had been so many who wanted to "give" him something — a job, a vaudeville show, a political appointment, a column — but it was Charlie — just hearing him talk was exciting — to whom he now deferred, who he was convinced was a multimillionaire, who, he trusted, would represent him and his interests above all. What was within Red that made Charlie such a necessity? *What did he see in him?* Something different from the people of Wheaton, from his father, from the college stiffs or the high-collared Chicago businessmen. Someone real, someone he wished to be, offering escape, someone who could talk the way Red could run, who for all his slick dandiness was tough, who didn't let poverty control him, who was self-taught, living by his wits, the language of rural America on his lips, a man like no other he had met. Red had considered other offers but this one was so neatly packaged. It would carry great personal risk. He would endanger his eligibility, invite shame, and kill job prospects. He might even make an enemy of Bob Zuppke. Grange evaluated Pyle. Hundred thousand dollars, he thought. That's a lot of money. He could move Pa out of their downtrodden apartment and pay off their debts.

"Sounds good," said Grange, still worried about the risk, "but I've got to do a bit of thinking on it."

"What thinking? Think of the millions of people who are crazy to see you in action! Millions of them all over the country! They'll jam the parks like they've never been jammed before! They want to see the Galloping Ghost in action — and they'll pay for it."

"Yeah . . ."

"And they'll get their money's worth. You'll be doing the thing you want to do most, play football, and you'll be making a fortune at it, to boot." Red was dreaming that he was happy. In the privacy of Pyle's office it sounded like a good idea. They shook hands. Pyle was victorious. They made a secret pact that they were now partners, but to anyone who asked they were merely friends. The secrecy of their partnership made Grange feel as if he had delayed his decision and the troubles it would inevitably bring. Thought of jointly, they went forward together, like a jockey and horse, Pyle stroking him but the whip was in the other hand, hidden but at the ready.

The first day of fall practice, September 15, 1925, came quickly enough. Grange and the rest of the boys were in Urbana, no longer practicing on the rutted ground of old Illinois Field; rather they had moved to the southwest side of campus where they trained at grand Memorial, changing in the top-notch 27 x 49–foot dressing room with the hundred lockers and the uniform-drying ventilation system. The coaches and officials even had a private showering area. (The one thing that Huff and Zuppke should have invested in was a field tarp.) Hordes of writers were coming to watch the two-a-days and to cover Grange. The Chicago papers were in a newspaper war. On one side of the most bitter rivalry was Col. Robert McCormick's *Chicago Tribune*, the self-proclaimed "world's greatest newspaper" and with its hundred thousand columns of annual advertising certainly its richest. The *Trib* was housed in a thirty-six-story castle near the Chicago River, complete with Gothic gargoyles, grotesques, and tower. Its rival was William Randolph Hearst's *Chicago Herald and Examiner*, which was in a stuffy warehouse sopping with newsprint and ink. Despite the modest accommodations for its writers, Hearst papers had a way of making you laugh or cry. The other Second City papers, the *American*, the *Daily News*, and the *Journal*, had their writers coloring the mundane goings-on. No one knew about C. C. Pyle. James Braden of the *Chicago News* wrote, "On the practice field Red is not so shy and seems to be a different fellow. His old-time quick bursts of speed are still there. He is in excellent physical condition and when given a ball to carry he readily shows why the Purple toga belongs to him. Red is the football king, Zup is the emperor. He struts about the field with that same stubborn shock of hair sticking up behind. His brows are drawn and his mouth is grim." Reporters never seemed to understand the importance of blocking and tackling.

The 1925 schedule was a killer. Grantland Rice got wind of it and wrote in a preseason column: "Grange starts the season with a war on his hand from the kick-off. What a season he and his mates face! — Nebraska, Butler, Iowa, Michigan, Pennsylvania, Chicago,

Wabash and Ohio State. And no one of them may be any tougher than Nebraska."

On the practice field the newspapermen would ask Zuppke about his senior star. Because it took away the focus from the rest of his miserable squad, Coach loved talking, in that German-Wisconsin accent of his, about the boy:

"I say without hesitation that Grange is the greatest player of the age. He is one of the greatest in all time. He does things that the average man would have to stop and think about. By that time it would be too late." The reporters laughed. "I believe that Grange has a sixth sense. I think that he can feel the approach of tacklers before he is touched. I have been on the sidelines and watched him dash right at the tackler, stiff-arm him off and then whirl around to evade a man coming behind him. Grange could not see that tackle.

"I honestly believe that the nerves of his legs are so sensitive that they communicate to his brain the approach of tacklers, and that he is to make lightning-like moves to escape tacklers. It may seem out of order, perhaps it is stealing Sir Oliver Lodge's* stuff and all that, but, nevertheless, Grange does it. He can't explain how he does it and he surely has me stopped."

Red credited the summer ice drudgery with making him feel in midseason form (realizing the benefits of off-season conditioning, Zup encouraged his other players to work in the rail yards or any other laborer's job that built strength), and he would need his hardened body because the other teams would go after him, but that was nothing novel. He expected more late hits, like the one that befell him in Minnesota and the regular late knees, elbows, and fists he had to endure. He had to be extra-durable this year because his line wouldn't be anything. Illinois's line didn't rely on size as much as quickness and technique, and Zup believed his recruits had neither. He needed to find and develop a whole damn line — center, guards, tackles, and end — to block for Red. He used a modified T formation, which he called the "Grange formation," which put Red way in the backfield and gave him room to make decisions and create on his own. But the men who had made it work — Frank Rokusek,

---

* Lodge was a noted British physicist who was known for his electromagnetic research, which helped pave the way for the radio. Lodge was also known for believing that it was possible to communicate with the dead.

captain and end; Dick Hall, tackle; Lou Slimmer and Roy Miller, guards; and Gil Roberts, center — were all gone. "This leaves us a scant nucleus for the line," understated Zup. It was even worse than that.

Harry Hall, the rangy quarterback, was considering dropping out. The critics were touting Red's kid brother, Garland, whom everyone called "Pink," but Zup knew better. Pink was faster than Red (he could run a 100 around world-record pace, according to Red) and he liked contact, but he didn't have Red's acceleration (Red was a "soundless rocket," said Zuppke), and he had a bum shoulder. Instead of his older brother's quiet determination and confidence, Gardie always had an easy smile and it was rumored that he was quite the playboy with a taste for fast cars: "I don't think he ever drove one under seventy miles per hour," said Red; "anyone who went past him was a personal insult." In a missive or two over the summer, Zup had told Red to keep up on his passing and kicking because he wanted Red to perform a multitude of duties. If Red could better develop his arm and his foot, then Earl Britton could move from his traditional fullback spot to guard. Britt was having serious academic problems, however. His best subjects were Football, which he somehow was allowed to take twice, Basketball, and Infantry Drill. (One semester Britt took Theory of Football and Football Theory, getting Bs in both.) But his spring semester the previous year was a disaster with two Ds and two Fs. Losing his on-the-field versatility would ruin the team. Luckily his workingman father wrote a pleading letter — and Britt promised to make up the work — and he was admitted to return. Since gregarious Britt was Red's best — and only close — friend on the team, Grange was relieved when the big boy was allowed back into school.

Along with the weak line and all of the eligibility problems, Zup worried about the pressure on the whole squad because it was Grange's last hurrah. Red had started as a lone wolf, but the coach had watched him grow into a leader. Red would come over to Zuppke's apartment. Zuppke would do most of the talking. "When you are in conversation with him a word, a thought, may touch him off, and he leaps away on a brand-new tangent," observed Grange, which was a way of communicating that was foreign to Grange's upbringing of silence. Zup would tell him one of his old yarns, like the one when Zuppke nominated himself for the presidency of the American Football Coaches' Association:

Army's coach nominated Fielding Yost. "A man as tall and straight and strong as the great timbers which grow in the North-land. A man whose heart is as pure and white as the snow flurries over the Dakotas . . ."

Zuppke then went on to nominate himself and turned to the southerners. "Do you want a damn Yankee ruling you? Where is that hot southern blood I've heard so much about? Why pick a man as tall and straight and strong as the great timbers, which grow in the Northland? Why not pick a little guy like me, whom you can push around?" Zuppke won, 500–1, and claimed, just to be inde-pendent, he had voted against himself. Zuppke and Grange would laugh. Red enjoyed the moments with his coach. And Zuppke no-ticed how Red was so kind and comfortable around Fannie, Zup's wife. Coach knew that Red had lost his mother. Just look at the three of them saying grace, talking, and enjoying the rapture of the hearth. *Follow me, son. I will lead you.* When Zup, Fannie, and Red were together it felt like family.

Zuppke wanted to create a special final season but he didn't have the goods surrounding Red, and the competition would be tough that year. There were not only the regular rivalries, and the upcom-ing Homecoming game against Michigan, but also the tilt against Penn, which in everyone's mind would be the year's duel between the East and the West, a veritable national championship decided on the field. Michigan had been a midwestern rivalry game; Illinois versus Penn would have national implications. Since Zup had never taken a team east, the Penn contest could make or break Robert C. Zuppke's reputation among the East Coast football critics and cement or crush Grange's legacy as he went against "real compe-tition." If it was possible, the publicity men were building up the boy even more. A poster had been created that showed Grange run-ning for his fourth touchdown against Michigan. The poster was in about every Illinois city building, bank, high school, and library. Three of the home games were already selling out; the ticket sellers were saying the coming games would be the largest football crowds in history, but the Penn game was already the hottest ticket in the land. The Illini boosters and the Chicago writers like Warren W. Brown (who were so tight with Zuppke that the "little Napoleon" had them introduce him on the after-dinner circuit — "sugaring," it was called, because it gave the writers a little pocket money) and the big eastern guns — Damon Runyon, Grantland Rice, and Ford Frick — were circling October 31 on their calendars, too.

As the Illini practiced, and school started on September 22, Red Grange was readying himself for the season, but he was also secretly plotting against many of the things he held most dear. The next morning Charlie Pyle had an appointment at the Chicago Bears Football Club. It was not an impressive enterprise. Charlie and his friend Frank Zambreno would be meeting with George Halas, the Bears' owner. George not only owned the team, which was a season of rainouts away from eviction; he played on the ragged, unkempt, preindustrial Bears. Halas prided himself on being a real son of a bitch. As a player, he was perhaps the best illegal user of hands in the game, said *Time* magazine. A hard taskmaster, Halas worked sixteen hours a day, seven days a week, interrupting his routine only for church on Sundays. He was a decent athlete in his own right. He was an end and halfback under Zuppke at Illinois. Signed as a right fielder by the New York Yankees in 1919, Halas played in twelve games and batted .091, injuring his hip going into third base one day. He would suffer the effects of the injury his whole life. (As for the Yanks, they replaced him with Babe Ruth.) Halas went back to football — as coach, trainer, ticket seller, publicity man, and player for the Decatur Illinois Staleys, later called the Chicago Staleys and, in 1922, named the Chicago Bears. Some of the original Staleys, who tended not to come from the most upright families, were still on the team.

Halas's teammate and minority partner, Ed "Dutch" Sternaman, also an ex-Illini player, sat in the office, too. Dutch had skin the color of blue cheese dressing and thin scraps of hair going across the top of his head. Halas had a tough jaw, contrasting with the babyish pallor of his skin. He was not quite the ugliest man on the football gridiron, but he was close. At age thirty he was losing his thin, lank hair. A habitually suspicious man, he didn't smile much, preferring to clench his teeth under a hawkish nose. Halas and Sternaman both knew that they wanted — *needed* — Grange, who was also a fraternity brother, but they didn't know what they would have to give up to get him. Perpetually short on money, they didn't have much to offer. They were hardly an intimidating duo, and they didn't know anything about his manager, C. C. Pyle, except that he was a "Champaign theater manager."

Charlie strolled through the dirty white limestone and terra cotta canyons of Chicago's financial district and into 111 Washington Street, home of the Bears, across the street from the oldest church in Chicago, the Gothic First Methodist Church's Chicago Temple. He hopped aboard the elevator — the door decorated with a pattern of Art Deco diamonds — and traveled toward George Halas's offices, already scheming to make them his own lair. Pyle greeted these nervously friendly men, in their dour suits, with a sideburn-to-sideburn smile.

Halas's nature went against grand poetic gestures, and the Bears, though a hometown team, rarely had more than a couple of thousand die-hards at a game, in contrast to the college brand of football with its grandiosity, its tabernacle of fanatics, and its cultural juggernaut as a maker of men. Halas, a chronic worrier in a cheap suit, was a part of a misfit league. But he was a pro football missionary, a gridiron monk. To keep his enterprise afloat, he would start a laundry business, one of many side jobs. He didn't care what the world thought about pro football, and he knew that one's very presence at a pro game labeled the ticket buyer as debauched. Pro ball was a cross between a small-town fair and a freak show. But Halas saw its potential. He loved the sport. What he didn't have were the skills to move it beyond its current and sorry state.

And now the three of them. At first Charlie and George chatted amiably, and that's when Halas started feeling sick. Pyle, Halas would later recall, was a "smiling, dapper man ... impeccably attired in a tailored gray flannel suit and gray spats with fashionable pearl buttons. C. C. also wore a derby and carried a cane. I think of him every time I see Adolphe Menjou in the late TV movies."

"Grange is ready to turn pro," Pyle told the young Bears executives. "He'll join the Bears immediately after his final college game, and we'll go on tour for a couple of months — schedule a string of games down through Florida and out to the West Coast."

Just like all of the other owners, Halas had sent his share of admiring letters to Grange in an attempt to entice him to the pros, and here was the Ghost's representative telling him he wanted to join the Bears. He was one lucky son of a bitch, except for one serious caveat — he had to deal with this irritating fellow Pyle. Dutch and Halas offered Pyle a flat one-third of the tour's net profits. Pyle waved off Halas's proposal as if he was swatting a moth, saying that the Bears should receive one-third of the net, with two-thirds going to the Pyle-Grange team. Pyle knew what he was doing better than a hustler understands an alley craps game. Even Charlie would admit that the Bears were the natural outfit for Grange, but it certainly was not his only option and he wasn't shy about letting Halas know it. Pyle could easily negotiate and place Grange with another franchise. Pyle controlled Grange, thus Pyle was in control. It had been Pyle's chutzpah and vision that were creating the pending tour, and the Champaign theater manager shook a fistful of telegrams from all of the other pro owners who would love to get into bed with Grange. Halas and Pyle negotiated — through Pyle's cigarette smoke — into the night and early morning. The barely audible clock on the Wrigley Building, across the lazy Chicago River, finally reminded them that they had been talking for twenty-six hours when they came to the agreement, staggering out of the suite with a handshake and a secret contract that Red would eventually sign. The Bears would get half of the net, but they would have to shoulder most of the expenses. The result would be profound.

Charlie immediately called Grange.

"Plan on spending Christmas under the sun," he told Red. "A few lovelies, a little football. The time of your life." After the meeting with the Bears, Charlie went on the road. Cutting a shadowy figure, he would travel around the country to create the tour, while promising himself to keep as quiet as possible. With his outstanding ego, Pyle found it difficult to keep his mouth shut. The porters would greet him in Chicago's LaSalle Street Station: *Mister Pyle! How are you today? Welcome to the Twentieth Century Limited. Let me take your bag. Mr. Pyle, what a niiiiiice suit.*

He *paid* the porters to pay him compliments.

Charlie walked, from underneath the waiting room's vaulted ceilings, on the soft red carpet, toward the Twentieth Century Limited. He smelled the coal, heard the hiss of steam, and eyed the other passengers. Pyle entered the train's plush club car, which was decorated in blue and gray. Very classy. *Mr. Pyle, they will be serving T-bones in the dining car, Mr. Pyle. Please, sir, let me know if you need anything! Would you like me to light that cigarette, sir? Thank you! Thannnnk you! Very generous of you, Mr. Pyle.*

If they failed to call him by name, to completely recognize him, there would be no *schmear*, not even a plug nickel.

Who was he anyway? Some sort of bond salesman? It didn't matter. It paid to treat Charlie Pyle like a big shot. And he would be one, for real, soon enough.

Bob Zuppke had no idea about Red Grange and C. C. Pyle. The very notion of it would have sickened him.

Zup intended to honor Grange this season by pointing his squad to one game, a game in which Grange could share his brilliance with the whole country. "If a coach can lift the boys beyond themselves, then he is a real coach," believed Zuppke. Even if the Michigan game had been the greatest performance in college football history, the East Coast newspapermen and fans still had their lingering doubts about Grange. It would take all of Zuppke's powers to beat the University of Pennsylvania, a team many considered the best in the country. The Illini, the most knowledgeable football men confirmed, would have a down year. Even Grange couldn't single-handedly beat the tough Big Ten teams, and the Illini wouldn't have a chance against mighty Penn, with its athletically gifted behemoths. "I have picked out the men who seem to have the most pluck," Zuppke said, forlornly. "But it doesn't look like as good an offensive line by a long ways." Zuppke would walk around campus, head down, depressed. Garland Grange's shoulder popped out in the freshmen versus varsity game, so he was a goner for the season. Zup was struggling with his role players. Merwin "Bubbles" Mitterwallner, a doughy-faced 230-pounder from Colorado who always sported a goofy smile, could take the critical center's role, but he was a wild card. One lone bright spot was Chuck Kassel, Zuppke's "Kangaroo" end, a hard tackler and an excellent receiver. But after his team barely beat the frosh team, Grange being creamed because of the porous line, Zuppke figured they would lose the season opener, October 3, against Nebraska and its tough-guy Weir broth-

ers — Edwin, the All-American tackle, and his brother, Joe. Grannie
Rice came to Champaign with Frank Craven, the actor. When Zup
saw them, he moaned, "I'm sorry you came to this game."

"Why?" asked Craven.

"My team has got away from me. They think they're unbeatable,
even before their first game. I can't wake them up. So I've given
them only four plays against Nebraska. Grange won't make a first
down."

When the Nebraska team wasn't barreling over him, Bubbles Mitterwallner was mixing up the signals and passing the football on the
wrong count, sometimes hiking it to the wrong back. In the Illinois
style of play, with its direct passing from center to ball carrier, the
quarterback did a large share of the blocking, too, and the center had
to hike the ball perfectly, which he wasn't. But it wasn't just Bubbles
being a dumbshit; there was plenty of blame to go around. Grange:
slap slap slap phew phew phew smack smack. He was constantly
brought down. Red never felt vulnerable on the field. Even with a
platoon of so-so teammates, he would overcome their deficiencies.
Zup would be out there stomping and gesturing like a crazed symphony conductor while Grange concentrated on his teammates'
movements and how he had to compensate for them. Nebraska had
reduced him to a spastic bumbler as he tried to avoid the storm of
tacklers. He would have to do something. Could Grange and Zuppke turn a team game into an individual one? Would this poem in
motion be reduced to a limerick in his final season? As Grange was
downed again and again, anyone could see that the squad looked
weak, cowardly, soft-shelled. Warren W. Brown of the *Herald-
Examiner*, whose florid descriptions usually painted Grange as a
demigod, wrote, "Halted all along the line of march through a soggy,
slushy field, whenever he exhibited signs of wanting to go somewhere, 'Red' and his mates went down to defeat, 14 to 0.

"Those pesky Nebraskans, fast chargers, sharp tacklers, didn't
seem to realize that the mob was there to see 'Red' run. They
stopped him as if he were Rufus McGonigle of the East Liverpool
Y.M.C.A. second team."

The Cornhuskers bragged that they hit Grange so hard that he
had wept.

Grantland Rice tapped out one of his elegant classics: "The color scheme was all red above the wet green turf of Illinois' field today, but on this occasion it was not the red of Red Grange. It was the shining crimson of Nebraska."

Fortunately the Illini had a breather the following week against Butler University, the Illini's yearly breather game. Red was back to form and carried the team, doing one of his prances 70 yards for a touchdown. Grange played forty-one minutes, carried the ball fourteen times, and gained 185 yards in the win. For the blindly loyal, the Nebraska game was seen as some ridiculous anomaly. Grange the magnificent engine was humming again. Iowa would be next. Burt Ingwerson, the Iowa coach, had been Red's freshman coach. Red gave him all the credit in the world for teaching him to run, and now his mentor would try to stop him. As the Iowa team, cloaked in black and gold, entered Iowa Field, the crowd clanked cowbells.

Red Grange had only a handful of games left. To the world his athletic career was ending. Too bad they would never see him again. The contradiction troubled Grange, who with the assistance of C. C. Pyle was forming his own ideas about the world of sports. He was still in his prime. Zuppke was talking about the purity of amateurism and how football trained men for distinction, but Red couldn't totally comprehend why his winged shoes were being clipped. He was an athlete, not a scholar. Just look at the thousands who had come to watch him against Iowa. He would entertain them. He would make both universities thousands of dollars . . .

The game was under way . . . Iowa dared common sense and decided to kick off to Grange, and of course he ran 65 yards for a touchdown. In the end Grange gained a total of 208 yards, almost without assistance, but Ingwerson's team beat Illinois 12–10 in the last two minutes of play. "The defeat was a heartbreaker, nothing less," said the *Illio*, the Illini yearbook. The Illini were now 1–2. Red could hardly believe that the adulation was still swelling for him. Civic leaders wanted to embrace him: free from guilt or evil, soaked with good old values, every yard gained a confirmation of rural honesty. Talking against Grange became a blasphemy — only a whoring bastard atheist would doubt him. Grange was outwardly humble, but he was starting to believe his believers. In his mind he was figuring out an indignant defense for his actions with Pyle. Although he was no romantic and didn't believe in the amateur ideal, rebellion against the three things he loved the most — Zuppke, his father, and football itself — was testing him. His face couldn't hide the strain.

Michigan loomed the following week. The Wolverines, with Fielding Yost once again coaching, had become a passing team. The University of Illinois's administrators were bringing in extra cops from Chicago to control the crowds, which were figured to be enormous and antagonistic. The papers were filled with celebrations of Grange, and some companies were taking out ads.

DON'T EXPECT US TO DO ANY WORK ON
SATURDAY, OCT. 24

WE ARE CLOSING WITH OTHER BUSINESS HOUSES
IN HONOR OF GRANGE

And his hometown had essentially closed down: "I, Marion J. Pittsford, Mayor of the city of Wheaton, Illinois, do hereby declare and proclaim Saturday, the 24th day of October, A.D. 1925, a holiday in honor of Harold Grange."

The *Chicago American* was even critiquing Red's reading of the part of Rosalind. Bubbles and Red had portrayed the leads in Shakespeare's *As You Like It* in a literature class.

Fielding Yost was fidgeting a bit, but anyone on the inside knew it was nothing more than a man trying to quit smoking cigars. Doctor's orders. The papers talked about him riding his team hard, and how the previous year's drubbing had "seared the heart of the veteran coach," but Hurry Up, as always, was plenty confident. Zup kept telling people that his team was set and then he'd turn around and fiddle with it, which is never a sign of much faith. Yost read the papers and he had scouts; he knew Zuppke had decided to bring Britton back to his old fullback position where he could run-block for Grange and hit those big boomers, but it was obvious that Zup was reaching. After the Wolverines arrived in Urbana, Yost hosted the reporters in the lobby of the Hotel Inman and good-naturedly demonstrated some plays for the men while Michigan alumni sang:

Sing to the colors that float in the light;
Hurrah for the Yellow and Blue!
Yellow the stars as they ride thro' the night
And reel in a rollicking crew; . . .
Blue are the billows that bow to the sun
When yellow-robed morning is due.

Yost, who had tasted so much success, considered his 1925 team the best he had ever coached. It seemed as though Grange's trouncing of the previous year's team had changed Yost. He was still tough on his players, but his sensibilities were different. He would open it up. He bragged about his three outstanding skill players: Bo Molenda, a bruising fullback; Bennie Oosterbaan, a receiving end, whom the *Chicago American* described as an "Egyptian" who can "slide into the air and pick off passes with his finger tips," and who would be a three-time All-American; before Oosterbaan went on his route, he would snap at his QB, Benny Friedman, "Just throw the cantaloupe close, I'll catch it." Friedman, a future Hall of Famer, was the best of the three. He was, said one newspaperman, a "cool and deliberate field general who can run, dodge and throw the oval with the accuracy of baseball. His passing and running, together with his general handling of the team, have stamped him as one of the leading quarterbacks in the country." Benny, a product of Cleveland's vibrant Jewish ghetto, was plenty cocky and he had the skill to match. Benny-to-Bennie would become a college sensation, and the combination was so much fun to coach, shaking Yost into a more open style, that Hurry Up stuck around for another year afterward, overseeing the construction of Michigan Stadium and permanently taking a desk job as athletic director in 1927.

Because of Grange's success the prior year, to everyone's surprise, the game was close and a typically low-scoring affair. Benny-to-Bennie didn't work when Grange was in the secondary. Michigan won 3–0. (Michigan would end the season scoring 227 points and surrendering only 3.) The starting elevens went the entire game (almost two hours) with no substitutes. Grange played well, but once again his balky line allowed the Michigan players to tackle him as fiercely as they had intended the previous year. Prepared to see Grange perform magic a year too late, the New York papers had sent their correspondents, who went away without much of a story, and yet Grange's luminescence couldn't be dimmed in the Midwest. Betty Walker, of the *Herald-Examiner,* covered the game for the paper's women's pages, unsuccessfully channeling Grantland Rice: "'Red' continued to be the Douglas Fairbanks-John Barrymore-Jack Dempsey of every football lover's heart," she wrote. "An ideal setting, despite the weather, was this Memorial Field. Southward as far as one could see stretched the mist-hung prairies of southern Illinois, while northward rose the handsome red brick buildings of the state university, their green roofs rising above the tops of the lofty elms. And now and then, men with water buckets stopped things long enough for the mud spattered athletes to drink." How long would the world continue to worship Red? That question would be answered in Pennsylvania the following week.

After the Michigan game a deflated Red would, as was his ritual, go to the Virginia Theatre — Charlie Pyle's realm — to escape, seek reassurance, and get his mind right again. Grange enjoyed Pyle's company. Charlie was fun to be around, and he was promising a new sort of life: money, for sure, but Pyle was really offering him independence. He realized Bob Zuppke, his friend and mentor, would never understand a guy like C. C. Pyle — a "doer." Zup was content to be an $8,000-a-year football man, but there was so much promise in the world, so much money to be had. Charlie provided an entrée into an exciting life, his own life. Red and Zup loved football — the excitement of the game — but Zup didn't really understand what it was like to have so much athletic talent, and then be told to retire from a sport you loved to play, and then to worry about your cop father who wasn't getting any younger, and who had taken out loans to get you through school. The ice route had helped build Red into a speedster with bulging muscles, but Red had forgone the easy money. It was, Grange believed, a selfish act. Pa had done the best he could for the Grange boys and Red felt obligated to pay him back. Everyone saw Red as a blue-collar kid, but he saw himself as a boy playing at games while others sacrificed for him. Zuppke held up Red as an ideal amateur: a boy who received an education and became a man before his eyes. But Red didn't feel like a man.

6

America's Hearts and Minds

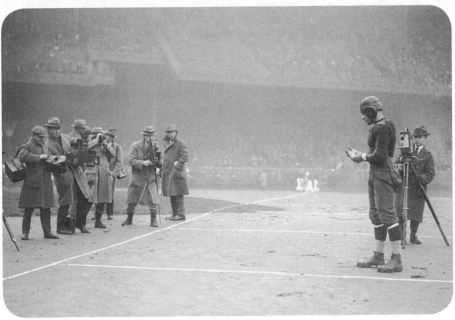

GRANGE FACING NEWS PHOTOGRAPHERS

T HE PRESSURE WAS ON. It was always on now. The fatal disease of rising expectations. Grange would look at the stream of faces — especially the ex-players who had sold their bodies to play the game; their flesh, his flesh — and feel it his duty to satisfy them through his performances. Technically he hadn't signed a contract with Charles C. Pyle, and so he was trying to convince himself that he was not violating eligibility rules, or his own morality. He was more intent at practice. His teammates always kept a distance from him.

"The Quakers play croquet!" Zuppke kept shouting at the men. The implications were clear. The Illini were working-class heroes, sons of the western soil. He wanted his team to out-hit their opponents on every play. Frank Rokusek, captain of the Illini team the previous year and now an assistant, had Zuppke's ear. He had scouted Penn four times this campaign. In the mid-1920s the teams used an unbalanced line, in which four men would line up in the backfield, strong to the four-man side, which was called a single-wing back. Rock said that other teams playing Penn would shift to the right and Penn would shift its entire defense to cover it, and the rumor was that the Penn players thought Grange could run only to his right. Zup hadn't liked using weak-side plays, where the tailback would take the ball and run to the side with only two linemen, but he was practicing it today and he planned on using it. Risky as hell. Considering the damage he had already endured this season, it could get Grange half-killed out there.

At about the same time the Illini were going through their practice paces, Penn was training on Philadelphia's Franklin Field. Coach Lou Young, Penn's steady yet uninspiring coach, had them concentrating on defensive drills to combat Grange. Adding to everyone's excitement about the game, Philly would be the center of the sports world, a goddamn Murderers' Row of writers, a bunch of reporters who would try to out-drink, out-gamble, and out-write each other. Their columns were filled with such vim and vigor for two reasons: creating heroes sold papers, and they usually had money riding on the contest at hand. This game would host the greatest sportswriters of the era. The mythmakers/breakers were licking their pencils, forgoing the annual Army-Yale classic, to write a nice little obituary about the boy from "out West." Earlier that year, many of them had schlepped to the Zeta Psi house on Urbana's East John Street: Grantland Rice; James Braden, the former Yale halfback with the *Chicago News;* Herbert Reed for the Hearst syndicate; James Cruisenberry with the *Chicago Tribune;* and the *New Yorker's* J. R. Tunis. They all got their sit-down with Grange — one by one they were granted an audience. They hungered for profile stuff — little angles on which they could hang a nice little feature. Tunis wrote that Grange was "colorless" off the field, and the other writers struggled over their Underwoods, too, trying to embellish his achromatic characteristics, hoping to unlock the mystery of his athletic competence, or at least find an interesting hook: a sob story, a sense of humor, a streak of irony, a bit of controversy. They went to L. M. "Mike" Tobin, the Illini's crack publicity man, who beat out press releases and his *News of Sports* bulletin like a mad gorilla. (Many of the lazier writers would simply ape Tobin's stuff.) The writers knew the fables, but they were trying to find the man.

Now as the pregame coverage started rolling, even the Chicago writers were hedging, questioning if Grange was really so great since this season had been a letdown, thus far. Since many of them had not witnessed his athletic feats, most of them were skeptical, counting them as the product of western hucksterism and weak opponents. *Grange is a great player but is he the greatest?* The *Chicago American's* vivacious Jimmy Corcoran filed a story that said, "The East awaits the coming of 'Red' Grange like the cat awaits the mouse . . . This season the poor old West has suffered so much humiliation by these eastern teams that our red head will find himself marked not only by the 65,000 who will view the game on Franklin Field Saturday but by eleven hot players of Penn who will endeavor to toss him back so far that he will end up somewhere near

Danville." When the writers started arriving in Philly, they were entertained by Max "Boo Boo" Hoff, a sallow man who had used his bootlegging money to build a fight promotion and nightclub empire. Boo Boo threw lavish parties for reporters, athletes, and chorus girls. After one of those parties during game week, Damon Runyon — who could be a loner and was the master observer of the betting class — took his 5½B feet for a walk. He observed characters through his metal spectacles, seeing how they were putting their money down. Runyon liked to paraphrase Ecclesiastes — "The race is not always to the swift, nor the battle to the strong, but that's the way to bet." Runyon noticed that the dope was against Grange, some people wagering he would not gain 10 yards from scrimmage. Grange, the greatest football player in the world, was an underdog.

But all of them were missing the bigger story: the relationship between Red Grange and C. C. Pyle. Through Grange, Pyle was secretly preparing to make professional football a viable sport, but both men knew how important this game had become for their futures. To become a box office sensation as a pro, Grange couldn't be short of spectacular on Saturday in front of the East Coast scribes.

In their buildup columns the writers were showing caution. Only Grantland Rice, who had actually seen Grange, showed boldness when he wrote, "Grange hasn't the support he knew in his sophomore and junior years, when he left a flame along the gridiron, but he still manages to step — he still is one of the greatest backs that ever played football. On this occasion he will run into a strong defensive team, but he has run against strong defensive teams before." Grantland Rice of the *New York Tribune* was the nationally syndicated dean of sportswriters. He could quote Emerson and Keats, and Grannie was considered so understanding that after returning from the Great War, he discovered that $75,000 that he had deposited in a bank had all been embezzled by a friend. "It's my fault for putting him in such temptation," Rice said. Grannie was from Tennessee, a voracious whiskey drinker and a beloved poet to millions of men. Rice composed one about Grange entitled "The Red Head":

> *There are two shapes now moving,*
> *Two Ghosts that drift and glide,*

And which of them to tackle
Each rival must decide;
They shift with spectral swiftness
Across the swarded range,
And one of them's a shadow,
And one of them is Grange.

Few men may seize a phantom
Who drifts above the chart,
But even spectral phantoms
Must have at least a start;
Men reach to find both missing,
But this is not so strange
When one of them's a shadow,
And one of them is Grange.

The Penn team looked very strong, but it did have one significant injury — Al "Little Albert" Kreuz, Penn's massive kicking fullback, had a knee swollen to the size of a small melon. Al, who was bald and looked to be about forty-three, was wearing a special brace, and the Penn trainer was saying he was done; but Al — the battler — was insisting to the press that he could play. Al Howard "Zip" Long, a baseball player who had only played once in a varsity football game, would replace Kreuz, who was lobbying his coaches to let him suit up. "Kreuz will not start and will not play at any time," said Bert Bell, backfield coach and future Hall of Famer.

Head Coach Young had led the Quakers for three years, resuscitating the team from its failed experiment with college football mastermind John Heisman. Young had made the fans forget the legendary Heisman, a drillmaster who had lost his squad — players had danced when Heisman was fired. "I have taught you all I know — and still you know nothing!" Heisman would scream through his megaphone during practice. Before departing, Heisman, who worked summers as a Shakespearean actor, had graciously said, "I expect Lou Young to produce a fine team . . ." Young's 1923 squad went 5–4, but the 1924 unit posted a 9–1–1 record and won the eastern championship, its only loss to a powerful University of California team. James Braden, a Yalie who was covering the upcoming game, said, "Penn is 25 per cent stronger this year than last." Many experts considered Young's team the best in the nation.

The Quakers played a seven-man front. Young had solid ends in Don Singer and George Thayer, who would be named an All-American. There were Joe Wilson and Ed Hake, the tackles; Bob Pike and Johnny Butler, the guards; and Karl Robinson, center. It was a big and strong line, but perhaps a little deliberate. In the Quaker backfield there was Al Leith, who called the signals; and Jesse Douglas, Charlie Rogers, and Howard Long filled out the roster. "This is a typical Pennsylvania eleven in that the fundamentals are so sound and the generalship so daring," wrote Herbert Reed of the Universal Service syndicate. Many writers considered it a foregone conclusion that Penn would win the national championship. It was a good, well-balanced squad — and their reserves were deep, too. On defense the Quakers, given their institutional pedigree, were known as an intelligent team. The ends would go directly at the runner, which worked on straight-ahead teams (like Chicago) but posed a risk against Illinois, which could curve around the ends. The strategy had succeeded against powerhouses Brown, Yale, and the University of Chicago, but if the Penn ends pinched inside too much, Grange would swing around them and have only the secondary to beat. With the Illini's young and rather pathetic line, that was a long shot even on a dry field. The Associated Press concluded, "On a wet field, I would say Grange is not to be feared."

The Illini left for Philadelphia a couple of days before the game, and as the Illini train chugged to Philly, the collegiate laughter was interrupted by reports over the telegraph that weather was descending upon the East Coast. Inside the Pullman it got real quiet. The team looked to Red. "Grange was a genuine leader, unique in his quietness, but a powerful force nevertheless," noted Zuppke. "His teammates respected his fighting heart and his gameness, because they had a closeup view of the beatings he took." But even if Red didn't seem to care about the impending snowstorm, it worried them all. It was one of those wet and driving autumn snows, and the flakes were soaking woolen coats, bringing curses from men who had forgotten their galoshes; kids would have some great slush-ball fights, the coal order would have to be upped, unraked leaves would dissolve into glossy pieces; the streets were a goddamn mess. Philly had been prepping for Grange. People warmed themselves in downtown shops and shook off the snow as they gazed at the Illini team photo; everyone was looking over it, trying to pick out Red, who in the photograph looked like a brooding Valentino. Expectations were lowered: Grange, with his weak line, wouldn't be able to run.

The *Chicago Examiner*'s headline shouted at its readers "SNOW BLANKETS PHILLY AND ALSO ILLINI HOPES." Their hearts sank a bit; they, too, wanted Red to show the East. Its correspondent depressed them even more: "Santa Claus himself would experience difficulty making ground over this neighborhood tomorrow. The game is certain to be played under the worst conditions of the worst football season on record, looking at it from weather and turf angles. Even if the snow stops, and at this writing it doesn't look as if it will before next April, Franklin Field will look like an Eskimo's back yard. That means that 'Red' will do no spectacular sprinting unless, of course, he has the secret of Santa Claus."

"This snow looks awful bad," muttered Grange, who sported bell-shaped trousers and a gray felt hat at "a saucy angle," according to the *New York Times* writer. Grange could sense the heaviness of the air descending upon him. There was a lot on his mind. He dreamed that his partnership with Charlie meant freedom. The anticipation already building toward fever pitch, as Red and his mates stepped off the train a large crowd engulfed them. They took their leather traveling bags and forced their way through the crowd — gold footballs on their watch chains — underneath the banners reading "Penn rules the East," which were blowing in the driving gales. They went into the awaiting taxis. They studied the slushy Philadelphia streets. Zuppke's car was hit. Another car had skidded into him. He was shaken up a little. "I hope my team doesn't skid tomorrow like that car did," he quipped as he sat down at the Bellevue-Stratford Hotel for lunch.

"Coach, what kind of team do you have?" a reporter shouted.

"A fighting team, but my boys are inexperienced. They have played in-and-out football this season because of their inexperience. We have lost three of our four games, but I will admit that against Michigan last Saturday the team showed considerable improvement. Grange and Britton are seniors, two of the other regulars are juniors and the remainder, seven of them, are sophomores. You can readily see that I have a very young team."

After the meal the team went to inspect Franklin Field. "Gosh," Grange repeated, "that snow's bad. We haven't had a decent break on the weather this year. The field's been slippery every Saturday." Inside he was preparing for pain, for the blackouts and rain of stars after he was hit. The boys stood by stone-faced as their coach went off. "This is terrible," said an exasperated Zup, testing the field. "Why not protect the field as much as possible and let the public enjoy Grange?" Zup berated the groundskeeper, demanding that he place straw on the gridiron, which the man finally did. Zuppke, who was concocting conspiracy theories, told anyone who would listen that in the Midwest groundskeepers covered the field the day before the game if bad weather was threatening.

Zuppke knew Penn wanted to take Grange's legs away. He was mad. It was a disaster. A complete disaster. His reputation and Red's reputation were in danger. Red looked over the field. It made him smile. For all of his internal struggles, Saturday would bring relief, a return to his childhood, of playing with his friends at Wheaton's orchard. He was an experienced mudder; in high school his coach made him roll around in the dirtiest, muddiest puddle, and the Illini team had already played three games this season in the stuff. Some of the fellas were even calling the 1925 season the Year of the Mud. He couldn't wait for the game to start. Red read the papers and knew the Penn team was in Absecon, New Jersey, getting ready. Their coach, Lou Young, had a face like a librarian's. He wore football pants and a black sweater. "I would rather have a dry field," said Young. *Yeah, right.* A gunky field played right into Penn's hands. Young was brimming with confidence. "If the ground is slippery it will slow up Grange, of course, but don't forget that it will handicap Douglas, too."

Douglas? Who was Douglas compared to Grange? Yes, Saturday would be fun. Guilt, pride, and the need to prove himself to the sportswriters, the Bears, and Pyle welled up inside Red. He was like a predator. Every little incident created a reason for the kill. The people poor-mouthing his team. Even the freezing rain that started coming down on Friday evening created madness within him. And then when Grange awoke, he heard that Penn's Coach Young had brought his team over from the Seaview Country Club about eleven o'clock and boasted: "We've got to beat Illinois today, and that's what we are going to do. My team will fight harder because Kreuz and the others are out. You'll see the best fighting team that Penn has put on the field this year whip Illinois." And listening to Zup, right before they left the Manufacturers' Country Club: "We have been licked twice this year, but you are going to see a much better team today than Nebraska saw or Iowa saw. I have been building a team for the last half of my schedule and we have been coming slowly. We will hit our stride today. In the previous games I experimented with various combinations. I think I have the right one now." Zup was focused despite fumbling a good cigar into the slush, gritting, "We will win." Zup's front teeth had darkened from tobacco. He always smiled with his upper lip covering his top teeth.

All led to this. Grange was out there to show what he was created for: Running. Hitting. Red readied himself, put on his Rawlings "Anti–Charley Horse" moleskins, leather shoulder pads, and sweater. Someone told him that there was an urgent message from a Millie and Charlie Vallette, his Wheaton neighbors, who had prom-

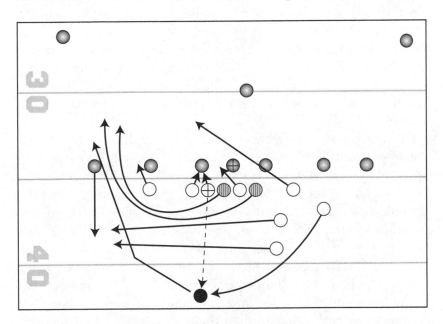

THE WEAK-SIDE PLAY.
Going to the weak side, without blockers, was risky against Penn's
defense, but the strategy gave Grange room to run and use his creativity.

ised him during the summer that they would attend the game. They had driven all the way to Philly for the contest but their tickets had not been waiting for them. Red had someone fix it all up, no problem, and the Vallettes had 50-yard-line seats for the toughest ticket in the world.

At two o'clock or thereabouts, on the last Saturday of October, the game began on Franklin Field, a venue with the ghosts of American athletics — the nation's first scoreboard (1895), first two-tiered stadium (1922), first football radio broadcast (WIP, 1922); and since 1899, Franklin was the home of the Army-Navy games, the annual contest attended by presidents. Right before the starting whistle, the Illinois band rushed into the stadium. The band had been waylaid because of a train accident, and the 150 student musicians, led by a golden-garbed drum major, had huffed and puffed to the stadium. On the Pennsylvania sideline cheerleaders wore new blue slickers and led the crowd with megaphones as Penn students pelted cops with snowballs. Among the VIPs were two of the world's most famous physicians: Lord Dawson — the English royal family's doctor who had just been given an honorary degree — along with his daughter, "Ticky"; and Dr. Charles H. Mayo, the most celebrated physician of his era, who had brought his son, Charles W. Mayo, a medical student at the University of Pennsylvania Medical School.

The field was still a mess — sticky mud with bits of straw sticking out from it, like a pigpen. The teams could hardly move their feet during warm-ups. It was starting to get cold again, too.

Up there, in the stands, was Charlie Pyle, watching it all. His gleaming eyes sparkled. If the Atlantic Coast, where the big money was, loved him it would mean unheard-of profits, of that he was sure, and it would make his entire master plan work. This was the first time the East Coast writers had covered Red in force. Hands were rubbed together. Charlie prayed. How could Red move in that stuff? Surrounded by still cameramen and the newsreel boys, the captains met each other in the middle of the field. Red pumped Joseph Wilson's paw. Wilson was Penn's captain. The Illini would receive.

"I want you to line up strong either right or left," Zup told Red. It

was like a benediction. Grange knew what was coming. Zup wanted
to shock Penn early. He would risk it all for visual beauty and the
tactics of surprise. The players had been trained not to rebel. There
were cracks of individuality forming but Zup still held them in his
power. If Grange listened, the team would follow. But really, Zup
could have called anything. "My coach," Grange would always call
him. Red Grange's eyes stared at Zuppke. Grange wore his blue
sweater with the orange 77 on the back. He always looked hun-
gry before a game; a little jittery, cursing at the cameramen, spitting on the ground, rubbing his hands together. No one liked to be
around him because he would snap at you. Zup went on: "Run Britton into the strong side the first two times. The third time, I want
ya to line up strong one way, generally, to the short side of the field."
Playing the wing with an unbalanced line, Illinois would usually
shift right and run right, shift left and run left. Today there would
be a change of plans. Grange nodded as Zup continued, "Then, I
want you to take the ball and go to the *weak* side. The first time
to the weak side." They ran the plays according to Zup's orders. Up
in the stands they wondered why Grange wasn't running the ball.
Why was he just a blocker? Britt came back to the huddle, gasping,
and said, "What have you fellas got against me?" The Penn defenders, Grange observed, "pert' near killed him." But the Illini players
knew it was all a setup. On the next play Grange took it to the weak
side and the field was wide open. As he galloped, his hooves dancing on the mud, 56 yards to the end zone, he thought, "I never was
as lonesome. I could be in Wheaton at twelve o'clock midnight and
they'd have more people in front of me than I did there. They're all
gone." The crowd was in shock. Grange had run so swiftly. The mud
trapped all of the players except him. They had never seen a player
run for so many yards so quickly. It must have been a momentary
lapse. They had only half believed the stories about Grange. They
were watching something that they could not quite comprehend.
Grange seemed to be conquering nature itself.

Before the spectators could catch their breath, Red took the
kickoff following his first score and ran it back 60 yards to Pennsylvania's 20-yard line. Among the hushed shock of the crowd,
there was a smattering of applause from the Penn fans. Grange
was handed the ball and drove his team down. The Illini scored.

What did the crowd wish for at that moment? For the Penn team
to rebound, or to experience Grange's artistry in the mud? There
was something beautiful about the juxtaposition — a group of men
covered with and stuck in glop, and yet here was Grange so grace-
ful, light, almost pretty, and oblivious to the impossible conditions.
The men out there were like horses, steam rising from their flanks.
Grange's jersey and tan pants were covered in the slop, but everyone
could tell who he was when he started running, dodging, sprinting,
hitting.

In the second period, after his team had been forced to make
a safety, he carried the ball over two-thirds the length of the field,
only to lose it on downs on Pennsylvania's 2-yard line. During the
next possession Grange carried the ball in three of the five plays and
scored again. A mist was entering the stadium and Grange looked
eerie down there. *He was a galloping ghost . . .* More and more Penn
fans were clapping for Grange. Something had come over Grange's
blockers. They were moving Penn men from their stations as if they
were toothpicks in their path, noted one observer. "It's not a bad way
to enter a game of football," said Grange, "to feel that your team is
supposed to be the underdog and knowing that every play calls for
all the strength you have." Later in the second quarter, Zup called
for Red to take a breather. He left the "weird, mud-bespattered pyramid of gnomes, removed his yellow head guard, revealing for the
first time his red thatch of hair, and started to the sidelines," wrote
Walter Eckersall. The crowd cheered, men removing their hats in
tribute and waving their 25¢ copies of *Franklin Field Illustrated.*
The scene defined masculine beauty.

At halftime, on press row, in his flashy coonskin coat, John O'Hara,
the writer, watched the Illini band form letters in the mud. O'Hara
had been experiencing a powerful melancholy because seven
months before, his father had died, leaving eight children and
a widow, and now John was responsible for supporting them all.
The O'Hara family was owed about $60,000 from Dr. O'Hara's pa-
tients, many of whom were impoverished Irish, German, Slavic,
and Anglo-Saxon immigrants; but the money would never be repaid, bringing hard times for the family living at number 606 Ma-
hantongo Street in Pottsville, Pennsylvania, where over the moun-

tains, eighteen miles away, was Shenandoah, from which O'Hara could see smoke from a subterranean fire; and minutes away was Minersville, where the professional football Pottsville Maroons played, while spectators, many of them workers in the anthracite mines, watched from wooden bleachers. O'Hara, at age twenty, was the oldest child but perhaps the least capable of leading his family. He was expected to show up at 8:00 a.m. every day at the *Pottsville Journal*, an afternoon paper, but he rarely met the obligation. O'Hara covered the football team, and he hoped his writing would get him to one of the higher-paying Philadelphia or New York papers where his heroes, such as Rice, plied their trade. Perhaps this game would help him make a mark. He watched as on the field the Illini band formed *P-E-N-N*, when suddenly a man dressed like an Indian ran from his hiding place just north of the Illinois stands and started an insane dance, as the band played "Hail, Pennsylvania." This was the unveiling of the Illini's mascot, named by Zuppke, Chief Illiniwek. A William Penn impersonator came forward and smoked a peace pipe with the Chief as the half ended. The halftime show was an attempt to create drama, but the real drama would continue after intermission. The people, the sportswriters — everyone couldn't wait for Grange's next act of illusion.

The Illini were in control immediately. It was into the third quarter and the kind of cold that made your lungs ache. The Illini were on the Pennsylvania 35-yard line, which was well within Britton's range. The game stood at 18–2, so keeping the game in their control seemed like a priority. Grange, wiping his hands on his pants, called the signals, and he thought it was the perfect time to fling the dice. "Flea-flicker," he told the boys. Grange looked over to Zuppke, who jumped off the bench, which meant to change the play. Zup sent in a sub to call it off, but the team would not accept the substitution. It was funny to watch Zuppke, the ultimate gambler, want to play it safe, to hold the lead, to not create chaos. They had the win, no need to risk it now. But Zuppke's risk-taking had rubbed off on Grange. Zup put his head in his hands like he was weeping.

No matter the point in the game, the flea-flicker was a dangerous call. Grange would go down on the ground as if he was holding for Britton to kick a field goal, but the ball would go to Britton,

Grange would get up and run to his right, and Britton was supposed to throw a lob pass to the right end, who was Chuck Kassel, and Chuck would throw Grange a lateral. They started the action, executed it flawlessly. Most of the Penn players ran one way. Red ran the other way. The bewildered Penn team couldn't seem to lift their heels as Grange's boots thumped past them, pivoting as he had described in an article for a boys' magazine: "It is a good deal like the basketball pivot, consisting of a rapid whirling and change of direction. You'll find that often if you're tackled in the line or in the open field, a twisting pivot will shake the tackler off, turn you out of his arms and permit you to go on for more yardage. The big fault of many backs is 'sneaking' with the ball. That means loping along half-heartedly instead of running for all you're worth." Straight-ahead runners dominated the sport; Grange would be the first player to use such hip-gyrating moves to such effect, revolutionizing football. Red was running with all his might, all right, and he also had this high-stepping style that made it seem like the mud couldn't smother his legs. The Quakers could feel it, a sense of dread, resonating from their own feet. Grange had knocked one of their teammates out of the game with a straight-arm. Their sinister intentions were replaced with respect. Red looked calm, unfazed, as he blew past them, their lungs chilled, a salty film on their lips. Red Grange took the flea-flicker in for a touchdown.

Grange left the game with the Penn fans cheering him. A steady ovation. Charlie Pyle was on his feet. He clapped. He smiled. He knew. "Millions of people would want to see in action the boy whom they knew only through the newspapers," Pyle thought, marinating in the secret knowledge that he was about to get filthy rich.

Red finished with 363 yards and averaged more than 10 yards per carry.

The final score was 24–2.

In its completely matter-of-fact assessment of the game, the *Pennsylvania Gazette* wrote, "It did not seem humanly possible for any individual to realize the expectations raised . . ."

Penn's Coach Young concluded, "Grange, in my estimation, is the greatest football player in the game. They can compare him with any of the greats of the past and they can place him alongside of Thorpe and others, but to me he stands out alone. I saw Thorpe play in his heyday when he was the hardest man in football to stop. But I firmly believe that Grange eclipses anything that Thorpe ever did."

It wasn't the ground-out yards, the long gainers, or even the touchdowns. Grange had done more than meet his advance billing; he had created something grander, and up in the press box, the nation's star writers were tip-tip-tapping away, selling Grange as if he was more than a man, perhaps sensing a shift in the very essence of football, a class shift to workingman glamour, an end to upper-crust eastern schools and their athletic old boys' club valor. Ruth and Dempsey and Jones were gods, and the writers were now putting Grange alongside those immortals. With these writers' words, and the photographers' beautifully rendered images splashed across the pages showing Grange above captions such as "The wilderness of mud" as the "Might of Penn Falls before 'Red' Grange and Ten Other Illinoians." *Tit-tit-tit-tit-tit-ti* . . .

Ed Pollock of the (Philadelphia) *Public Ledger* rhapsodized: "Countless columns have been written about Red Grange, but words cannot stir the imagination sufficiently to present a picture that is even close to reality." *Tit-tit-tit-tit-tit-ti* . . .

Damon Runyon of the Universal Service: "This man 'Red' Grange of Illinois is three or four men and a horse rolled into one for football purposes. He is Jack Dempsey, Babe Ruth, Al Jolson, Paavo Nurmi and Man o' War. Put them together they spell Grange. At 2:05 o'clock this afternoon, by the watch, this man, 'Red' Grange broke out against the University of Pennsylvania football eleven, and at 4:30 he had 65,000 men, women and little children positively dumbfounded by his performance. They finally reached the conclusion that this man Grange is something more, or perhaps one should say less, than human. Perhaps a throwback to some Saurian age when they played football in the ooze and slime. He is melody and symphony on the football field. He is crashing sound. He is poetry. He is brute force." *Tit-tit-tit-tit-tit-ti* . . .

Harry Cross, the *New York Times* correspondent: "His left arm is a rod of steel. When he shoots it out straight at the onrushing opposition they bowl over like so many tenpins . . . Everywhere in the melee of mud-smeared players the golden yellow top piece of Grange stood out like the helmet of Navarre." *Tit-tit-tit-tit-tit-ti* . . .

Ford C. Frick, the Indiana native working for the *New York American*, the Hearst morning paper, wrote: "Sixty-three thousand human voices took up the cry at Franklin Field Saturday, booming it in mighty cadence across the mist-swept gridiron; sending it roaring in mighty reverberation against the sullen gray clouds that hovered low to watch the spectacle . . . And there he went — a daring, shimmering, elusive will o' the wisp, writing across the mud-strewn wastes of Franklin Field, Autumn's brilliant page in another season of gridiron history." *Tit-tit-tit-tit-tit-ti . . .*

Gordon Mackay of the *Philadelphia Enquirer:* "A Man o' War in moleskins, Red Grange, on whose back stuccoed with mud, flared the '77' of his alma mater, bore aloft the torch of triumph that was the beacon to light the trail of the Fighting Illini to victory. To describe Grange in his glory is to rob the language of its adjectives, and to strip the mother tongue of its superlatives . . ." *Tit-tit-tit-tit-tit-ti . . .*

And John O'Hara, the young man who had seen football players in a setting that the other well-known writers had never witnessed — inside his late father's doctor's office as their legs were set, their shoulders jammed back into sockets — perhaps understood Grange better than most other writers, and he might have produced the most realistic, and touching, tribute: "Grange went over to the bench, leaned over and spoke to Zuppke, who put his hand on Red's shoulder while thirty-two assistant managers tried to bundle him up. Grange nodded and then began his jog trot to the dressing room. All alone, the slow trot down the seventy-five yards to the exit, and there wasn't a man or woman not standing in the whole stadium. And if I was any judge, there wasn't a dry eye, either. There he was, the boy who had come through when the chips were really down, dragging his blanket behind him, and it was wonderful. The men on the field could have pulled pistols and shot it out and no one in the stands would have noticed, because we were all looking at Grange. Somehow or other I felt that the eyes of the whole East were on that solitary figure, and for some reason or other I was proud of him."

Tit-tit-tit-tit-tit-ti . . .
Tit-tit-tit-tit-tit-ti . . .
Tit-tit-tit-tit-tit-ti . . .

Readers couldn't help but marvel at him. Through the newspapers' own correspondents or one of the syndicates, descriptions of the game would find their way into most of the country's newspapers — the new American Bibles, with a captive, believing audience, the radio a growing, but fledgling, medium. Red Grange no longer belonged to Wheaton, or to the people out West; he was in the process of becoming America's player, as the writers frantically handed their copy to the telegraphers. Here was greatness.

In the locker room Joe Green, Grange's backfield mate, whose nose was split wide open, stormed into the dimly lit room.

"Red, old man, I'm proud to call you captain," he cried.

"Ah, shucks — we just got a-going, that's all. They were a good team — as good as we've met this year — well, we just got a-going."

A crowd of boys peered through a basement window and clamored for a glimpse of the Ghost.

"Nothing to see, boys." Red laughed, in a heavy, gruff voice, but he stood up and the kids ran away pleased.

After the Illini dressed, they went to the Bellevue-Stratford for dinner. "We upheld the honor of the conference, didn't we?" Zuppke bragged, who was now calling his team a "November team" because it had started slowly but come on at the end of the season. He had pulled off the upset and proved himself as one of the best — if not the best — strategists in the land. "I guess I sacrificed myself dearly in conference games, but I saved 'Red' Grange. We pointed for this Penn game. You know that. You know that what we accomplished here today means more for Illinois and for the conference than anything else we have done, or may do this season.

"These eastern critics know now that there is still football in the conference. They thought Red was stopped. He was just resting, that's all . . . He had to satisfy those sixty-three thousand. He did.

"I guess my reputation as a coach wasn't worth much after those three defeats we have suffered out West. But the reputation of 'Red' Grange means more to me."

7

A Passage to Manhood

RED GRANGE AFTER HIS LAST COLLEGE GAME

BEFORE RED GRANGE COULD even process the heroics of the Penn game, he realized something was different in his life. Grange had never seen or imagined such chaos. The frenzy had reached an even larger scale. The team was on the train heading back to Champaign, and in the back of Red's mind were thoughts about his relationship with Pyle and how it would eventually trickle into the world. The public's retribution concerned him, but that wasn't a major worry at this moment. The newspapers gloriously describing the Penn game had been printed and put on the streets. The bundles of newsprint were barely dry. Red held on to a question-mark gaze as he squinted through the train window. At every stop that afternoon and into the fading evening Red could see men and women and little children all bundled up in their Sunday best, standing on tiptoes in the snow, peering into his train window just hoping for a glimpse of him. Back in Champaign-Urbana, twenty thousand students and townspeople had lined the tracks to celebrate the man who had, according to one writer, "rattled the effete East." The train was two and a half hours late but still they waited, distracting themselves from the cold by singing songs until the headlight of the train emerged from the cornfields. When it was about a mile or two from the city limits, town cannons blasted, guns cracked, and fire works rocketed into the sky. They all chanted:

We want Red!
We want Zuppke!

He was exhausted and embarrassed, and so Red slipped from the sighing machine and bowed his head into the crowd, trying to escape the mob scene. Red sneaked through the coal-scented coats for a block until they recognized him. They hoisted him onto their shoulders and carried him two miles to his frat house. Once there, Red hurried inside, but the rabble kept chanting until he finally came to the window.

"We-er-had a fine visit down East," Red stuttered. "I don't know how to thank you fellows for everything, but the team deserves the credit. And we're certainly going to do everything in our power to lick Chicago next Saturday." Three more games in his collegiate career. Three long weeks. The Ghost ducked into his room and did not return. But the next day, and in the days that followed, they went to him with a growing intensity, trying to get near him, to express their love before it was too late, before he became another huckster in a business suit. The throbbing crowds, the attention — in comparison, he predicted, the small potatoes pro game would give him some tranquillity.

The season had been lost early on, of course, but Illinois versus Chicago was always a major in-state battle. The now-legendary Austin "Five Yards" McCarty would be playing for the Maroons, a team that was battling bitterly with its alumni, who were showing up at practice each afternoon and accusing their team of being yellow. Calling a Maroon athlete yellow was an inside joke. Back at the athletic beginning of the University of Chicago, the football team had worn yellow, but the color kept running, creating the effect of a person who was not controlling his bladder. Because of their tepid performances, opponents — and now their own fans — were bringing back the slight. In the past couple of weeks the pressure had mounted even more when Graham Kernwein, Chicago's halfback, had the goddamn audacity to smile and hum during pregame warm-ups for the Penn game, a contest Chicago lost 7–0. The alumni dubbed the team a bunch of singers, and the papers had piled on by nicknaming the team the "Maroon Ladies."

But the real story behind the game was Grange. The Grange mania was uncontrollable. Zuppke had to close practice because of the "co-eds, sporting eds, movie photographers, still photographers, radio announcers, big businessmen trying to exchange tickets on the fifty-yard line, big politicians, big financiers, big butter and egg men . . ." went one account; another said, "Foreign debts, local politics, graft scandals — they all yield to the epic of the football season, the annual struggle between the Maroons and Illini"; and yet another described the crowds as "a mighty maelstrom of humanity, fed heavily by an exodus from Chicago, almost as remarkable as that ancient flight from Egypt." Nineteen special trains of fourteen cars each were coming from Chicago, and the roads between the metropolis and Champaign looked like ribbons of maroon, blue, and orange, as the big-city fans flew their respected colors. The governor and Senator William McKinley were in their private train cars heading to the game. Tickets were going for $25, sometimes $50, and five thousand others would see the contest at the Armory on the Gridgraph. On the night before the fray, the Illini holed up in the Champaign Country Club. Some of the boys were playing cards. Joe Green, a gash still visible on his nose, played jazz on the piano while a few players sang "Don't Bring Lulu": "We all went to the party, real high-toned affair, / Then along came Lulu, wild as any Zulu . . ."

"Aw, give us some of your own stuff, Joe," someone said.

His thick hands ran over the ebony and ivory with surprising authority. Joe was playing "The March of the Maroons," and there came a howl of laughter.

As rain hit the clapboard country club, Zup sat by the fire with Justa Lindgren, a star tackle on the 1901 team. Justa was Zuppke's line coach and most trusted aide. Zuppke's brother Paul was there, too. Matt Bullock, the quiet trainer, was talking with Frank Rokusek, captain of the 1924 team, about going on a hunting trip. Zup was surrounded by his boys, his family. The season had been a success because of Red's redemption in the Penn game. Zup had risked it all for Red. After arm wrestling another player and winning — "it's just my superior strength," Red joked — he autographed photographs of himself for the newspapermen, who would give them to their kids, friends, editors, wives, or girlfriends. Red wore a smashing tan suit and tan shoes and went to work blunting the Maroons' motivation. Referring to the knocks they were taking in the press and from their alumni, he said, "That's no way to talk to a team or a player. As to the Maroons or any other team, for that matter, being yellow, those Chicago alumni were all wrong. If a player has a yellow streak in him, he wouldn't even appear on the field."

Who could forget Jack Trice, the Negro Iowa State standout, who had broken his collarbone in the first half of a game two years before, kept playing, was trampled during one subsequent play, and died two days later of respiratory problems?

At game time the field was a complete mess, another quagmire in this Year of the Mud, and a chilly northeast wind swept through Memorial's columns of the dead. In the newsreels people would see drizzly images of men bathed in mud, sliding into ponds and then lakes of water; no one, not even Grange, was visible. When Red Grange slopped onto the field there was a "roar that could have been heard back in Chicago," wrote the *American*'s Harold Johnson, but the Galloping Ghost had a God-awful day, carrying the ball seventeen times and gaining 51 yards. Besides a drizzly rain and terrible field conditions hampering his play, Red had a charley horse in his left leg and just couldn't get anything going because the Maroons — whom no one was describing as yellow after a gutsy effort — had stymied him, thanks once again to Stagg's defensive alignments. Because of the team's ability to stop Grange, the Chicago alumni would not have to hang black crepe around their school — even if it was just a moral victory. Despite Red's play, the Illini won 13–6 because Britt had hit punt after gorgeous punt, averaging 50 yards, and scored one touchdown, the other coming after Kassel blocked a punt and Art D'Ambrosio, an Illini end, fell on it in the end zone. Zup never gave much credit to Britt, but after the game he told him that for the first time in Britt's three years on the team he felt compelled to take off his hat. Red, who admired his friend, would say, "Without Britton there never would have been a Red Grange . . . but nobody knows the name of Paul Revere's horse."

Like any other player in his position, Red should have been appreciating the honors and soaking up the applause for his collegiate swan song, but he felt vulnerable. The lies were starting to pile up. Zuppke started hearing nasty whispers about Grange and that wretched professional football. Zup had a personal vendetta against pro ball: just four years previously it had caused him humiliation and almost cost him his job. Nine of his own players had betrayed him by playing in a pro contest down in Taylorville, Illinois, against ten Notre Dame stars who played for the town of Carlinville, Illinois. In direct violation of college rules the players were paid, and an unheard-of $100,000 was bet on the game. The Chicago gambling syndicates were involved, meaning the Capone gang had a stake in it. The Associated Press found out about the contest and Coach Zuppke and his friend, Notre Dame coach Knute Rockne, whose names were synonymous with the amateur ideal of college sports, suffered national embarrassment. The game happened four years ago, sure, but the talk of it had continued unabated. Some of Taylorville's townspeople were still accusing Zuppke's staff of scouting prairie teams and inducing the best prospects with money and gifts. Zuppke scoffed at the allegations and felt especially hurt that the stories had hit the press; after all, the reporters were not exactly on the payroll, but they were given their fair share in Illini-run speaking engagements, tickets (which could be resold for a pretty penny), and almost total access. The season after the controversy, 1922, had been horrible: *a 24–0 drubbing by Michigan . . . a loss to tiny Butler University . . . five losses in total . . .* But the season's failure also brought Zuppke one of his most treasured mementos. After the final game the team sent Zuppke a letter: "Whatever our faults, many people were good enough to say that we never quit. If this is the truth, and we believe that it is, we learned the spirit of never quitting from you, our coach."

Grange's brilliant 1923 national championship season had brought glory to Zuppke and erased the Taylorville game and the poor 1922 season from the public's mind. Grange had helped save Zuppke reputation.

To Zuppke's immense pleasure, Grange always denied interest in the pro game. A star like Grange going pro was not only unthinkable, because it would tarnish the good name of the University of Illinois; it would be personally hurtful because of Zup's growing closeness to the boy. Then Red, after he was asked his future plans, came out with a bombshell: "I haven't made any plans whatever to play professional football. I haven't signed a contract nor have I made a verbal agreement to play, and right now I really don't know whether or not I would accept an offer to play for money."

Zuppke wanted to see Grange and Earl Britton immediately.

"If you are ineligible, turn in your suits," Zup screamed at Red and Britt, who was also rumored to be turning pro.

"I'm no more professional now," said Red, "than I was when I was on Burt Ingwerson's freshman squad."

"That's not what they're saying," said Zuppke.

"I don't care what they're saying."

"What about the automobile company?"

"I don't know what you're talking about."

"You haven't signed anything?"

"Nothing."

"How about this promoter Pyle? Lots of talk around about you and Pyle and some sort of contract."

"Charlie Pyle? The man who runs those moving picture houses?"

"You know very well who I mean!"

"He's a friend of mine," said Grange, quietly.

"You're being sold on the pro game."

"I haven't signed anything yet."

"But you will."

"I don't know."

"Don't do it."

"I haven't made up my mind yet."

"You'll be crazy to go into that mudhole of a game."

Zup, disgusted, told Red to sit out practice for a couple of days because he had become a distraction. He wanted Red to talk with George Huff and to go home and talk with Lyle Grange. It was a troubling reality to Zup, who realized that Kant was right — God, freedom, and immortality were reflections of a society. The world, Zup's idea of the world, was out of step. But Red? Anyone but Red.

"We would rather Grange wouldn't play professional football for his own good, but we have no control over his private affairs," Zup sighed to the gathering storm of reporters. Then the story about the auto dealer that Red and Charlie had tried to shake down over the summer went from rumor to news story. In their slow but sure rhythm the press was getting started on him; the stories mutating. The dealer told the press about the shakedown. Writers started speculating about Red and Charlie. They believed Red had signed a contract with Charlie Pyle, which was against eligibility rules. Inside Red was panicking, but he denied it all. Newspaper readers seeking spiritual nobility may have wondered about Red Grange, and they wanted to know about this Pyle character. Charlie, hunted down in balmy Tampa, where he was "secretly" making arrangements for Grange's pro tour, was indignant. The public could easily read the stories about Charlie Pyle and start coming to conclusions. Pyle — a ballyhoo man — flashed a dangerous smile when informed that Red had denied putting his name on a contract.

"I have nothing to say yet," said Charlie. "If Grange denies having signed, then he must have some reason for doing so."

Contrary to his public stance, in private Charlie waved a paper with Red's signature on it. Red was his property now. The public's judgment would be rendered soon. Would they blame Red? Would the vast majority support him or just not care? On campus the students, who expected Grange to respect the university and end his career nobly, were angry; jealous promoters were doing their best to discredit the upstart Charlie. The newspapermen called Pyle "mysterious" and tried to justify their intuition by talking with his associates. A publicity man hired by Charlie but who had bolted to a competing concern had been persuaded to blab about their partnership, claiming Grange and Pyle had signed a contract. And Calvin Barth, an Indianapolis manager of the Warner Brothers film company and a friend of Pyle's, said, "I know Mr. Pyle too well to suppose that he would begin an extensive advertising campaign for Grange's appearance in the South unless he had a written option upon the half back's services." No one was safe from the thirsty reporters. University of Illinois President Kinley passed through Chicago, where he was corralled about the Grange matter: "I talked with Harold last week and he told me he was not tied up with anybody and I believe him," he said. Kinley found the celebrity worship irritating — "his first duty is to his studies, and that duty, with his athletics, takes up all his time and strength," he said privately. The university had to hire a stenographer to answer the twenty-five to one hundred letters Red was receiving a day, and Kinley was constantly getting dumb letters suggesting ways to honor Grange; one letter writer said a life-size statue should be erected, perhaps a nude likeness "to show the wonderful physique of Mr. Grange." To the faculty who wanted to condemn Grange, Kinley said that he would not dignify the "sad matter"; rather he wanted Grange to learn a lesson on his own. To the more persistent Grange bashers, Kinley quoted Gamaliel: "'If this counsel or this work be of men, it will come to naught: But if it be of God, ye cannot overthrow it.'"

Red *had* made the university and the conference a lot of money.

At season's end 370,000 people would have watched him play, filling athletic coffers, creating coaching reputations, and giving the Big Ten national prestige. Grange would be given the benefit of the doubt when he was called in by George Huff, the cherubic athletic director who looked like a carnival barker with his straw boater and too-short dress ties that always rested on his prodigious belly. The two men talked for an hour. Afterward Huff described the meeting to the newspapermen. "I don't like the idea of professional football at all and I have repeatedly told Harold to have nothing to do with Pyle; I hope Grange never again puts on a [football] suit after he finishes college. It is by no means a crime to play after leaving school, but Grange has so many better opportunities before him. I believe I convinced him that it would be wise to proceed cautiously." In other words, pro football was beneath a man of Grange's stature.

But Red heard something else in their meeting. Lots of people underestimated the genial and slow-talking Huff, but he had entered the University of Illinois at age fifteen. Grange would remember Huff, who had a smile that went to St. Louis and a worldly pragmatism, confiding, "I won't attempt to advise you — but I left school before graduation to join the Boston Red Sox. A true amateur is a man whose father never worked. You have to go to England to find them." Just a couple of years earlier Huff had lobbied, but failed, to pass a conference rule permitting college football players to play off-season pro ball. Huff sent Grange to Wheaton to talk it all over with his father. But before Red left the twin towns, the *Champaign News-Gazette* invited him into the pressroom and grilled him about the rumors. "You print any damn thing you want," stormed Red, as he grabbed his hat, "but be ready for a lawsuit if it's not truthful." The pressure was making him crack. To most of their fellow ink-stained wretches, the *News-Gazette* reporters had gone way over the line. The bigger writers didn't want to blast Red. Hell, there was a cottage industry in the boy! About the upstart *News-Gazette* James Braden of the *Chicago Journal* sniffed: "Grange was in the vortex of the storm and an attempt was made to 'strong arm' him into certain admissions. As an individual in the land of the free, Red resisted these efforts."

A gaggle of scribblers was in Wheaton to meet Red as he pulled up in his borrowed car. "I'm still pretty much of a kid," he told the note takers before strolling across the street and ascending the stairs to the Grange apartment. "My dad and I have been pals. He has paid my way through school and I wanted to talk it over with him before making my decision. But I haven't signed a contract for anything. It would be a violation of the university's rules and until next Saturday's game is over I'm going to be loyal to my school and give it all I have. After that game, I'll be ready to talk business. I've had a lot of offers but I don't like to sell things. I think I'm a rotten salesman. But I do like to play football. Some of my advisers have frowned on professional football, but the way I figure it that's my own business and my father has left it to me to decide. After all, I'll soon be forgotten down on the campus and some of the fellows who are now my best friends wouldn't loan me a dollar 10 years from now if I was broke. And I haven't much money." Everyone knew Lyle didn't want his son to quit school a semester shy of graduating, and the former lumberman was plenty upset with his son. There in the apartment with the flimsy curtains, the dust-filled bachelorhood, the Grange men trying to make ends meet, with Garland recovering from his shoulder surgery, Lyle lectured his boy, warned him about Charlie Pyle. "Character and not money is what the world needs today," said Pa. "Money is nice. But between the two character is the more important."

"I like football," said Red.

"I know."

"What's wrong with making a profession of the thing you like to do most?"

"Nothing, except, from what I hear about it, professional football isn't much of a profession."

"Nobody is advising anybody to stay out of professional baseball, is there? That's the way it's going to be with professional football."

Pa looked out the window at the shuffling newspapermen.

"Do what you like, son. Do what you think is best." Lyle was letting his boy go.

We are quick to defame someone's ingenuity and audacity, perhaps because there is such a universal absence of both. Red listened. Character meant something, sure, but it seemed like everyone preaching about it was someone with money. He had options if the football thing didn't work out. The local Republicans wanted to run him as a congressman-at-large. Red was only twenty-two but he would be old enough in 1927 when the regular congressional session started. Enough with the way they had always lived. Enough with the scrimping and saving. Enough with everyone else making a fortune from his talent like he was some sort of sap. Enough of borrowing his pal Doc Cooley's car, the jalopy that he had driven to Wheaton and that was parked outside. Why was John L. Griffith, the commissioner of athletics in the Western Conference, deriding him? They had investigated his amateur standing and had found nothing, but Griffith had still criticized the pro game. "The college spirit is lacking in professional football," he said. "The players are not willing to risk injury to themselves just to enable an outstanding start to make a good showing." *Spirit? What'd Griffith know about spirit?* Why couldn't he play a little pro football and make enough money to pay off his debts and buy a $500 raccoon-skin coat? Fifteen contracts from various promoters were stacked in a pile in the apartment. Why couldn't he build his father a proper house and make it something special with a poolroom where Pa and Gardie and their pals could bum around?

Before he returned to Champaign, a sympathetic reporter for the *Evening American* had breakfast with Red and Garland.

"One thing is sure at the start," Red began. "I am not going to carry ice. I may play professional football. You know a football player when he has left his team is as dead as yesterday's newspaper. If I am to make any money playing football I have got to do it now. I can't wait. I need the money, I'll admit that. Father has helped me and he's in ordinary circumstances. You may tell the readers of the *American* that I have not signed any contract to play. Nor have I talked over any of their propositions with them. That would be unfair to Coach Zuppke and to my university. You know I owe something to him and to my school. People think I am going to quit school. I expect to graduate. I owe that much to myself. You know that I am behind in my work right now, football practice having taken up a good share of my time. I'm not so good you see. If I play pro football after Saturday I will have to take an extra semester of work to get my diploma."

What about this man Pyle who says you have signed a contract with him?

"If I signed a contract with him or any other man would he be apt to tell anybody about it before the proper time?" He wouldn't say any more about Charlie because he didn't want to bury himself alive in lies.

Do you have a movie contract?

"I have had several written offers but have sent them all to my father and I think he has them all here somewhere in the house."

How much have you been offered to play football?

"An eastern team offered me $50,000 for three games. But I can't understand how I can be worth that to them. I am a little suspicious of these big offers. There is one thing in this professional football game that lots of my friends fail to understand. Granted that I have been an unusual player in college but I might not be a success in the professional racket. The fellows who play pro football are older, stronger, more experienced than I and the fellows I am now playing with and against. I might be a flop. This pro business isn't any cinch it appears to me. The same thing goes for the movies. I don't know anything about acting. I might be a flop there, too. Guess I had better go slow and not lose my head. All this publicity and newspaper talk about things that I don't know myself makes me want to go slow. The only thing I ask is that my friends stick with me and wish me luck."

After breakfast the three men went to the jail to meet Lyle, who was known to never lock the jail cell doors. When asked why, he would tower over the questioner in reply, showing that prisoners wouldn't dare escape.

Zuppke had lost the boy to Pyle *and* professional football. *Had the boy lost his damn mind?* It was the personal betrayal that would hurt the most. It felt like Grange was joining the lowest rung of the sports world. It was embarrassing. Zuppke had to hold it together and coach Grange in one more game. At Saturday's end their run would be over. For the past three years Zup had made a career — and some good money — talking about Grange *(Michigan ... Chicago ... Penn ...)*. The father-son, teacher-student image so wisely conceived and promoted by Zup was being spit away. Grange was denying Zuppke a coach's glory. The university wasn't exactly investigating Grange, but it needed to conclude that his relationship with Pyle did not violate any rules, because the total gate for

Saturday's game was $150,000, and no one wanted to jeopardize it. "Grange has satisfied us that he is not a professional athlete and he is eligible to play football against Ohio Saturday afternoon," said Huff, trying to put the matter to rest.

"Ohio is not making an issue of the eligibility of the players of its opponents," said the Buckeyes' A. D. Lynn St. John.

Putting on a brave face before boarding the train, Coach Zuppke gave a purse-lipped speech at the Champaign station: "We will do our best to shake Grange loose in this game Saturday, after that he will have to do the rest. All the players are in good physical shape and we have a good chance to win." Zuppke had never felt so defeated.

The train, chugging rhythmically on oily wheels, was supposed to bring respite to Red, a last adventure with his teammates: Chuck Kassel's pink cheeks and flop of hair, Britton's constant chatter, Bullock's hunting stories, the porters in their brave solicitude, and the clownish alumni who were inevitably and regrettably a part of it all. The writers were aware of the contradictory stories coming from the Grange camp, but they were not willing to face them. The reporters were well taken care of and they were more than a little reluctant to push Grange off the perch. It was the beginning of the sports journalists' tug o' war between glorification and destruction.

James Braden, the *Journal* writer, was aboard the train en route to Columbus. He ignored any controversy, choosing to telegraph a cheerful story: "Fifty-five players, coaches and supernumeraries make up the Illinois party, and this morning everybody was feeling in the best of spirits. Even Zuppke was ready for breakfast, and he and George Huff recalled the old-time methods of travel that a squad had to undergo. The players were up at 7:30 a.m., had a good breakfast and lolled about the Pullmans reading and talking. Most of them remember the enthusiastic sendoff received at Champaign last night and the many telegrams which old alumni have been sending in during the last twenty-four hours."

The game had become a farewell party. The *Herald-Examiner*'s Warren W. Brown wrote, "There is to be a football game here tomorrow between Illinois and Ohio State, but what of it? Eighty thousand people, from all parts of the West and from various spots along the line of march that leads to New York, are here, or on their way here, not for the Illinois-Ohio State game. It's Grange's game.

"It's not what Illinois does or Ohio State does. It's what Grange does that counts with the 80,000.

"Newspaper men of New York who haven't missed a Yale-Harvard struggle for more years than they would care to admit, are here to see the Red Rover stalk across the collegiate chalk-lines for the last time. It's Grange's game. His last game. You cannot get away from it. And who, pray, wants to? The hullabaloo that has kept up for the past week regarding Grange's career after the final play tomorrow continues unabated. Only Grange can say what the future holds for him, and he, disgusted as numerous others with the uproar that greeted the introduction of promaterial Mr. Pyle into the action, says nothing, and wraps himself in silence and the folds of a new raccoon coat. Not that Harold the Red is cold. Quite the reverse, indeed. He is hot.

"To those it may be interesting information that Harold the Red today volunteered the information that on Thanksgiving Day he, in company with Matt Bullock, the Illini trainer, was going out to shoot ducks. If Mr. Pyle is to be in the party, or if he is to get his manager's percentage of the kill, Harold the Red did not say. Nor did he say whether the Chicago Bears would run interference for him when he took up the attack on ducks."

Red posed for a picture with Zup and for one with Chick Harley, the former Buckeye star. Some of the older hacks remembered that Harley had become a pro after he left Ohio State, but no one heard much about Chick anymore.

Zuppke was in his usual pregame grim mood. "My fellows think they are on a picnic," he lamented. "All the way over on the train, they never talked at all about the game. They hadn't their minds on it. They talked about Grange. I don't know what they'll do out there tomorrow. I wouldn't want to say."

The reporters crowded around Red. A hundred reporters were there. "What about C. C. Pyle?"

Red kept smiling, wanly, the fame bearing down on him.

He was living a secret life. Luckily it would end soon. The whisperings of his teammates and the press were turning to shouts. Everyone was studying him for signs of insecurity. Red had plenty: willful naiveté, the absence of a mother's love, anger from a dismissive Zuppke. The two men — surrogate father and son — could hardly face each other. Cynicism contorted Zuppke's face. Red's voice was starting to crack, taking on a shallow timbre. Maybe the Bears, a quaint little group with one reporter (maybe) covering them and a handful of fans, would give Red a much-needed break from all of the attention. He prayed it was true.

On Friday, the day before the game, Zuppke's blowy nature turned truly solemn. He was tired of fending off the questions and he had struggled all week to keep his team focused on the matchup against the Scarlet and Gray. After the team arrived they had a long afternoon practice. Zup, gnarled but energetic, chased them up and down the field and prodded them with an angry "You're a bunch of singers, not football players." Even in the dressing room after the workout he howled about their carefree attitude and wound up by blaring, "Why, you've almost got me on the verge of breaking out in song," comparing them to the Maroon Ladies. There was a parade, and the organizers had asked for Grange, but Zup dressed up another player to impersonate Red. No one seemed to know the difference.

Saturday's game was Ohio State's Homecoming, complete with a freak show as part of the pregame festivities. The game's winner would get Illibuck, a live turtle. The game was played at Ohio Stadium, which everyone called the Horseshoe because of its open-ended design, the concrete architecture feeding a dual purpose — the curved seat banks bring the spectators closer to the field but also protect them from the miserable wind, which whips off the Olentangy River about one hundred yards away. While the architecture created a sense of belonging to the university, to its higher ideals, it was far from conformist. The structure's signature was a templelike dome with forty-five gold rosettes on its ceiling, their classic beauty giving visitors a reflective pause: football had a connection with the ancients; just stroll inside the black gates and proceed under the gray arches to feel them come alive. Anyone with a ticket was pleased to have a seat, of course, but thousands more hungered to be inside. About one hundred fans who were unable to secure tickets spent Friday evening hiding in the stadium's amphitheater before being thrown out Saturday morning by watchmen.

Ohio State announced that ten thousand general admission tickets would go on sale one half-hour prior to kickoff, so fans began camping out Friday evening, and by Saturday noon five lines stretched from Ohio Stadium's southeast corner to Neil Avenue. Despite a heavy police presence, forty or so urchins cleared the fences using a homemade rope ladder.

The paid attendance of 84,295 was, at the time, the largest crowd to attend a sporting event in the country. One writer described the scene as a teeming wall of humanity with an increasing volume that "gave the listener a feeling of awe." Never mind that Ohio State had also lost two conference games so neither team was in contention for a title. The Grange controversy was bubbling over before the game, but it cooled down quickly enough. They had all come to see him. No matter philosophies about amateur athletics versus professional, or even the people who simply thought Grange might be blameless but a simpleton to get involved with the pro league; when Red took the field, people stopped to appreciate his gift.

True to his uncanny ability to rise to the occasion, Grange electrified the crowd each time he touched the ball. Early in the game his running set up the ball on the 2-yard line. On the next play everyone expected Red to run it in for a TD. It was what they wanted. Red had other ideas. He decided to give the ball to Britt, his protector, his Falstaff, the man who not only blocked so brilliantly for him, and who yanked the enemy off of him when they were piling on, but who usually played the entire game from start to finish as if Zuppke was trying to exhaust his good-natured personality. Once that season he had been pulled at the end of the game. "You fellows needn't think you're so great," he said; "even I got out of this one." A player had replied, "Zuppke must have thought you were dead." Britt's touchdown plunge put the Illini on top, 7–0. Ohio State scored a second-quarter safety when Illini center Robert Reitch missed a signal and centered the ball over his own goal. Later that quarter, Grange threw a 13-yard TD pass to Charles Kassel to complete a 60-yard drive, giving the Illini a 14–2 lead at intermission.

The Buckeyes made a game of it in the second half. Quarterback Windy Wendler passed 22 yards to halfback Elmer Marek, who beautifully sidestepped two defenders and dived across the goal to bring OSU within 5 late in the third period. The crowd was an agitated throb of voices. They were always looking for Grange's number. Pointing. 77. *The Galloping Ghost!* His nose had a slice across the bridge. Blood streamed down his face. Tough kid. 77. There he was in the pile. 77. His vulnerable flesh. *Ugh ugh ugh.* A leather boot to his kidneys. *Ugh ugh ugh.* Red never left a game but he went to the sideline now. Red had been kicked in the kidneys so hard that he was momentarily forced from the action. It really hurt. He could barely breathe. *Ahh Ahh Ahh.* He was bending over like a parenthesis. *Ahh Ahh Ahh.* Matt Bullock, the trainer, inserted and sewed in some sponge rubber to protect him from further damage. While the sideline tailoring took place, the Buckeyes shoved over a touchdown. Red returned. It was killing him, but he could breathe a little.

The crowd was once again pointing. Red would avenge the brutal cheap shot. It was the fourth quarter. Zup ordered Britton, the man who had sacrificed stardom because of his loyalty to Illinois, to call the signals in the final quarter. "He has been my Mexican general for three years and he might as well call them now," sighed Zup. (Britton, true to his kind and loyal nature, would be instrumental decades later in organizing testimonials for Zuppke.) In the fourth the Ghost intercepted a pass and ran 42 yards from his own 20 to end an Ohio threat. Two minutes later Grange made another interception at midfield on the game's final play. "It was a fitting conclusion to one of the most celebrated careers in all of college football," wrote one observer. "It was his day, his game, his triumph," wrote Warren W. Brown. Red, in his last venture on the collegiate chalk marks, carried the ball from scrimmage twenty-one times, and his net gain, in yards, was 113. He ran back three punts for a total of 25 yards, and one kickoff for 13. He completed nine passes for gains totaling 42 yards. In the fourth quarter he intercepted a pass and reeled off 42 yards before being horse-collared. Piece all of the statistical information together and Grange gained 235 yards. Illini publicist Mike Tobin let everyone in the press box know Red had finished his career by running for more than two miles in yardage and making thirty-one touchdowns.

Underneath the goalposts, the sportswriters crowded around Grange. They were sorry to see the boy who had given them so many column inches go. They had ripped pages from the thesaurus to describe him: "The Will o' the Wisp," "The Titian Typhoon," "The Sorrel-Thatched Meteor," "The Red Rocket," "The Fiery Comet," "The Crimson Tornado," "The Red Streak," "The Fleet Phantom," "The Illinois Cyclone," "Mercury's Ghost."

"I'm turning pro," the Ghost muttered. *"My father advised me to use my own judgment . . ."*

Within five minutes after he had galloped off the gridiron into the receding mist, his face still streaming with the heat of battle, he made his official announcement:

"I am going into professional football to make money out of it," he blurted. "I see nothing wrong in playing pro football. It seems to me to be the same thing as playing professional baseball. I have to get the money now, because people will forget all about me in a few years. I am still loyal to Illinois, but I don't think I owe my college anything more. I had to pay a price to play football. It was hard work, and I had little fun in or out of season."

The *Herald-Examiner* immediately started doing the math.

The Bears would bring in only $14,000 gross without Red. With Red they could play to a capacity crowd of thirty-five thousand. At the usual scale, $2 per ticket, the revenue would be $70,000. Deducting the average or expected gate, there would be $56,000 left, of which Grange would receive 45 percent.

In dollars and cents that meant Red would receive $25,200 and his flat salary of $2,000 — totaling $27,200 (in today's terms, using the Consumer Price Index, the relevant amount of money would be $320,673), with Red and Charlie splitting the total. Illini students almost immediately started boycotting Pyle's theaters.

Grange looked beaten. The knock in the kidney was a real killer. Within the confines of the locker room, he gazed forlornly at his dark blue sweater. The peach-colored tag said in red lettering, "O'Shea Knitting Mills Chicago." He had felt that tag on the back of his neck for four years. Turning the sweater — darned holes peppering it — cradling it in his hands, he revealed the back of the jersey, the blazing orange "77." The photographers took their shots. He would never wear a college uniform again. His childhood buddy Lyman "Beans" DeWolf was waiting for him outside, car running. Red wouldn't be joining his teammates on the train.

"Grainche, let's go for a drive." It was Zuppke who wanted to give one last-ditch effort for his star's troubled soul. They hailed a taxi outside Ohio Stadium, eighty-four thousand shadows moving into the early evening, Zup telling the driver to *just drive!* as he tried to compose himself and give his pitch. He talked for an hour as the taxi kept traversing the stately streets of Columbus. The worst of it was that Grange was giving up his diploma for the cheap huckster Charlie Pyle. Football formed men to succeed in life; it was not an end to itself, he preached, echoing the ol' epigraph about Waterloo being won on the fields of Eton.

"You're making a mistake."

"You're making a living out of teaching and coaching football, so what's the difference?"

They argued. Darkness fell. Zuppke had lost him somehow. How had that happened? This boy, whom he had brought along, was slipping away. Grange was young. Grange still loved his coach; he couldn't quite understand his distress. Lyle Grange had told Red to make up his own mind. Red had made a decision. He needed Zup's support. He needed his help. Four short years ago Grange was a starry-eyed high school kid meeting the eminent Coach Zuppke. Now their roles had shifted and Grange felt like he was overpowering the man, but he couldn't help himself. It was against all conventions but conventions didn't make sense right now. The argument would take a brief respite this evening, but it would go on, in other forms, for decades.

They returned to the stadium. They left each other. It was over. Zup's body fading into the distance as he joined his team, Red hopped into the car and Beans DeWolf took him to a Columbus hotel. The place crawled with reporters, with women, a dangerous breed of people, and Red had to sneak away, climbing down the fire escape, and then take a cab to the railroad station, where he would depart for Chicago and for his passage into manhood.

8

||||||||||||||||||||||||||||

A Pro

GRANGE SIGNS TO PLAY PROFESSIONAL FOOTBALL
*Left to right: Chicago Bears owners Dutch Sternaman
and George Halas, Grange, and C. C. Pyle.*

T O GET SOME REST and escape the reporters, Red had spent the night at Chicago's Belmont Hotel under an assumed name, but now he was at the center of a frantic rush into the new Morrison Hotel — an enormous place on Clark and Madison. The ads read, "Tallest in the World — With 2 Floors at the Top of the Tower for Theatrical Guests Exclusively. 1,944 Outside Rooms — $2.50 Up." Through the mob scene, half-glimpsing the lobby's lacy marble and cast-bronze ornateness, Red moved past the bathrooms, where attendants were brushing suits for two bits, and on to Room 1739. All the papers were there, ready to play it big. "A madhouse," said Grange, now a seasoned veteran of mob scenes. And Grange's new partners, George Halas and Dutch Sternaman, were waiting for him like a couple of homely high school girls eagerly — and blessing their insane good luck — readying themselves for a date with the handsomest boy. Grange's father couldn't make it. Red's relationship with his father had been strained and there wasn't room in Lyle's life for such frivolity. And, of course, Zup wouldn't have been within a long pass of the place. (Years later Grange would say, "I don't know how Zup feels about George Halas; we have never discussed the matter.")

Charlie, who had kept his word on everything thus far, sat on Red's left and called Grange "my boy, Red," which didn't seem to bother Red, who thought Charlie was a good egg, "a millionaire several times over," and fun to be around, always bragging about the Ghost's big games and taking a real keen interest in his ideas. He could tell stories that a guy like Red liked to hear, all about Hollywood glamour pusses. Coach Zuppke enjoyed his nip at the bottle but he always believed the boys should be in bed early and he liked sheltering them so they didn't become bun-dusters. Red was still preaching a steady diet of milk and getting to bed by eight o'clock, but he knew being around Charlie would change his habits. Zup had kept him so sheltered, and Wheaton and Champaign were such small towns; Red was anxious to become a man. He would rely on Charlie to teach him about the wider world. And for Charlie it was a gosh-darn honor to pick up a check at the Belmont or pay for a drink at the Oyster House, and Red could be sort of cheap about that kind of thing so he liked it. Charlie always told him to order the most expensive thing on the menu, and Red would do it even if he didn't want a filet mignon; he felt like that was what a big shot was supposed to do. Red was already starting to come across all sorts of characters. He would meet a fella named Ralph Capone, who wore a nice blue coat and tie, his big brother Al sitting silently in the corner, and Ralph asking the Ghost, "How's tricks?" The conversation would eventually come around to "doing business" together. "I have a contract with C. C. Pyle," said Red, smiling cautiously, "and I cannot do anything until he OKs it. I can only do what he allows me to do."

As Red, Charlie, Dutch, and George took their seats in the suite, some other owners still thought they had a chance at the Ghost. Two promoters from Rochester were vainly racing on a westbound Pullman to Chicago, and Tim Mara, the bookie who owned the New York Giants, was also en route. It was said that Mara carried a suitcase full of cash; his son, Wellington, nine, was back home holding a vigil, praying that his father would sign his hero. Tim was in desperate straits because his Giants were going broke and he needed a star. It wasn't easy to make money in such a slipshod league.

Halas had a lot on his mind, too. Although he had ended the 1924 season with $3,474.03 in the bank, he was putting his beloved Bears into the dubious hands of C. C. Pyle. There was always money pressure; and adding to the importance of solvency, his wife, Min, had given birth to a baby boy two months earlier. (Showing the fly-by-night nature of pro ball, under "Profession" on the birth certificate George wrote "Realtor.")

Red now put pen to paper; the gathered press held their breath for a moment, as the sound of a radio tuned to a religious service oozed through the suite. It was Mayor Thompson's WHT, where

Paul Rader, the Baptist preacher, discharged fifteen hours of old-time religious programming every Sunday.

And round my heart still closely twine
Those ties which nought can sever
For I am His, and He is mine
For ever and for ever!

Harold Johnson, the *Chicago American* reporter, shouted a question, "What are your views regarding professional football?"

"Why I cannot see that there is any difference between the game as it is played on college gridirons or on the fields used by men who turn their attention to the sport for financial reward," answered Grange, sounding more like C. C. Pyle than himself. As Theodore Dreiser wrote in *An American Tragedy* (1925), "The line of demarcation and stratification between rich and poor . . . was as sharp as though cut by a knife or divided by a high wall." The era had its frivolity, but that was only a slice of society. In the rancid slums, where men lived and worked in mind-numbing jobs, there was a desperate need for escape, and Grange wanted to appeal to the common folk; but he used the stodgiest language possible, as if he was trying to sound like a college grad.

"There remains undischarged my obligation to my father. Possessed of a scant supply of this world's goods, he has given me an opportunity for an education at a great sacrifice. Then there is still imposed upon him the burden of my brother's education.

"I have received many alluring offers to enter fields of enterprise in which I have had no training or experience. But I believe the public will be better satisfied with my honesty and good motive, if I turn my efforts to that field in which I have been most useful, in order to reap a reward which will keep the home fires burning.

"There are countless thousands interested in football who seldom have an opportunity to see a college game. These devotees of the sport cannot take Saturday off and make a long trip to Champaign or some other point, in order to witness a college game. Many are excluded from college games, too, because of the limited number of tickets available to the public. These people in order to satisfy their desires must perforce attend professional football games which are held on Sundays, when and where it is convenient for them to go.

"Therefore I have resolved that I will play professional football. I will play with the Bears because they are a Chicago team.

"Mr. Pyle has acted within the recent few weeks as my good friend and adviser. Today he is my manager."

A relief. The truth. The denouement. The official wait for judgment began.

Charlie, wearing a double-breasted suit, was now on stage, shiny eyes staring at the newspapermen. In his cathedral voice, which always had a puckish tone, he said, "Considerable speculation and misinformation have been going the rounds during the past several days as to my relations with Harold Grange. As his friend, I undertook to act for him as an adviser and emissary.

"With all the numerous offers being made to Mr. Grange, it was necessary to reduce them to a sensible selection. Recognizing this need, I visited the managers of professional football teams in Florida, advised with promoters and schemers, as well as bona fide producers of motion pictures, interviewing them by scores, ascertained their offers and ability to make good and in every way I attempted to ferret out the good prospects from the worthless ones.

"I traveled a great deal, spent much time and defrayed all my own expenses, in order to make this investigation. After considerable work and examination, I came to certain conclusions as to what Harold Grange's future course should be. I laid my conclusions before him and he is now making his decision in respect to them.

"He has appointed me his manager. Today we have entered into several contracts for professional football to be played in Chicago and other cities.

"Mr. Grange has at no time sullied his pure amateur standing by any act of professionalism. He waited until his last game was played and today the contracts for his future services were drafted and entered into. I believe Harold Grange has made a wise decision in following up his splendid college career by engaging in professional football while his popularity is at its zenith.

"There is a large body of the public clamoring for an opportunity to see him play, who never had a chance during his college days.

"Joining the Chicago Bears, Mr. Grange will be continuing to play under the same teaching he received at the University of Illinois. He will give lovers of the professional football game the same sterling efforts he gave to the followers of the college game. He is destined to be as great a success in his newly chosen field as he was in the one just brought to a very successful conclusion."

Pyle's task was to maintain the Grange hero worship and the titillation of stardom. Fame is an essential truth, more salable than amateurism. But without the real drama of important games (a built-in aspect of the college game and any sport that matters) Grange could be written off as a novelty act. Pyle would not allow the interest in Grange to die even if it killed his client.

It was the Grange and Pyle show. Halas, known only to the small subculture of pro football fans, was not even quoted. Papa Bear had a game to play and coach against the Packers that afternoon, but the tickets for Grange's first contest were so hot that before the morning was done — this was unheard of! — every box seat was gone, and the grandstand was nearly sold out. Grange and Pyle sat on the bench for the Packers game. Red wore his new raccoon coat and police had to be brought in so the crowd didn't mob the field. When Red was avoiding the chanting fans, he studied the pros. Joe Sternaman, Bears QB, was particularly impressive. Little Joey, five foot six, 150 pounds, was once described as a bantam rooster mixed with a pit bull. A shifty runner, Joey was an excellent drop kicker, a skill he learned by kicking a ball through a fork in his backyard tree. Grange took a special interest in Joey because he had played under Zuppke until he was kicked off the team for participating in the Carlinville-Taylorville scandal.

"This is the first time I ever have seen Joe Sternaman play," Grange told the press hounds, "and if he travels at that pace in all his games I'll sure have to play harder than I ever did in the conference to keep up with him. He certainly is a wonderful quarterback and one of the greatest broken field runners I have seen. You can just bet they play hard football in the professional circuit." Little Joey had a good game, but the crowd seemed to be crazier about the back of Grange's head. Halas traditionally *schmeared* a *Chicago Evening Post* writer $25 a game, but he didn't seem to need that kind of payola anymore. The papers were even burying the Babe, one writer saying how "Ruth was the incarnation of Thor, but he had been replaced by a fleet-running back in leather helmet, a Mercury of the gridiron and as the older pictures fade, Red Grange takes all of the limelight away from the athletic heroes of yesterday." He hadn't even played a pro game yet.

There was fun to be had, too.

Building his image as a quiet warrior, Red would say, "I don't smoke, I don't drink, and my meals are paid for. I do like to have a good time, a dance in a cabaret now and then, but I contracted to stay in training and I am going to do it." That was a bunch of slush. The lovelies were everywhere, keeping Red going at all hours. *Red! Red! Score one for me, Red!* The girls on the pro circuit had a little more polished determination. Despite the ruggedness of the pro games, Grange's fame would bring women through the turnstiles. Sometimes, because this was 1925, the women were unaccompanied in the stands, which was not unusual for football, a game that has always embraced its sexual component to confirm its manliness. Mostly, they were prowling the hotel lobbies. Red noticed that some of the older guys seemed to have a system. They had been on the football circuit for years and they would just disappear after the games, do their stuff, and show up at the train station before the Pullman rolled on down the tracks.* Pyle, the biggest lady-killer, would hang around Red, help him keep the conversation going, and stake out his share. "The greatest ladies' man that ever lived," Grange said. Red liked to go out, too. He enjoyed the clubs. Music was his thing, listening and dancing, watching the girls shake, all decorated with flowing beads, in their little dresses, the cloth rising and falling to reveal talcked flesh. It had all started from the first moment he turned pro. When he dined at Chicago's Terrace Gardens, the gals swarmed him. "He hardly noticed me there were so many girls there," pouted Rosemary Deering, a serious-eyed slim dancer, who tried to swim through the other beauties to get near him.

But the lovelies would cause problems for the boy. "Red didn't go out, he couldn't go out," said one insider. It was true in spirit. Red would disguise himself with a wig and a big fat cigar and sneak through the lobby, maybe find himself in a nightclub dancing. But those outings became few and far between because he would create

---

* "Well, shucks," Grange would say later in life, "drinking and sex were not just recently invented, you know. We had a lot of guys that were better swingers than [Joe] Namath will ever be. They found places in New York that he hasn't located yet."

a mob scene — men gassing to him about football and women interested in more intimate pleasures. It got so out of hand that Red
started ordering his meals in, trapped in his hotel room playing
penny-ante poker, listening to the *shh-shh* of the carpet sweepers.
Along with his entourage, hotel clerks and hat check girls became
his closest acquaintances. Maybe too close.

Red Grange was the standard-bearer of Wheaton's moral culture, and now its native son would display his gift on sacred Sundays among the drunken betting rabble; and worse, he had hopped
into a feathered bed with a crook. He was making a mistake, sure,
but for the most religious among them it was worse than that. This
character Charlie Pyle would stand to make a fortune, too, and that
peeved everyone. Why? *Why?* There was something beyond reason
at play. The town elders were frantically plotting to wrestle Harold
back into their fold, so they hired Ray J. Cannon, an attorney from
Milwaukee, who said, "My personal opinion is that Grange needs no
manager." If Grange did hire someone for his affairs, many hoped
he would go with A. H. Schatz, a Wheaton innkeeper and wannabe
sports star manager, but a dubious character by Wheaton standards who went by his vaudeville stage name, Johnny Small, and
who claimed that he and Red had a verbal contract — "made it several years ago," he kept telling the journeyman reporters who were
flocking to Grange's hometown. Johnny Small claimed that he had
secured a venue for Red's vaudeville debut, in which he would play
an iceman, and he arranged a newspaper column for Grange. (Mr.
Small would sue Red for fifty large.) The town pooh bahs, the men
who had given him banquet after banquet, were simply waiting for
Red's nod, but for some reason the boy, whom some of his neighbors were sneeringly describing as "his highness," wasn't replying to
their messages. Red struggled with it. He was easily hurt. When entering manhood it isn't always easy to like where you're from.

As Red traveled to the Champaign Country Club on Monday
night for Illinois's annual postseason football dinner, he had to endure all of this nonsense. He referred all of his business matters to
Charlie, who was hired to protect him and give him breathing room.
Charlie was proving to be a zealot. With all of the chaos around
him, Red looked forward to the football love fest where he would be

handed his "I" sweater, see his old teammates, pass the captaincy to the next man, and maybe even utter a few words. Newspaperman Warren W. Brown, everyone's friend, would be a speaker, and there would be a lot of reporters covering the celebration. Zup would ramble on, recapping the season, giving the audience one of his after-dinner gems. Zuppke's anger had undoubtedly subsided.

Red was naive. The more Zup thought about Red turning pro, the more livid he became.

Before Zup went on stage, Red was asked to give a little talk. Having abandoned his teammates in Columbus, he felt compelled to explain himself. "There was nothing better than playing for Illinois, but now that I'm through I will do the next best thing and play with a team that has many old Illinois men." He wanted to make it all right with everyone. Red knew that Coach was still smarting from his decision, so he sent a peace offering: "That can't compare with the pleasure of three years under Coach Zuppke." The speech was sincere and received applause, but Zup's face, historically open and kind to Grange, turned pensive, as it had when he was losing control on the practice field. The little man stood, quieting the room.

"Remember, Harold," Zuppke began, "I have no fight with professional football, and if you choose to enter it, that is your business."

Turning to others at the table, Zuppke sneered, beginning his dudgeon:

"But Grange is green, greener than when he first came here to Illinois. He must watch out for persons who will try to make their own fortunes out of his tact and his talent.

"Suppose he does get $60,000 for his professional football services? Will he be able to guard that from those who will seek to take it away from him? Wouldn't he be better off, in the long run, if he took up some substantial business and profited from it? He must remember that old saying of 'Easy come, easy go.' But above all, he must be careful of his companions, his associates. He must not fall into the hands of — yes, men who are eager to use him for their own advantage."

Red waited for it to end. He did a slow burn. After signing with the Bears, there was panic. Bears owner George Halas knew football but the whole league was essentially a disgrace to the sport. Now Red planned to make something out of it to prove Zuppke wrong. Zup was offering him up — predicting his decline, misery — a glib whiff of his starry death:

"Grange has been an asset to the University of Illinois, but the University of Illinois has been a greater asset to him. And the saddest thought that I have in this whole business is that Grange will no more return to the University of Illinois to graduate than the Kaiser will return to power.

"The Grange we know, and the Grange we have watched for three years, is a myth. As time goes by those runs of his will grow in length with the telling. And soon they will be forgotten. I remember when I saw Heston,* the great Heston, and thought there would never be another like him. I saw Pogue,† the flashiest, shiftiest runner we ever had up to this time. I thought there would be no more like it.

"They all passed on. Grange will pass on. He will be forgotten. There is a saying that if a homely man comes into a room, sooner or later a homelier one will enter. And if a good-looking man comes in, some time there will be a better looking one. Football, with its stars and individual stars, is like that.

"I tell you that no other $100,000 player is going to be on one of my teams."

Like that, Grange had become an opponent. There must have been words in Grange's head, but he was silent, his anger coagulating. You went into college football knowing the score. You fought for your school, then if you wanted to stay in the game you coached, ref'd, or put your byline on a ghostwritten expert opinion for the papers, but you never played again unless it was a benefit game for some crippled kids. You played out your senior year and you were through with the moleskins. But why were you taking orders from a college coach? What would happen to Robert C. Zuppke without all of those boys who followed him like a father? Who was Zup? A man living half the off-season in the Biltmore, drinking speak-

---

* William Heston was a lightning-quick All-American halfback for Michigan at the turn of the century.
† Harold Pogue was an All-American at Illinois. Zuppke considered Pogue, Potsy Clark, and Grange to be the three best backs he ever coached.

easy schnapps as he told football yarns (most of them about Red Grange), and driving a fancy car, and he was one of the humblest of them, living in a smallish apartment at 305 West University, which, unfortunately for Zup, looked out at C. C. Pyle's Virginia Theatre. Maybe without the likes of Red Grange those brand-new football stadiums would stand empty and Zup wouldn't have his ten grand per and the additional money he made from his Zuppke School for Coaches, and the little Dutchman and Hurry Up et al. would not be known by their childish nicknames by every man reading the sports pages over breakfast. Red didn't say any of it. He could not articulate it; his mind was like falling dust. Red Grange clutched his hat and walked into the night, away from the hurt, never picking up his letter sweater.

The following day Zup laughed it all off — rage turning to regret. Using the age-old my-remarks-were-taken-out-of-context excuse, he told the Associated Press, "I defy anyone to read into the newspaper accounts of my words any reproof. I did say that the saddest thought I had was that he would not return to graduate and I am afraid that he will not. I did warn him that with money often it is a case of easy come and easy go, and I did urge him to be careful of his companions — advice I would give my own son if I had one."

Sometimes Zup just couldn't keep his big mouth shut. It was Pyle, upset by Zuppke's damnation by association, who struck back. He was ready for a fight. The world was an awful, solemn place and Charlie simply made it interesting. And for this Zuppke went after him and his star client. It was part of the game but it still bothered the thin-skinned promoter. Pyle gathered the press and told them that Grange was not being taken advantage of, and in fact, his friend H. E. McNevin, a Champaign banker (who in reality was being sued for improper financial dealings along with Pyle), had set up a savings account for Grange.

Meanwhile, back in Chicago, Grange went to his first pro practice. The Bears took a slow lap around the field and walked another one. They didn't hustle, but when they practiced their plays they hit hard, Halas cursing at them. Halas didn't talk, he barked. He coached by intimidation, and he expected his men to play angry. Big George Trafton, the Bears' center, put his arm around Red and told him Halas liked his men to be on time, go light on the complaints, and hit hard during the games — cheap shots were perfectly respectable if there wasn't a penalty against the team. Trafton — hulking, funny, profane — would teach Red the tricks of the pro trade. As with his friend Earl Britton, Red liked to surround himself with roly-poly men who would speak for him and tell him jokes. Halas would see the connection and assign the two men to be roomies on the road.

George "the Brute" Trafton wore number 13. He was a bad-luck kind of player. Grange would fondly call him the "toughest, meanest, most ornery critter alive." He had been born in Chicago on December 6, 1896, the son of a cop on the take who had abandoned George and his mother. Trafton, six foot two, weighed 230 pounds, and he enjoyed using his bulk to crush the smaller, lighter players of his day. He was the first center to snap the ball with one hand, probably because he was missing the index finger on his left one. On defense he roamed — like a modern linebacker — and he was known as the first man of his size to prowl with such quickness. If an opponent gave one of Trafton's teammates a cheap shot, he was sure to return the favor with a forearm massage to the face, always delivered with a puckish grin. (Later in life when Dick Butkus was getting press for his brutal style, Trafton would scoff, "Compared to me, he's a pussycat.") Give Trafton a Tommy gun, and he could have been one of Al Capone's men — in fact, he lived next door to Al's brother Ralph. Inside the Brute's home it was no less chaotic. After discovering his "gigolo-ing" at a Loop hotel, his wife cracked a ginger ale bottle over his head. She denied hitting him with an alarm clock, a chair, and a carving knife but told the papers that she regretted her aim was so poor.

Trafton was in the army in 1918 and had played for Notre Dame in 1919. Two people would bring tears to the Brute's eyes; one of them was Knute Rockne. Rock had big plans for Trafton and believed George's abilities would make him a Notre Dame legend. In his gut Trafton knew he shouldn't do it, but he needed the money so he played in an off-season semipro game. George thought of Rockne as the father he never had, but the legendary coach for whom George would have done anything heard about the violation, called him in, and expelled him. After leaving South Bend, Trafton joined the Staleys, forerunner of the Bears, in the first year of the American Professional Football Association (it was renamed the National Football League, or the NFL, in 1922). When the team moved to Chicago in 1921, Trafton — the team captain — went with them. It was said that Trafton was strongly disliked in every NFL city, with the exception of Green Bay and Rock Island. In those places he was hated. "I spilled a lot of blood in my day — and it wasn't all mine," he would say. Trafton's reputation belied a man who was, in many ways, just a big dumb kid. (Westbrook Pegler called him the South Bend Tornado with a footnote that a tornado was merely a vacuum surrounded by wind.) He always bought the drinks, or, more accurately, his Irish-born mother (the other person who could get the Brute blubbering) bought the drinks — she gave him $50 a week to get by since Georgie seemed to have holes in his pockets.

After the training session, a dusty and perspiring Halas brought a pile of sandwiches and milk bottles. *What the hell?* Halas setting out a picnic raised some eyebrows. To a Bears player who once pleaded for an advance "to buy my kid milk" Halas had replied, "What's his address? I'll send him a quart." Despite worries about C. C. Pyle's involvement in his beloved team, George Halas was in a giddy mood. Red Grange brought him vindication. It wasn't just that he had Red Grange on his team, which he was imagining might make him a fortune, but he also appreciated the kid's attitude. For the rest of his years, when a young player would start getting cocky, Halas would bark, "Red Grange was a pretty good country halfback but he was never cocky."

In Halas, Grange saw a football man through and through. He owned, coached, and even played on the team, but he was only thirty years old. He was more like a blustery big brother than a coach. The team was happy to have Red on board: he would bring them some attention and some money. And they had heard that he was practically one of the owners of the team. They would need to figure out this kid. Red was welcomed but unsure. Halas ran a good practice. He knew his football, and his intensity surprised Grange, but the whole thing felt rinky-dink, like a second-rate circus, nothing like the organizational structure and money of the college game. What had he gotten himself into?

9

|||||||||||||||||||||||||

Cardinals vs. Bears

A HUGE CROWD WATCHED RED GRANGE'S FIRST PRO GAME

R ED GRANGE AND THE CHICAGO BEARS put on their uniforms, stripes of orange on blue, the orange a nod to the University of Illinois, where George Stanley Halas had gone to school and played football, the dark blue a reminder of his naval service. George Halas had his battered nose in just about everything — ticket sales, buying medical supplies, getting the drinks. His actions were predicated not so much on kindness as on cheapness; he was a small-business owner trying to make ends meet. The players were coming into the locker room, but Halas did not meet-and-greet them. They might have called him George or Halas or even Coach, but most of them just said "Hi-yuh" to the man who signed their paychecks. George wasn't much on socializing; his pleasure came from smart football and breaking down his opponents to the point where they showed fear. His men had all spent a lot of time together on Pullmans, in dumpy hotel lobbies, in the occasional speakeasy, and undoubtedly in brothels when the road trips wore on. Many of the guys were roommates, living at a North Side hotel, not far from Cubs Park, where practices were scheduled each morning between the brick walls. Halas, *Time* magazine would write, taught them all the lost arts of tripping, kneeing, elbowing, gouging, slugging, biting. When Halas had the money he would pay each man $10 per practice, $100 a game on average. Ed Healey, the brilliant left tackle, a talkative Dartmouth grad, was getting dressed; as an opponent he had once tried to hit Halas during a game so George, liking his spirit and his play, signed him to the Bears. Jim McMillen, left guard, who like Halas had graduated from Illinois with a degree in civil engineering, put on his jersey. At six foot one, 215 pounds, McMillen had been the captain of the unbeaten 1923 Fighting Illini, clearing the path for Red's All-American debut. Some men played cards. Some read the sports pages. Up until Red's arrival not many people had seen them play. They were football hobbyists.

Sitting in the Cubs Park dugout, Red forlornly studied the bear cub struggling in front of him. The Bears' mascot was tied to a wooden peg and it pulled on the chain, around and around, in mad fury. It was part small-town fair, part freak show.

As the Ghost trotted onto the field, wearing his new jersey, the crowd stared at him. Never had there been more people at a professional game. Many of the attendees had never seen a football contest, and until a few days beforehand they wouldn't have wasted a dime on one. Jimmy Corcoran, the irrepressible *Chicago American* columnist, described the mad rush: "The panic is on! Everybody wants tickets, tickets, TICKETS! Babies wow-wow in the bassinette this morning and prattled for tickets, frosty faced millionaires on the Board of Trade want tickets. The washlady wants tickets. The coal man does. The grocer does. The bootlegger does. The painter, the baker, the candlestick maker, the old clothes man, the street car conductor, the soldier, the sailor, the organ grinder — They all want TICKETS. Two hundred thousand people want to see Red Grange plus the Cardinals and the Bears play football Thursday morning." The Cork was having a little fun with the story, but he was right. The cops were out in force to try to control the mob. Hours before the game they had already cuffed seventeen scalpers who had made phony ducats and thrown them in the paddy wagon, heading to the Town Hall police station. Some smart-ass said that half the thirty-six thousand saw the game from the press box; some of the newspaper reporters who weren't covering the game but just *had* to see it jammed into the press area to the point that they were thrown out. They had all come to see Grange but they were morbidly curious about professional football, too, a spectacle darkened with shade. *Hadn't there been a championship game in Evanston a few years back that turned into a riot as the two teams battled in a postgame fistfight? Weren't the brutes merely actors in a fixed charade? Why would Grange associate with these lowlifes?*

There were 2.7 million people in Chicago, and its major papers like the *Tribune* (608,130 daily readers), the *American* (459,663), the *Daily News* (400,696), the *Herald-Examiner* (334,289), and the *Journal* (123,026) were telling the Grange story to their 1.92 million loyal readers. All of the hacks, the Chicago guys and the fellas from the smaller or ethnic papers, had spent the week boning up on the players, introducing themselves to Paddy Driscoll, the Chicago Cardinals standout who was the best player on the pro circuit — "We are almost willing to confess that we knew little about the great warrior until yesterday when he parked himself in front of a base burning stove in the dressing room," admitted the *American*. To the few Cardinals die-hards, who hailed from Chicago's South Side, Paddy was an Irish brother — tough and crafty; someone with whom they could imagine walking the streets, cudgel in hand. As if to show the darker side of football fandom, it was known that the mobsters loved Paddy, and the Bears worried about tackling him too hard because the gun-packing gangsters sometimes sat on the Cardinals bench and they didn't mind coming out onto the field either.

The Chicago Bears played an early version of the T formation, in which the forward line is balanced so the guard, a tackle, and an end line up on each side of center with the quarterback close behind center, the halfbacks about 4½ yards behind the tackles, and the fullback the same distance behind the center. It is a formation that is best for a squad pounding the ball through the middle. Grange had only a couple of days to practice the scheme, and it was not a good match for his outside running style, but in his first Bears game Red struggled because of Paddy Driscoll, who was a virtuoso kicker. From the start Paddy refused to boot to Grange. The Bears fans were plenty pissed, but Grange didn't seem to care, the game releasing the week's tension. He loved being alone and in action, and he was never more alone living by his athletic wits than on a football field, where the crowd seemed to disappear before him.

The game was typical of that era — lots of punts to pen the opposing team. Paddy mistakenly kicked the ball to Grange a few times. Red returned three punts for distances of 25, 15, and 20 yards. He advanced the ball about 35 yards while running from scrimmage, and he intercepted a Cardinals pass. Grange realized quickly that the game was faster, and the men wanted to knock you straight into the hospital.

"They cheered when Grange gained ground; they cheered when he lost ground," wrote Don Maxwell, the *Chicago Tribune's* sports editor, who assigned himself to cover the game. "They went into vocal hysterics when he trotted on the field, and they almost mobbed him when he left it." Charlie had done it. He was right. The people loved Red no matter what.

The people and even the sportswriters took something away that day. Here were man-oxes who ran into each other with a certain grace, and they weren't dogging it. About Ed Healey, the Bears tackle, someone said, "He's everywhere." "When he hit 'em, they remained where they were," wrote Maxwell. And anyone thinking Grange was some college cake-eater only had to watch him straight-arm one of the South Side sons of bitches — looked like a Dempsey jab.

The game ended 0–0. Didn't matter. The Cork wrote, "It was Grange-Grange-Grange. The day of heroes isn't over." And the *Trib* opined that the fans attending the tilt would become regular paying customers.

A pistol shot rang through Cubs Park. The Cardinals all came over to shake the Ghost's hand, and a few minutes later a crowd mobbed the field trying, in a frantic rush, to get close to him. Red was happy but winced as thousands pushed toward him, trying to touch him, to look into his eyes, and to see if he was really human. Fifty blue-coated cops formed a flying wedge and escorted him into and through the dugout as he escaped through the door labeled PLAYERS ONLY and sat himself on a rickety wooden chair. There, in the dressing room, Red touched a large red bump under his left eye and smiled. "A rough game? Not at all," he said. "'Twas a great game. I gave everything I had, but those fellows are mighty good players. It's going to be harder going in these pro games than in the university games. I only had two practices with the Bears. I hope to do better in a week or so." George Halas cried after the game as he looked at the gate receipts.

Grange made $12,000, which he split with Pyle. Manager and player had Thanksgiving dinner together to celebrate the debut. They both felt good, especially Charlie. In Grange he had a star, and in George Halas he had a taskmaster. It was a wicked combination. Halas would drive his men to the brink and Pyle would take advantage of that overexuberance. Charlie knew what needed to be done. Charlie knew what men have on their minds: women, and the glory of fame. Men, masses of men regardless of class, would want to see Red — at least for a little while. But all stars have a limited run. Actors lose their looks; athletes, their skills. Charlie was impatient. Charlie made a squinty assessment of the books and concluded that the team would have to play at every chance without rest days. He would create an unbelievable schedule. Each man was on a crusade, each for his own purposes. Charlie and Red talked about the money they would make, how they would take the country by storm with mere pro football games, and how they had to plow ahead while the getting was good. Charlie was masterminding not just a barnstorming tour but the outlandish idea that pro football was a legitimate pastime, the equivalent of baseball. It would take all his skills.

Charlie had big ideas, but he suffered from little cash problems. The day after Charlie and Red's Thanksgiving feast, the men were served legal papers; the Chicago Morris Plan Bank filed a garnishment action against C. C. Pyle because Charlie, who claimed he was a millionaire, hadn't paid his rent — he owed $2,828, and as Charlie's new partner, Red Grange was named in the suit. There would be more problems ahead.

In the days that followed, Red slowly started figuring out that Charlie was not all he said he was, but there was no going back now. Red wasn't much on investigating someone. He trusted his gut. Despite his ingratiating smile, Pyle's expression suggested future prosperity. The fame and money *were* intoxicating. Red and Charlie were coconspirators now. Red decided not to look into it. The whisperings were loudest in Champaign. It was the Virginia Theatre. Charlie had not been straight about it. It was, in fact, the product of Pyle's latest scam. It was right there, a narrative of deceit, in the court papers. But Red stood by his friend, not really examining it. To understand Charlie Pyle, turn back the clock a few years to 1921. It would tell you a lot about Charlie and the risks involved in doing business with him.

Pyle came to Champaign, Illinois, and hooked Almon W. Stoolman, a clean-shaven former baseball catcher and a pillar in the Champaign community. Stoolman, who had sported white hair since his early twenties, was, by some accounts, the second-largest builder in the United States. Stoolman had built his first house at age fourteen, and since 1915 he had won bids on many plum jobs, including a $152,176 massive brick mansion created for the University of Illinois's president, the Masonic Hospital, and about every sorority and fraternity house in Champaign. In fifteen years as a contractor, Stoolman's revenues were over $35 million. Almon was a man who doted on his daughter and could afford Capper & Capper suits. There was a lot of money to be made in construction, especially in a growing place like Champaign, where he knew everyone and had a spotless reputation. Since 1900 Almon had been married to Lois, a University of Illinois graduate (1903), who helped him in the business and thrived when she was in the midst of her active social life, such as traveling to Pi Beta Phi sorority functions. When the Stoolmans were not working, they raised their precious only child, Elizabeth, whom everyone called Virginia.

Back in 1921 Charlie had let it be known that he would be constructing a grand theater. Stoolman wanted in. Pyle couldn't have asked for anyone more appropriate for his needs. Almon's impressions of Pyle were favorable, too. Almon, forty-three, was certainly not naive; most contractors understand the strata of human nature better than most. Charlie was certainly a different egg — self-made with, at best, a high school education — but he dressed like a dandy and he could talk. Don't even get him *started* on the Lewis and Clark outdoor extravaganza that he once ran. Almon was a builder, but like most contractors after a job is completed, he had to win yet another bid, which could be a grind. Partnering in the theater business sounded easy enough and like a good gamble: he could make money on the theater forever. Charlie Pyle seemed like a potentially propitious partner because of his varied but appropriate experience. (As one of Pyle's acquaintances remarked, "He would cheat and steal but man-on-man he was a perfect gentleman.") Pyle had manly qualities and men liked hanging around with him, listening to his whopping ideas, and he could sweet-talk the wife, too, making even the homeliest matron feel pretty, light, and alive.

Feeding Almon's ego, Charlie had come up with a great idea: Charlie Pyle wanted to show the world that this theater represented the future. It would be named the Virginia, after Stoolman's daughter.

So they signed a deal and became partners.

Within a few weeks Lois, who did Almon's accounting in a leather-bound ledger, was questioning why Charlie had not put any money into the common account. Stoolman had efficiently hired dozens of subcontractors, and he had laborers knocking on his door to work construction on the theater. And then someone in town told Almon that the land that the "greatest theater in Champaign" was supposed to occupy had never been purchased by a Mr. Pyle. Couldn't be true. But before Almon had a chance to confront Charlie, H. E. McNevin, a big-eared son of an Irish immigrant, asked to see him.

Pyle and McNevin had made a secret pact that McNevin would receive some shares in the company for a teeny-weeny favor. Stoolman met with bankers all the time. Even though they failed on a daily basis, it was always a smart strategy for a contractor to be in the good graces of the local banks, which were getting desperate. Larger financial institutions were putting them out to pasture because farm loans were disappearing, as people moved to big cities. Instead of putting money into the bank, people were gobbling up stocks and bonds. About five hundred commercial banks suspended operations between 1915 and 1920, and nearly six thousand went bust between 1921 and 1929, many of which were concentrated in the rural Midwest. A good angle for exploitation in the 1920s was the banking system, and Charlie preyed on the newfound willingness of banks to take risks or go broke. But even the local lenders in Champaign were reluctant to issue bonds for the theater. McNevin, sitting in the bank at 10 Main Street, the one with the two enormous paintings entitled *Work* and *Play*, told Almon he wanted to borrow $10,000 *from* Almon, which he would in turn invest in the theater. Almon loaned him the money, and then McNevin walked down the street and presented it to Charlie, who immediately purchased the land. Eventually, angry bondholders would accuse them of creating their secret partnership "unlawfully, fraudulently, maliciously, wickedly and feloniously to conspire a large amount of money by means and by use of the confidence game." A white-collar pyramid scheme or good ol' American hustle, either way Charlie didn't come out looking so good.

On April 27, 1921, Almon met with Charlie. In the accounting books the columns were not adding up and concerns were aired. Al-

mon asked, point-blank, "Do you have the money for the construction work?" Stoolman was bleeding $1,000 a week.

"We have more than $40,000 cash in the bank, and we have
made arrangements for the issuance of bonds to raise the remainder of the money." There was a little caveat: "The bonds have all
been sold, but there might be some delay in collecting the money,
but at the most, and for this reason only, you might have to wait for
the $75,000. I will have that money for you within ninety days." It
was a lie. The bonds hadn't even been issued and none were sold.
The construction costs were devastating Stoolman's finances. There
were bills due for heating and ventilating ($30,000), electrical wir-
ing ($15,000), plumbing ($8,500), sprinkler system ($5,000), vac-
uum-cleaning system ($1,500), temperature control ($1,500) . . .
The Rudolph Wurlitzer Company of Cincinnati was wisely demanding payment before it would deliver the organ. And Pyle insisted
on top-shelf accouterments. Did the showers in all of the dressing
rooms really need to be of the highest-end marble?

And then Charlie disappeared. Pyle was supposed to be paying bills, but he was nowhere to be found. Where was he? Chicago?
New York? On another project? Visiting his mother? (Pyle had once
asked for money from Stoolman, claiming that his mother was on
her deathbed and he needed the money to visit her. Mrs. Pyle would
live until 1939.) No one could seem to find him. Someone let Stoolman know that Pyle hadn't sold a single bond. When Pyle finally
made his way back to Champaign, he had a perfectly good expla-
nation. It was the bank's fault. *It* had not issued the bonds. Charlie
would make it all work. *Yeah, sure.*

Stoolman was in deep. He then learned that Pyle owed $10,000
to one bank and $5,000 to another one, and that the banks were
threatening liens against Pyle, which would have shut the unfin-
ished theater down. Like it or not, Stoolman and Pyle were partners,
and so Almon reluctantly bailed out Charlie and paid the banks the
$15,000. It was probably quiet that night in the Stoolman house-
hold, the one filled with Mencken and Sinclair Lewis first editions
and a whiskey bottle hidden in the closet.

Soon enough Almon discovered that Charlie had sold only $100
worth of bonds, and those were to Pyle's stenographer in Chicago.

There was a confrontation. Charlie was big and tough but Almon was no coward; he had grown up in Champaign's tough East Side and never backed down from any gang of ruffians. Charlie broke down and said, "I have no financial backing. The theater is lost unless you save it."

It gets cold in Champaign in the winter. The cold mist over the cornfields seems to go right through a wool coat. Almon, leaking money, hat in hand, knocked on his neighbors' doors. He wasn't exactly a beggar, but he was begging for a hand. He had taken out an advertisement in the *News-Gazette:*

An important message addressed particularly to
People of Moderate Means
You are given the opportunity to become a part owner in
The Beautiful New
Virginia Theatre
$20,000 worth of Bonds
offered in denominations
of $100 on easy payments
— if desired . . .
Act Quickly
A. W. STOOLMAN

Throughout October and November and into December he sold bonds, promising that any bond buyer who was dissatisfied would get a refund with 7 percent interest added on for good measure. He sold $90,000 worth.

On December 28, 1921, the theater opened. The subcontractors might have been worried and pissed about nonpayment; Stoolman — if he hadn't already had prematurely white hair, he would have sprouted some — must have been paranoid about being destitute. People came to the theater, but the box office success didn't outweigh the concern of Stoolman's bondholders. Some of those people of moderate means had been learning about Pyle's shady dealings and they wanted out of the deal. Stoolman made good on his promise; he repaid $8,000 worth of bonds, but Pyle had brass ones. The money on the sold bonds created interest. Pyle worked with McNevin to funnel that money to his own personal bank account.

Trying to leverage his ill-gotten ownership, Pyle would audaciously sue Almon Stoolman for control of the theater. Charlie had put in about $10,000 of borrowed money and some sold bonds. With the land purchase, loans, and material and labor costs, Stoolman had invested close to half a million dollars. Charlie had run a pretty good scam.

In the autumn of 1923, while Grange was running toward All-American honors, the men were in court fighting over the theater, and the case was still winding its way through the court system and into public conversation. Even a man like Pyle, so sure of himself, must have realized that he would have a difficult time talking his way into ownership of the theater. And in came Grange, like God's gift.

And now, moving time forward, Charlie had Red Grange in his clutches. No one could touch him. After spending Thanksgiving together, and getting served court papers, Charlie convinced Red that the lawsuits were a horror of exaggeration. Truth be known, title deeds and bonds were of no consequence to Red. And the criticism of Pyle pricked a primal nerve. Red would defend his friend. He wasn't going to get into the details of Charlie's life. He wasn't going to listen to gossipmongers and complainers. Red was working off gut intuition just as he did on the field. Even if Red did find out something, what was he really going to do about it? He had signed a contract. They had a pact. There was a lucrative barnstorming tour in front of him. Charlie Pyle was all right by Red Grange.

In the calculus of fame the equation was simple: Charlie was turning Red's popularity into cash. Red, the marble-mouthed jock, needed someone to express his inner voice. Charlie did his job well, and then some. Charlie was getting some hard knocks, but mostly he was filling the papers with floods of publicity of which pro football had never dreamed. The public was no longer laughing about it. No one was laughing at Red. Charlie was pulling all the strings. Red realized, maybe more than anyone, that a man like Charlie, an American huckster, was dangerous but necessary for a man like Red Grange.

Pyle had been right about the public's love of the Galloping Ghost. There was another game three days after Thanksgiving, before another capacity crowd at Cubs Park, which meant that the Bears had played to some seventy-five thousand people in less than a week, the largest crowds that had ever seen the pro game. The Bears faced the Columbus Tigers in a snowstorm. Absent were the college ritu-als — the band, the traditional chants, the pomposity — replaced by an unrelenting need to see the game's star — and monumental gam-bling. Pro ball had a more cynical side to it but it was also more honest. Red played, of course, but in the third quarter he did not return to the lineup because he needed a breather. In the end the Bears squeezed out the victory, 14–13. The crowd, betting the Bears' side and working on a tight spread, chanted, "We want Grange!" with their blood-roar.

PART II

10

The Barnstormers

BARNSTORMING TEAM

T HE TRAIN WAS FILLED with men gurgling, coughing, and guffawing, and with the smells of coal, cigars, and food. The men called their private car the Dog House. *Ruff! Ruff! Ruff! Ruff! Ruff! Ruff!* At this early point in their journey, they were happily barking like dogs. In many ways they were living like ill-kept canines. Charlie was turning out to be a classic tightwad. The trainer's room reeked of wet wool uniforms. Pyle wouldn't spring for extra uniforms and wouldn't make arrangements to properly wash the one set the Bears owned. Like the crazed fans who now followed their every move, the men, who had been no-names a few short weeks before, were still in the early, giddy throes of being a part of something big, basking in the light of Red Grange. They didn't complain.

It all pleased Charlie. He was an old vaudeville man. He knew that entertainers had to entertain. To bankroll his dreams he had created the nearly suicidal schedule. Red and the Bears would have to sacrifice themselves for him. Everyone had the chance to get rich. There were many games. The pace was relentless and ruthless. As long as there was money to be made, Charlie Pyle would put a contest on the books. People warned Charlie that it was too much strain on Red, but Charlie was willing to take that chance. Charlie had the intractable habit of seeing flesh as replaceable. Red didn't read anything into Charlie's motives. It seemed like C. C. Pyle was looking out for him. They were making money. The public still hungered for Red. He held a place somewhere between football and fantasy. Grange had moved beyond the shame of deceiving Bob Zuppke, the University of Illinois, Wheaton, and the rest of them. His sense of boyhood entrapment was disappearing. Red sat back and relaxed a little, hunkering down to meditatively observe his new life. As always, George Trafton was in good spirits. Red could half hear him telling one of his many yarns. Joe Sternaman and Lawrie Walquist, who had played in the Carlinville-Taylorville game that had so embarrassed Illinois, were chatting away, dressed in their finest woolens.

As for Grange, he needed to step outside himself more. The quiet, unassuming college-boy act wouldn't play in this arena. Fer Christ's sake, the kid had chaperones. Any time he got up to stretch his legs, the players would make all sorts of racket, cracking, "Here comes Rudy!" They were dogging him, comparing him to Rudolph Valentino, because it was rumored that Red would spend his summer in Hollywood making a movie, one of the football flicks that had become the movie colony's latest fad.

Despite the manly bullshitting, Grange — iconoclastic yet innocent — didn't revel in it, and forty years later when the men on this train tried, as half-crippled gray-hairs, to reconnect, Grange was one of the few who showed little interest. Red didn't totally fit in. He was still a kid. Red had become the Odysseus of football, a metaphor, shockingly, not utilized by the gaggle of writers covering Grange, a boy smothered by his own thoughts and an aching shoulder. Damn, it was difficult to get through to him. Red revealed a faint smile — obviously strained if you knew him; all the responsibility, mounting every day, made the boy uncomfortable, and he was now reaching a state of loneliness that could be achieved only in America.

It wasn't for want of company. Don Maxwell of the *Tribune* said that Grange "has more managers than touchdowns; all Red lacks is a bouncer." Charlie and Doc Cooley were always keeping him secluded from the reporters. Doc, whose real name was Marion, was a college chum who followed Grange like a puppy. His father was a real doctor, Dr. E. B. Cooley (born in 1867), who was also along for the ride. The elder Cooley, a Republican operative, had other reasons besides medical care or being a chaperone; Dr. Cooley was behind the backroom machinations to put Grange — the college dropout — on the Republican ticket as Illinois representative at-large. Whenever the other three men weren't around, B. F. "Dinty" Moore, a high school pal of Red's, was there to do Grange's bidding.

They were on their way to Philadelphia to play their fourth game of the tour. Outside the steamy windows frost-covered fields were making way for hulking factories. It was dead winter.

After struggling against the Columbus Tigers, one of the worst teams in the league, the Bears had traveled to St. Louis, where they had played a game earlier in the day. Red's good buddy and college teammate Earl Britton joined the Bears there. Britton had dropped out of the University of Illinois and signed a $60-per-game contract. Bob Zuppke's nightmare was complete. Red had already made pro football a fashionable career choice. In St. Louis the Chicago boys crushed a team sponsored by a local mortician, the Donnelly All-Stars, 39–6. Eight thousand people showed up. "The Donnelly aggregation was pitiful to behold," wrote Harry MacNamara of the Universal Service syndicate, who concluded that all Grange had to do was "take the ball and start in the general direction of the line of scrimmage."

Charlie and Red weren't concerned about Columbus or St. Louis. They knew that a big showing in Philadelphia and New York would make or break the tour. For Pyle, the East Coast games would field-test an elaborate idea that was bubbling in his mind. He believed he could do a better job of running the league than the existing owners, and he thought New York was an untapped market ill served by the New York Giants. A grand showing by Grange in New York would give him leverage when it came to building pro football into the empire he believed it could be.

They were now nearing Philly, where only a couple of months earlier — yet it felt like an eternity — Red had run so famously against Penn. The Bears would take on the Frankford Yellow Jackets in Shibe Park, an eleven-year-old baseball stadium, designed in a French Renaissance style with brick walls and terra cotta trim and a domed tower with a roof made of green slate. It wasn't Franklin Field, but Shibe held some Illinois-Penn déjà vu because it was covered with three inches of rain — and sounds from the past.

As Red walked onto the soggy mess, the capacity crowd, including scouts from the New York Giants, heard the faint and eerie thunder of marching-band music playing on a Victor Talking Machine. After his performance in the Illinois-Penn game, the Illini band had journeyed to Camden, New Jersey, and recorded "Hail to the Orange," "Illinois Loyalty," and "Oskee Wow Wow," and now the

Victor people were giving Red a machine and a selection of records. It was a publicity stunt, but it was the best gift the Ghost had ever received.

Philly was fine and all (the Bears won 14–7 in front of thirty-six thousand people), but everyone was excited about New York. Red had conquered Chicago and Philadelphia. If New York fell under his spell, the whole country would acknowledge him as the country's greatest athlete and biggest draw. *It would be the fifth game in eleven days.* The Giants players and their boss, Tim Mara — who were scouting Grange — hopped on the train to the city with the Bears. Charlie Pyle and Mara started arguing about the poor state of football in New York City. "There a private feud started which cost both men many dollars," said Dr. Harry March, the Giants' general manager. Look at the publicity and the money Charlie had already made for the owners. Charlie had eight thousand people coming to a meaningless game in St. Louis, for pity's sake! No one else had created such interest in the sport. The powers that be didn't realize what he could do for them. In fact, they — exemplified by Mara — were a little dismissive. Charlie didn't like it and he lustily started planning his revenge. Grange's visit to New York would show them that Charlie Pyle owned the prized commodity.

In 1925 Rodgers and Hart had their first hit on Broadway. The show featured "Manhattan," a sweet little number that made the city feel like an intimate setting for lovers with the subway that "charms us so / When balmy breezes blow," and cleverly witty rhymes — "As black as onyx / We'll find the Bronix." Like many ballads of the day, the song had a Charleston rhythmic pattern, which fit the lyrical vernacular of the street ("goils and boys") and also gave the dance-mad public something to sway to. The song created a sweet dreamland, an "isle of joy," they called it. "Manhattan" sang to the exuberance of the city but also the nation. New York, proud and self-obsessed, was, is, the maker of myths, center of the nation's culture, the First City, for better or worse. In 1925 it was a city without the Empire State Building and the Chrysler Building to glorify its skyline, but it was still the tallest, most alive city in the world, with Broadway and Times Square, the chophouses, Chinatown's restaurants with their pale yellow lights and stone mosaic floors (where opium vied with chop suey, it was whispered), the Fulton Market wagons with paintings of fish on the side; the Jews, Italians, Chinese, Germans, Irish, blacks, and God knows who else; the smells of the Old Country, the cars whizzing by on the circle of Bowling Green and Broadway, the singsong of the trolleys, the taxidermy and hat shops, the Cotton Club, Sardi's, the cab joints, the pushcarts hawking Florentine silver bracelets knocked down to 80¢, the fire escapes zigzagging down the sides of buildings, the nickelodeons dotting the tenements, the lights — the lights! — changing from white to gaudy colors: "LIVE CHORUS GIRLS CHESTERFIELD CIGARETTES 'TAKE MY TIP THEY SATISFY.'"

And now New York would get its mitts on Grange — see if they liked the kid, see if the rest of the country was full of it. Pro football wasn't exactly something that excited Gotham. Baseball and boxing, hell, even indoor bike racing and professional wrestling had more juice. Before owning the New York Giants, Tim Mara had not even seen a football tilt. Mara, whom one writer described as a "large, florid-faced Irishman with unfailingly good humor," was a New York bookmaker who was more familiar with the sweet science and the ponies. One day in 1925 boxer Gene Tunney's manager, a friend of Mara's, came into his office and said it would cost $500 or $2,500 (the story changed depending on the day of the week but $500 was probably the correct sum) to have a pro team in New York. Mara figured that any pro team in New York should easily be worth thousands of dollars north of two grand so he bought it, but "the football team, to put it mildly, was not a financial success," recalled his son Wellington. Mara had hoped to sign Grange and create the franchise around a name player. When Red was in the last throes of his college career and talking out of both sides of his mouth, Mara had raced to the Midwest to sign him, but Red had to settle for a deal with Pyle, a man Mara would both respect and despise. Mara was not happy about losing Grange to Pyle but he was gracious in defeat. "Pyle had more imagination than Barnum and just as much daring," he would concede.

It was said that you could never tell if Mara was doing well or going broke, but every sportswriter in town knew that the Giants had been a failure for Irish. He was in the red to the tune of $20,000. After the Giants-Bears game was announced, Mara and a couple of

friends handled the rush of requests from Mara's office in the Knick-
erbocker Building. Allison Danzig, a *New York Times* writer, said it
was "almost a riot to get tickets" — which stood in sharp contrast to
the pre-Grange days when pro football was, Danzig explained, "just
sort of tank town stuff; you could hardly give tickets away because
no one wanted them." The clamoring for Red became so loud that
one hundred reporters planned to cover the event.

With the Illinois-Penn mud game a not-so-distant memory, the
New York reporters had already created a mythology around
Grange's college career, but he was yet to create the same aura in
the pro league among the sports intelligentsia. For national affir-
mation, Red and Charlie needed their approval.

The newspapermen probably first heard about the Grange and
Pyle Show at the Yankees office. That is where they would go to
punch the bag with the players and managers and get their story
ideas. After a workout they would ramble next door to a kosher deli
on 42nd Street. Pretty much everyone, all the gin-drinking, poker-
playing writers, breakfasted there. Ring Lardner, Granny Rice,
Heywood Broun, Damon Runyon, Ford Frick, Marshall Hunt, and
Westbrook Pegler used it as a regular hangout. Ring, a loner, was
always off in a corner. Granny, smiling underneath his gray fedora,
was the nice guy, loved by his readers but seen as a likable light-
weight among the other scribes because he would never bite into a
real story. Rumpled, black-haired, lipless Broun — a Harvard grad
and columnist for the *World* — hankered to be on the stage and he
had even tried his hand at it, but he couldn't cut it in that racket.
Runyon, the bespectacled half pint, could be a loner sometimes, but
when he talked people listened, because he could describe someone
in two words better than most could do in eight hundred. Frick's
claim to sportswriting fame was as a lightning-fast typist — he
bragged that he could write his stories in eight minutes flat. Marshall Hunt of the *New York Daily News* could regale you with Babe
Ruth yarns because he was the Bambino's ghostwriter and the paper paid him to spend every possible second with the athlete, pall-
ing around with him in the off-season on vaudeville tours and fish-
ing, golfing, and tubbing with the star in Hot Springs, Arkansas,
even signing baseballs while the slugger was out on a booze and

broads binge. The most talented writer among them was Westbrook Pegler, who at $250 a week was one of the highest-paid scribes and also the profession's angriest. Pegler would be kicked off the Notre Dame campus for life for daring to quip that words flowed out of Knute Rockne's mouth like "champagne out of a battered oilcan." Peg had more talent than the rest of them but his personality could grate on you. Even the Algonquin Round Table recognized the professional sports watchers as brilliant at what they did. Sure, the *New Yorker* looked down on sports as a "trivial enterprise" involving "second-rate people and their second-rate dreams and emotions," but the magazine would concede, "The quality of writing in the sporting pages is, in the large, much superior — wittier, more emotional, more dramatic and more accurate — to the quality of writing that flows through the news columns. What news reporter is equipped with the feeling for sensuous color that one finds in Grantland Rice, for example? He can give a methodical and rather stupid baseball game all the glamour and vivid flame of a gladiatorial combat."

Now it was Grange's New York moment. The game would come under serious press scrutiny because it was in the horse latitudes of the baseball off-season. Along with beautifully rendered, sepia-toned Rotogravure photos of lost children, grisly accidents, and loose women, the 2¢ *Daily News* had been plastering Grange's likeness all over its ink-drenched pages, and the advertising side of the paper was getting into the act, too: a $32 Hart Schaffner & Marx suit advertisement read, "It's like 'Red' Grange: This new-value suit 'stands' out." Jack Farrell at the *Daily News* was calling the Ghost "the most famous red head since Cleopatra." And the *News*'s Will Murphy, who had witnessed the Penn game, called Grange otherworldly. "Not wholly WHAT the man does; it is the amazing WAY in which he does it," he wrote. "To suggest that Grange has something of a ballet dancer's grace and something of the blithe celerity of a healthy antelope is to stray far from the accepted phrases of football. But it's true, and it brings no reproach of femininity upon the handsome Red. Isn't he an iceman in the summertime, and who ever heard of a sissified iceman?"

"Probably never in athletic history has a sport event attracted any more attention than this," wrote Ford C. Frick with the Hearst papers. "Even the Carpentier-Dempsey fight, though it drew a greater gate then the football game will, was no more discussed.

And it's a certainty that no professional football game ever drew so many columns of newspaper publicity or attracted so much editorial comment. Estimates made by middle western newspaper men show that Grange, since he turned professional, has received more than 3,600 columns of newspaper space. His name is almost as well known in England as in America, and throughout Europe he is regarded as the superman of American athletics." For all intents and purposes, Frick was building up an essentially inconsequential game, but one that had profound consequences for the sport itself.

Grange attracted crowds, but it seemed like he also brought rain clouds. The week leading up to the game had been a wet one on the "isle of joy," soaking the knobby-kneed tenement kids on their roller skates, the men pulling their coats up and covering their ties that went no lower than their bellybuttons, the Punch and Judy shows boarded up, the pickpockets and Princesses of the Pavement gone inside for their day's work; the restaurant smells, all steamy, made the sidewalks more pungent: goose liver, rabbit and pigs' knuckles, flaming crepes, soups, caviars, and cheeses; the drizzly East Coast rain making the "LUCKY STRIKE: IT'S TOASTED" sign practically invisible. Mara worried that the contest would be mired in mud, and the newspapermen writing about the pro game with derision, or worse, not at all, would pounce if no one showed up. It wasn't just the weather conditions, of course; the event *had* to be pulled off. Pegler showed the stakes for the popularity of pro football as well as Grange's vulnerability to a New York crowd: "In his quiet career delivering strictly fresh country ice to the back stoops of Illinois homes, Red Grange may never have developed those calluses on his soul which protect the spirit from the slings and arrows of the raspberry choristers just as the wads on his ribs protect him in the shocks and falls of football," typed Pegler, who went on to say that the teams had better make an honest showing or New Yorkers might think the pro game a fraud. Then came the first ray of (reflected) light for the game whose organizers were so desperate to make it in New York. The Maras received a call at three in the morning and someone screamed at Tim, "Look out your window! Look at the moon!" The rain had stopped. Tim was so excited he did not go back to bed. His kids hadn't been able to sleep anyway because they would actually get to meet their hero, Red Grange.

The Giants were 7–3, winning the last seven, and the Bears were

7-2-3. But most New Yorkers did not care if the Giants took the league championship (they wouldn't), let alone if the Giants were a football team or a burlesque act. Gamblers were everywhere. From the Giants' sideline, which was always on the sunny side of the bathtub-shaped Polo Grounds because Mrs. Mara didn't like to sit in the cold shade, fans could see the stadium decorated like a bouquet: gold, blue, green, purple, yellow, and scarlet bunting. Basile's Regimental Band supplied the music, a number of rooters wore feathers in their hatbands, and raccoon coats dotted the stands. Grange, wearing his dark 77 jersey, was escorted by fifty police officers, and the Mara boys were down on the field, more excited than they had ever been. It was the place to be, in America's most influential city. Sixty-eight thousand people were there, with two thousand on the sidelines. Charlie Pyle was giddy. If he could get half this crowd every week for a season, he could make a lot of money. Right there and then he knew that New York — where every showman dreamed of success — was there for his taking.

During the game the scrums had been the costliest yet, with both George Trafton and Ed Healey getting dinged, and Grange getting the bejesus beaten out of him, the Giants going after the Grange family jewels. The pro game was much tougher than the college variety. George Halas believed ferocity destroyed an opponent's will, and the referees tended to look the other way even during the cruelest of fouls. No matter that Grange had a natural humility; opposing players, and even some of his underpaid teammates, were jealous of his outsized image and the bulging bank account. They wanted to prove their worth by knocking him down to size. "It was a tough game," Halas understated. "They were tough," recalled Earl Britton, who was playing in his first pro contest. "This was when we knew the pros played for keeps. Just before the half they got George Trafton's knee. Andy Lotshaw, [the] trainer, straightened it out, taped it up, and George played all of the second half. You do not find men with guts like that today." At halftime Earl and Red sat on a trunk, listening to the Bears gripe. This was no Zuppke halftime speech. Halas was callous because pros dished out a lot of complaints. "We have a ring-side seat for when the fight starts," Britt told his friend. The people bearing witness on this game couldn't accuse the players of loafing — they were smacking each other in the solar plexus.

Football is, at least in part, an expression of a sadistic anger inside of us and people crave a good hit. Pegler wrote: "Deep in the second quarter, as he knocked down a Giant pass, Red was slugged with a Firpoesque slam on the back of the headgear by Williams of the Giants, [who] wound up like an old bar room fighter throwing the 16-pound cuspidor, and let Grange have it. Red stumbled unsteadily but did nothing about it, and neither did the officials who were about as hostile to fist fighting as Tex Rickard* is, all afternoon. After he returned to the game in the fourth quarter, Red was kicked on the forearm by Tomlin of the Giants' front line and it wasn't long after that till Joe Alexander, the Giants' center, stopped him in a line play and squatted on the ground with Grange in his lap, trying to twist his head off to see what kind of sawdust he's stuffed with. The officials told Alexander he oughtn't to do that but didn't charge him anything for it." Joe Alexander was a physician who had been a two-time All-American. He worked at New York Hospital during the week and would play football on the weekends, sometimes jumping on a train to Pennsylvania's coal country. Alexander, a Jew, was one of the first players Tim Mara brought to his team in 1925.

The day's meager warmth disappearing, the fans stomped and jeered when Grange, wearing a soaked and muddy uniform from the game in Philly, wasn't playing. Halas, not much older than Grange, would have liked to rest the boy, but Pyle wouldn't allow it. And Grange would never admit to physical weakness. It wasn't the money. It was who he was.

"Run, you red-headed bum!"

The energy had leached out of his body.

Pegler wrote, "Red played through the first quarter, almost through the second and most of the final quarter, returning to the game after a generous rest at the noisy demand of the massed customers from whose aggregate contribution he was said to be receiving $30,000 [the equivalent of $287,500 in today's purchasing power] for himself and his managers."

Red's game highlights: an interception run back 35 yards for a touchdown, and a 22-yard pass reception. The Bears won 19–7.

For Red and the organizers, the tilt had been a wild success, even

---

* Tex Rickard was a well-known boxing promoter.

beyond the monetary gains. The pro game earned legitimacy. For all his 24/7 obsessing over football — Halas was a man, after all, who bragged that all he did on his honeymoon was talk football — Papa Bear came away from New York with a sense of redemption that he hadn't had in the smaller Midwest cities: "That gave pro football the impetus that we were looking for ever since we started the league in 1920," he said. The local dailies on Monday went with three columns of Grange coverage on their front pages.

"Football became a game for all of America," said the *New York Times*'s Allison Danzig. As New York goes, so goes the rest of the country, and Grange and Pyle had produced a seismic mental shift. With some exceptions pro ball, for all intents and purposes, was a midwestern, medium-sized-city game. Up until Grange's showing, New York was the pro football backwater, but the game helped convince league leaders that money could be made in the large eastern cities.

Because of the dollars and acclaim that the game brought, it would be called the game that saved the Giants. Mara was no longer in the red. Everyone was riding high. It felt like professional ball had been created. Little did Mara know that he would soon be on the frontlines, battling Pyle and Grange for the control of professional football.

Back in the dark and comely Astor Hotel on Broadway and 44th Street, where the Bears were encamped, Red fought a chill, soaking his limbs and then adding to his bank account. George Halas and Red had come into Charlie's suite and damn, C. C. was happy, grinning as he shaved. Pyle had every right to feel confident. On the rare nights that he wasn't out with a lady friend, Charlie was going through the hundreds of telegrams, most of which asked Grange for one thing or another. Outside, on Broadway, was "tremendous jazz interpreted by light," as one writer put it, the flickering penetrating the curtains. Charlie always watched Red like a trainer studying a Thoroughbred in the paddock before a race. "Son," said Pyle, brandishing his straight razor, "this is the blade that knows no brother. We are going to take a deep cut at the dough on Old Broadway, let the gyps fall where they may." Pyle was an opportunist with a hint of crudeness, but the newspaper writers did not treat him sanctimoniously because they knew his type. They worked in or about

Times Square, a bustling den packed with burlesque shows, rou-lette rooms, heroin pushers, Gypsy phrenologists, midget troupes, $5-at-the-door stag parties, where "$30 Scotch," mostly embalm-ing fluid, could be had along with down-on-their-luck chorus girls. The beauty, for Pyle, was that the companies were coming to him. Their checkbooks were wide open. In a lifetime of trying, it was the easiest money he had ever made. Within two hours Pyle collected $25,000 in certified checks for Red Grange endorsements. He had to turn down a bonanza from a cigarette company because Grange didn't smoke. "That Grange would have been the perfect football player if he had only learned to inhale," said a laughing Pyle, who gave Red a $50,000 check.

Babe Ruth, the most popular athlete in the world, paid Red a visit, too. Red could hardly believe it. Babe was a hero.

"Kid, I'll give you a little bit of advice. Don't believe anything they write about you, good or bad. And further, get the dough while the getting is good, but don't break your heart trying to get it. And don't pick up many checks. Don't let them birds get you down, kid. You've got to expect that in this business. All you gotta do is run for another touchdown and they'll yell their brains out for you."

It had been quite a day for the Wheaton boy. New York. The game. The money. Thus far 181,000 had watched him on the tour, and he was just getting started. Every time he showed his face there was a screeching frenzy. But there was more. That night, just af-ter ten, he went on WEAF, which was being hooked up with radio stations in a dozen other cities, including St. Paul, Cincy, Washing-ton, Philly, and Pittsburgh. "Hello, folks," he said. He coughed. "I caught a little cold up at the Polo Grounds this afternoon, so if I'm not quite as clear as you would like I'll have to ask you to pardon me." Grange's voice was tight. "They tell me that I am playing to a larger audience this evening than ever before in my life — perhaps two or three or four million people. Well, it seems like a pretty big honor. And it certainly is a big responsibility. Football is like life. One fellow carries the ball and gets most of the credit. Yet ten men have helped to push him through and without them he could not have gained an inch."

He talked about the spirituality of sports, and how money was not his goal.

Hadn't Grange been making a cool $250 a yard carrying the

oval in a mere barnstorming tour? Most people didn't make $250 in a month. Everyone in the chattering class was talking about the irony of the speech. Hell, even the Harvard football players did a burlesque act, wearing red wigs and the number 77 in dollar signs and carrying ice tongs. Comparing football to the everlasting soul seemed high-hatted for a fella like Grange, the leader of a gang of "football minstrels," as writers called them.

But the speech resonated with Red's audience. Unlike his stilted remarks in Chicago when he turned pro, his words over the radio enthralled listeners who understood the spirituality of the games. What was it within men? What made them love him? What within them made them desirous to be him? Stripped down, Red's 170 pounds were well defined; his biceps were 14¾ inches, no different from any day laborer's; his brooding face was darkly handsome. Football had changed; it was no longer a game for kids who went to Yale or Harvard. Grange was speaking for the folk.

Red's barnstorming had made him into such a star that magazines targeted at intellectuals started to take their potshots, many of them pretty clever. On December 30, 1925, the *New Republic* ran a satirical faux Q & A with Grange, with the sole purpose of making fun of his intellect, or lack thereof:

> *Mr. Grange* — Spiritual? Wait a minute . . . Spiritual . . . Oh, yes, I remember! But between you and I some other fellow must of wrote that up and I spoke it for the radio. I just spoke it, that's all.
>
> *Reporter* — I won't mention that. If you said it you meant it, no matter who thought it up. Now what did you mean? Can't you elaborate that sentiment?
>
> *Mr. Grange* — I suppose I meant something like what it said. Fix it up to suit yourself.

The *Outlook,* yet another magazine that was missing the grander significance, scolded him as "redoubtable and now rather pathetic."

The *New Yorker* lamented about former college stars who were now "merely middle-aged executives, tired business men, unknown for the most part even in a football crowd at Princeton, at Cambridge, at New Haven." Needless to say, the rest of America was not taking these journals seriously, but anyone familiar with the issues realized that the New York anti-football crowd was basing its minority arguments on snobbism (as if being *merely* a business executive was a badge of dishonor), and worse, many of the journalists were disingenuous, humorless uplifters so absurdly serious about the game's cultural ramifications that they were blind to the game's true meaning: that it actually represented the country's values and its fundamental need for violence, more than baseball ever had, or would. Red Grange was causing debate outside the sports pages. He was part of the national dialog. Will Rogers, the influential writer, humorist, and social commentator, supported Grange. Writing in his popular column, he said, "Red knew something these Editors and College professors didn't know. He knew how many pounds of ice you had to carry before you got one $." Paul Gallico, the influential down-market *New York Daily News* writer and editor, spoke fluent French and German and was the son of Paolo Gallico, a pianist with the New York Philharmonic. Gallico was comfortable in most worlds, among all classes, which was a gift for a journalist writing about America, a country that closes its eyes and believes itself void of classes. About Grange, Gallico would write that his critics objected to "all this gorgeous jack falling into the hands of socially inferior persons who were in the thing only for gain, and didn't even pretend that they were doing it because they loved it."

Before leaving New York, Red should have been set for life simply for playing a month or two of football and signing a handful of endorsement deals. America hungered for his greatness and humility. Despite the grueling games (they had already played five in eleven days) and the relentless pressure, the money was staggering. Grange's appearance at the Polo Grounds netted him $36,000, making him $82,000 to date (by comparison, Babe Ruth made $52,000 a season, probably totaling $100 grand with endorsements; Calvin Coolidge earned $75,000), and, as promised, Pyle had made the boy (and himself) rich with outside contracts: a sweater ($12,500), a doll ($10,000), shoes ($5,000), cap ($2,500), souvenir football ($2,000), and other permissions ($6,000), which added up to $38,000. Within five months a Grange candy bar netted the pair $59,000 in royalties. Red sent his first grand of earnings to his father; the gesture made the front page of the *Chicago Evening American*'s sports section. More quietly he purchased some land in Wheaton so he could build Pa a house. Some fuddy-duddy editorialists and college types still harped on his greed and derided him for turning pro, but it was difficult for any workingman to hold it against him. "You can't eat cheers," Red said. It seemed that Red would hold on to his money, not because he was an excellent businessman as much as because he was an above-average cheapskate. Red had told Pyle to put him on a drawing account of $100 a week. "Every cent outside of that," Charlie told reporters, "is deposited in the Illinois Savings and Trust at Champaign.* A week ago I gave Red the usual $100, and yesterday I asked him if he wanted another $100. 'Oh, no,' he told me. 'I still have $70 of last week's allowance left. And, besides, the trainer owes me $10.'"

On the surface it all looked like a smooth operation. It wasn't. The engine moving the train was hardly in good working order. Red had let Ford C. Frick, a reporter for the Hearst papers, hang out with him on the train ride from New York to Washington, DC. Frick's editor, Arthur Brisbane, the most influential editor in the city, a dour-faced man with determined eyes, like someone ready to scold, whom everyone (behind his back) called "Double-Dome," had gone to the Polo Grounds game. Monday morning, first thing, he sent for Frick and said, "I want you to follow this guy Grange around the country."

Frick gently described Grange as "tremendously human, in his quiet shy way, just a little bit nervous and bored by the laudations which suddenly have come his way. And the pace has begun to tell. Deep lines showed about Red's face yesterday, and the piercing eyes were strained as Red sat pensively by the Pullman window with his best pal. That best pal — in case you are interested — isn't Earl Britton or C. C. Pyle, or any human member of the Chicago Bears. It's a portable phonograph — a squeaky, whining sort of machine. Yesterday afternoon 'Red' played it almost constantly during the five-hour trip." Frick described Grange as a loner who didn't join the card games or the "general hilarity of his comrades"; rather he just sat — and listened and gazed out the window "with tired eyes and a face that betokened exceeding merriment. 'Gosh I'm tired,' he said

---

* This was the same institution closely associated with Pyle's investments and the legal wrangling over the Virginia Theatre.

plaintively. 'I wish I could get away somewhere. Why can't people leave me alone?'" He was a bona fide dead man. Shaky, tired, drawn, dehydrated, wounded. He could barely be reanimated. Yet Charlie pushed him onto the field. It was too much. But Red couldn't say no. There was a contract. There was his loyalty to Pyle and to the game he loved.

Red's Pa was worried. Charlie had his men along for the ride, but Red's good friend Beans DeWolf hadn't been invited on the journey. Pa insisted that Beans join the troupe in Washington, DC, to act as Red's traveling secretary and paid companion. Beans and Red were pals, of course, and when the call came to rejoin his friend, Beans, who was toiling at the Union Tool Company, went to DC immediately. Beans was well versed in the art of taking care of sportsmen: he had worked for the *Chicago Tribune*'s Col. Robert McCormick as a whipper-in — a person who keeps all the dogs in a pack on a fox hunt — and he had caddied at the Chicago Golf Club for Robert Lincoln, son of Abe.

Charlie and Red needed Beans. *It was the sixth game in thirteen days*. Charlie and Red were doing too much, each in his own way. When they stayed at a hotel they would average 200 letters, 157 phone calls, 60 telegrams, and 39 interview requests a day. Someone had offered Red $1,000 to get in the boxing ring, which Pyle promptly turned down — one of countless offers, mostly absurd. They were constantly fending off fraternities, distant relatives, reporters, friends, promoters, and women. Some of the girls were lovesick; others wanted publicity. They had a little inside joke. Charlie would say, "Have you had your little lawsuit today?" Con artists, according to Charlie, were suing Red. "Just schemes to cut in on Grange's income or get some 'promoter' cheap publicity," Pyle complained without any irony. Charlie did handle most of it, holing up in his hotel suite or on the train and sifting through the correspondence, fending off the reporters between his daily rubdown and haircut. A reporter would ask Red some innocuous question and Charlie would jump in: "Red is not in a position to give any opinion on that." Some of the irritated writers were calling him "Chime-In Charlie." When Grange was resting or did not want any more attention, Pyle would sidle up to the Ghost and unload one of his fantastical dreams. "Look at this, Red. I had some plans drawn up for a covered stadium with a roof and all the aisles have escalators, see?" Pyle showed him the blueprints of an enormous indoor/outdoor stadium — think of it! "The minute you step out into the aisle after a game it takes the people away. We could empty the stadium in about two minutes. And each seat has glass in the back with a crank so people can crank a piece of glass in front of 'em, see? And the further back you are the higher the magnification. It's like looking through binoculars. And the roof opens and closes. There's only one problem, it would cost about $3 million to build." Charlie would come up with junk like that all the time. Within Pyle lurked an inventive, brilliant mind, but some said he was like P. T. Barnum without the attention span. Red was in awe. *An indoor football stadium! How could someone have that much goddamn imagination?*

After the journey to the Nation's Capital, where the Bears would take on yet another "all-star" team at creaky and unusual Griffith Stadium, whose center-field wall detoured around five houses and a tree, George and Red met Senator McKinley and went to 1600 Pennsylvania Avenue. McKinley was a big football fan. He had attended most of Red's college games and it seemed like he was at Illini practices half the time. The senator figured President Coolidge would want to meet the great Red Grange. Red would always use the White House meeting as a funny anecdote and nothing more, but there were ghosts in the room that day.

In some ways Grange's very rise to popularity came from the weekly football deaths that were concerning the nation twenty years earlier. Right in the White House, where Grange would meet Silent Cal, once sat Teddy Roosevelt, one of the greatest football fans of all time and a man responsible for changing the game into one built on speed. On an autumn day in 1905, two years after Grange was born, Teddy held a meeting with the football coaches of Yale, Harvard, and Princeton to talk about reforms. Roosevelt loved the game — hell, ten of his Rough Riders had stated football as their profession, his own kids played at football-mad Groton, and Roosevelt had been writing for two decades about the sport. In 1893 he penned an article for *Harper's Weekly* in which he called for an end to professionalism in the college ranks and implored umpires to "prevent slugging or any kind of foul play." A good fistfight was always tremendous fun, and broken bones and crushed skulls were all part of the game, but as football increased in popularity, the brutality was becoming a mini-pandemic. Several states had outlawed the game and any literate person could not escape the almost daily report of football fatalities everywhere else. The most serious injuries, and the fuel for Teddy's anger, came from the massive dog piles underneath which boys were being kicked and punched so hard that they were sustaining internal injuries and even dying on the nation's fields.

On October 9, 1905, the very day he was lecturing the Ivy Leaguers, a Chester, Pennsylvania, boy had been rendered unconscious from a blow to the stomach, been revived, and then was booted in his helmetless head and died. As the coaches of the country's elite universities, these men dictated the rules, but instead of changing them for the better they were dawdling — tradition and all that. Muckraking journalists were sniffing out the story, writing about tramp players, prized for their outlaw ways, who would jump from school to school like hired goons. Columbia planned to ban the sport, and Harvard had threatened to. "I do not wish to speak as a mere sentimentalist, but I do not think that killing should be a normal accompaniment of the game," the president said. "Brutality and foul play should receive the same summary punishment given to a man who cheats at cards." The next day Secretary of War William H. Taft threatened to expel any West Point cadet who played "rough football," and university presidents showed up at games the next weekend and promised to disband the sport if outright violence was condoned. As for the chastised Ivy Leaguers, they left Washington on a train where they drafted a fair play pledge, returned to their respective institutions, and pretty much did nothing.

As always, the Ivy League season was marred by brawls on the field and off. A little more than a month after Roosevelt's tirade, another player died. Harold Moore played for New York University. He had tackled a Union College player and as he fell to the ground another player kneed him in the skull. He succumbed four hours later. Shaken by the boy's death, NYU's chancellor decided that enough was enough and he called a meeting to reform the murky sport, modeling the rule changes — striking with fists, elbows, or knees or deliberate kicking would even get a player disqualified — on Roosevelt's recommendations. At the country's universities and elite prep schools there was an immediate impact as the game became less of a deadly scrum, but there was a greater country out there. These were brutal times and a thirst for blood does not diminish because of a presidential decree or a bunch of mortarboards signing a piece of paper with policies laid down by a rules committee. But the rule changes eventually trickled down to the folk — and helped open up the game for the likes of Grange.

If Roosevelt had been president in 1925 he would undoubtedly have been interested in meeting Harold Grange, but Calvin Coolidge — a different type of man, complexion like an egg — did not seem to share in the rest of the country's open-jawed admiration of the football star. The meeting with the boy, and the publicity to follow, was one of the first episodes in which a president used sports as a way to connect with voters. McKinley, Halas, and Grange entered the Oval Office. During the tour George Halas and Red Grange had started to understand each other, but they weren't really friends yet. Red was aligned with Charlie, so George wasn't allowed to get too close to the boy.

"Mr. President, this is Red Grange and George Halas with the Chicago Bears."

They shook hands. The president's hand was like a cold potato.

"I'm glad to know you. I always did like animal acts."

"Thank you very much," said Grange, trying to keep a straight face. When they stepped outside Grange and Halas busted out laughing.

The Bears beat the Washington All-Stars 19–0, but Grange didn't get any long runs. To assuage the crowd, Grange kicked an extra point after a touchdown. The *Washington Post* would declare, "Red a Sheep in Bears's Clothing." Red played only in the first and final periods and carried the ball a scant ten times against a squad that everyone was calling a pickup team. His runs totaled 16 yards but he was thrown for 10 yards in losses. The two forward passes he attempted were grounded, and he was unable to get near a pass intended for him, reported the Associated Press writer, who added that Grange seldom made tackles and loafed when he was on the field. Grange left the game with a wrenched arm, a puffed nose, and

Red Grange and his Wheaton High School team.
Grange is in the front row, third from left.

Red Grange and the 1924 University of Illinois team.
Grange is in the second row, far left.

Red Grange,
Bob Zuppke,
and Earl Britton

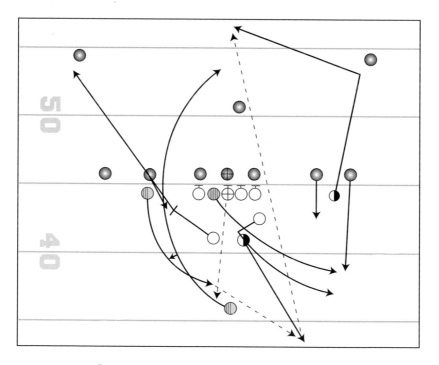

"FORWARD PASS AFTER A TRIPLE PASS."
University of Illinois coach Bob Zuppke was one of the most creative
coaches in an era known for conservative play.

UNIVERSITY OF ILLINOIS SPORTS INFORMATION

In addition to his skills as a runner, passer, and defender, Grange was an excellent kicker.

UNIVERSITY OF ILLINOIS ARCHIVES

STADIUM DEDICATION
U. OF I. HOME-COMING
ILL. 39 MICH. 14
OCT. 18 1924

Memorial Stadium at the University of Illinois was built during the college stadium boom of the 1920s. This photo was taken on dedication day, when Red Grange started on his path to national fame.

Red Grange's
last college game

Lyle Grange, Red's father,
and Red Grange

After he turned pro, Red Grange built this house for his father.

Grange would spend many an off-season in Hollywood.
Here he poses with the actress Marion Davies.

Helen Flozek and
Haroldine Grange

Grantland Rice, the dean
of sportswriters

Football great Bronko Nagurski

Pro Football Hall of Famer
George Trafton, the most
feared player of his era

George Halas on the sidelines

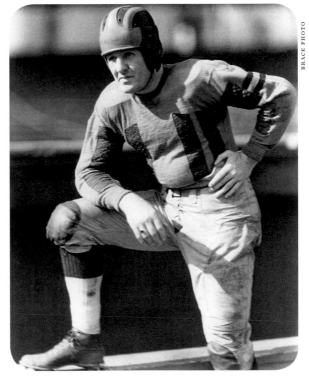

Grange during the
Depression, toward
the end of his career

Bob Zuppke with his
dog, Red Grange

Red at rest

a bruised mouth. Red was worn down, sore, tired, his body unable to recover. Halas had let Charlie subject his men to torture. It was getting worse. The Bears had lost another key player to injury — Joey Sternaman, their quick playmaker, the man who impressed the aficionados. Joey had banged his knee, and his hotheaded brother Dutch was tossed for fighting.

Inside the Dog House there was growing dissent. These men loved to play football to their very marrow, but there were no more joyful *ruff-ruffs;* the train started feeling like a mobile hospital. The men, resting in their billet, ached in every last recess, a dull unpleasant chill, and dreaded the prospect of playing tomorrow on Boston's Braves Field. They were unhappy. Most of the guys were making $60 per game. The fame wasn't enough anymore. Ford Frick, whose practiced empathy helped get people to talk, sat alongside Red. He described Grange as "the most famous, and by the same token, the most harassed young man in America." Frick said Red had emerged from the Pullman "here this morning, his face lined with wrinkles of weariness, his eyes red and heavy from exhaustion ... Red Grange can't eat, he can't talk, he can't go out for a stroll down the street without being, at once, the center of all eyes ... Youngsters, their eyes bright with adoration and hero worship, rush to touch his clothing; adults, still youthful at heart, come in to pat his back, to shake his hand to engage him in conversation ... Perhaps somewhere there is an end to human endurance, and unless this writer is sadly mistaken, Harold 'Red' Grange, the wonder man of the gridiron, is nearing the end of that marvelous nervous energy which has carried him thus far in a campaign which is unparalleled in athletic history."

Collier's simply stamped him as the "saddest young man in America."

Game seven. Day fourteen.

The Boston game was played on a field swollen by frost. Damn, it was cold, and who could blame the fans for getting oiled up a bit? They paid good money to see the Ghost but what they saw didn't add up. Red looked slower now, his gait tilted to one side, shoulders hunched, as if the marbled muscles had simply given up. Where were his high knees? The wraithlike slipperiness? *More action!*

More action! they screamed, showing obdurate stares. They didn't have to throw flowers and chocolates, but you would have thought the mob would cut the boy some slack. This wasn't like a baseball tour, where they could see their heroes in many a game; pro football, and Grange in particular, was more of a one-shot deal. They had paid good money and endured terrible conditions to see the Galloping Ghost, who was keeling to one side in his stiff and frozen uniform. An average man wouldn't even have been on the field, but one writer said Grange was a flop, and Pegler wrote, "Pursued, waylaid at every step of his progress around town, ambushed in his own room at the hotel, and bombarded by photographers' flash bombs even when he was washing his ears in the Pullman at six in the morning, Grange is now a listless figure, with dull eyes and dark lines in his boyish face. The Bears apparently realized that he was no man today to play the bruising, agonizing game they had to go through on this frozen ground and they used him little after the first quarter." This only created anger in the crowd of twenty-five thousand, who seemed to be lying in wait to screech their incoherent curses. At one point Grange threw a downed ball to the referee and the crowed cheered derisively. And in the third quarter when Red — who had run back a punt for 10 yards and had five carries for 11 yards — retired to the dressing room — a group of fans mocked him. Beans, Charlie, Dinty, or Doc (no one seems to remember) took a smack at one asshole. "A brawl began that surged over a full acre and needed lots of cops," wrote Peg. Charlie wasn't happy with the less than enthusiastic newspaper coverage and he confronted Pegler at one point and said, "Dammit, you drink my whiskey and then rip me up." (No one ever said how that one turned out — neither man was afraid of fisticuffs — but soon afterward Pegler was ghostwriting for Red.)

None of this dissuaded Charlie. He was in his element. Criticism, lawsuits, and threats of violence just emboldened him. He loved being in the fray. He had a greater purpose in this. Money begets power, and Charlie wanted to make enough to create his own sports empire. Charlie had big ideas and to fulfill them Grange would have to keep playing. That's just the way it had to be. Charlie had always understood Red's nature. He was impressed with Red's desire for brilliance and his frantic need to get himself out of poverty. Red's pain threshold was incredibly high. Charlie wasn't blind.

He saw the hits Red was taking. He knew Red was experiencing blackouts after he was getting knocked in the head. He assured Red that it would all be worth it.

After the game Babe Ruth, a big football fan, strode into the locker room, found the Ghost, and tried to cheer him up. From the beginning of the tour, Red had started providing the picture men with a concocted smile, but with Ruth by his side, it was genuine, like the smiles of the gleeful dirty-faced kids who sidled up to Red. Ruth, the biggest celebrity in America, was calling on Grange again. The papers were all saying that Red had supplanted the Babe as the most popular athlete in the world. Ruth, thirty, had just finished the 1925 campaign, which had been a disaster for the Yankees (they finished next to last) and for Ruth, who missed part of the season after mysterious stomach surgery, some people whispering it was syphilis. Late in the season the Babe had been fined $5,000 and suspended for nine days for curfew violations: Ruth was gluttonous in food, smoke, and sex. Red devoured the sports pages, which when they weren't touting college football were writing about the baseball gods, and here he was hanging out with the ultimate American deity. Sensing Red's breaking body, fragile psyche, and sensitivity to criticism, Ruth had come to counsel the boy; he knew what the pressure could do. The Babe said, "Hi-yah, kid. How you doing?" Grange was hurting. "Sit down," ordered Ruth. "Maybe you'd better lie down."

And now the Bears were on the train, rattling at thirty miles per hour toward Pittsburgh because Charlie had arranged another goddamn game for the next day. Charlie couldn't see beyond his own bank account. No one intervened. Not Halas, not Red's Pa. They just let Red be. He was a man now. But he wasn't. Not quite. Red couldn't bury his boyhood obedience training so he didn't complain. He should have. There had been three different games in three different cities in three days. Red, with his waxen expression, told Doc that he could barely move his arm. Charlie didn't seem to care. He was in the ecstasy of his own scheming.

Game eight. Day fifteen.

Now it was just ridiculous.

Lawrie Walquist had a fractured small toe on his left foot, and the Bears linemen were so banged up that they were playing match and the loser had to start, so they put Andy Lotshaw in the lineup on Pittsburgh's Forbes Field. Andy, the Bears' trainer, whom everyone called Iodine, had a body that was starting to resemble a pear and he had never played a lick of football. Iodine had straight blond hair atop a dog-eared catcher's mitt face. He had a regular job as the Chicago Cubs trainer, but in the off-season he made some extra dough with the football Bears. Working for Halas was practically charity work, though. Half the time the Bears' owner didn't have money for tape. Lotshaw had spent the tour in the train's ladies' restroom, which had been converted to the sick ward. Iodine stumbled around for about a half and just about got his neck broken against a team with decent skills; some of its members were alumni of Pop Warner's Carlisle Indian School machine. In a drab city on a drab day, the Ghost gained 3 yards off tackle and threw five passes, one of which was intercepted. The magic had been beaten out of him but Red soldiered on, digging for something despite the catcalls that he was yellow. On a first-quarter punt, Red collided with someone and his arm went limp. He cradled it. The injury had been with him since St. Louis but he had played through it. After the Boston fiasco his arm hurt so much that he just wanted to lie in bed forever. The six thousand fans started booing as he went for a rest. Doc Cooley fluttered nervously by Grange's side as they escaped into the dressing room. After getting the arm wrapped, Red returned to the bench, a plank of wood on the sideline. Underneath his raccoon coat, which couldn't shield him from the Smoky City's boo birds, Red's right arm had been torn loose and broken blood vessels were causing hemorrhages around his shoulder. Red needed help, or the tour would be over. Iodine was playing so they asked the Pittsburgh baseball club's trainer, Dr. Gustav Berg, to check him out. Berg could patch up anyone, but he was not so optimistic, telling the eager reporters that Grange wouldn't play for two weeks at the very earliest.

It should have ended then and there. Charlie should have called it off. Halas should have done something. *Eight games in fifteen days*. But the men were overcome by greed and grand plans. Confined to his room in Pittsburgh's Schenley Hotel, Red stoically described the injury as nothing more than an old bruise. That's why they didn't end it. Red was no cake-eater. He promised to play in Detroit on

Saturday or in Chicago on Sunday. Halas ridiculed chronically in-jured players. When reporters asked him about Grange, Papa Bear guaranteed that he would play in a few days.

Walter Eckersall, who had chronicled Grange's college games for the *Chicago Tribune* and had ref'd many of them, seemed disgusted by the charade: "Every team the Bears meet is a comparatively fresh outfit and each is primed to get Grange. It would be hard enough for Grange to cut his usual capers under this condition, let alone playing four times a week in addition to traveling and not receiving the proper amount of relaxation.

"Then again the former Illinois star is pestered by all sorts of hero worshippers, the worst pests in the world. In fact, it is a small wonder Grange has not cracked before."

The team left Pittsburgh, bound for Detroit. Red had his arm examined again. He promised the press that he would, at the very least, play in Chicago on Sunday. He sat on a bed answering ques-tions in a listless manner and constantly rubbed his injured arm.

"All right, put it in splints; do anything so I can get some sleep. I haven't had a bit of sleep for two nights because of the pain in my arm."

The physician found the upper part of Grange's appendage swol-len twice the size of his other one. The arm was broken out with red spots along its entire length and at the back of his shoulder was a lump described as large as a baseball.

Meanwhile, on the train from Pittsburgh to Detroit, Halas called a team meeting. George Halas hated the disorder of this journey. He hated Pyle, who was making money off his team without do-ing hardly anything. Halas loved the money but he was not happy about the disparity. Pyle didn't play the game. He didn't know the rush, the trancelike feel of executing a perfect play, the hot tears in your throat when someone really takes you down, and the feeling of dominance when you see raw fear in your opponents' eyes. Ha-las saw football as warfare. Pyle was a carpetbagger. The weary but angry players talked from 10:30 a.m. to 3:00 p.m., bitching about Pyle, the author of this hell, saying that the one man on the train who knew the least about football had made the fucking schedule. Should they play the Detroit game? Would anyone come if Grange wasn't there? They were pissed, some at Red because he was letting Pyle control him like a dime store marionette, but in the end they decided to suit up. They were upset, but if they were in Red's position they would have done the same thing, and they respected Red's stoic toughness throughout the ordeal. In the end they were obedient. "As to games scheduled but not played the player shall receive no compensation," read the stingy NFL Uniform Player's Contract. To no one's surprise, the object of the invective was nowhere to be found. *He was a piece of work, that Pyle!* When trouble brewed, Charlie was as slippery as deer guts on a doorknob. When his third wife, Effie, divorced him in 1936, Judge John C. Lewe asked her how Charlie treated her.

"He was gone most of the time," replied Effie, who had been married to Charlie for twenty-two years.

While the Bears went to Detroit, Charlie was headed for the orange groves of Los Angeles to get a game going there. Charlie had an air of indifference to the players' griping. He had experienced it all before and football players were child's play compared to actors. He also needed to seriously avoid Detroit. Anyone who read the papers knew that Red Grange, managed by C. C. Pyle, was coming to Detroit, and C. Howard Crane, the preeminent theater architect and erstwhile designer of the Virginia Theatre, wanted Pyle to pay his outstanding bill. Charlie owed Crane $1,217.98. Crane filed the lawsuit trying to snag, or maybe shame, Charlie while he was in town. Charlie had given him the slip once again. It was a hell of a mess. Grange was made a garnishee defendant and James Conzelman, owner of the Detroit Panthers, a former Staley, and future Hall of Famer, was forbidden to distribute the gate receipts for the game. Other defendants named in the suit were Dutch and Halas. Pyle had never reneged on paying Grange, but Red noticed something about Charlie that was odd: Charlie would fight like a badger with someone over a couple of nickels, but then he would take the same person to a nightclub and not even think twice about wasting $500 on him. When it came to money, Charlie was definitely off.

Pyle's first Los Angeles appointment was with William Wrigley Jr., who had a ballpark in Los Angeles and as the owner of the Chicago Cubs knew something about Grange's drawing power. Pyle was also going to Hollywood to make a movie deal for Red. Thirty grand a pop for a football game was one thing, but there was some real money in Hollywood. Hell, Valentino's contract paid him $7,500 a week! And Rudy didn't need to risk his neck to get it. Red would never make it as a legitimate actor, sure, but it didn't matter. "I'll give them the best I can," Red would say, "and I guess no one can do more than that. When I get in the pictures, there's one thing about it, I won't try to be a Charlie Chaplin or a Douglas Fairbanks. I'll just be Red Grange." That would probably be enough for America. They couldn't get enough of Red. His heroic image had become too big to cut down. A movie would make him even bigger.

Stupidly, perhaps, or maybe because he was receiving $13,000 per appearance, Grange raced to Detroit's Navin Field on a west-bound train. *It was the ninth game in seventeen days.* He would try to give it a go in Detroit, but his arm was swathed in bandages. It hurt like a son of a bitch. Doc cut through the tape and revealed an arm swollen and purplish. Grange couldn't go and the Bears got their asses kicked, 21–0. At halftime one of Grange's entourage grabbed a megaphone and went to a spot before the stands: "Laaaa-dies and gentlemen!" yelled the ballyhoo man. "I take great pleasure in introducing to you our great gridiron hero, pride of the United States — Harold E. 'Red' Grange!"

With a whoop and a roar the crowd surrounded him. The photographers took shots.

"Don't frown like that — smile!"

"Aw — " said Grange in protest, but he smiled.

"Take your hat off!"

"Aw, it's too cold," pleaded Grange.

Grange took his hat off.

"Hurry up — it's cold."

Only 4,111 showed up to see a bad game on a gooey field. Thousands of other people had demanded a refund and Grange and the Bears paid *out* $18,000. To ease Pyle's fears that his Man o' War was coming up lame, Grange sent a telegram to Charlie at the promoter's Biltmore Hotel suite in sunny California. In the luxurious room Pyle had a secretary taking dictation and another person helping him with the Grange business, and some reporters were hanging out. The telegram bordered on the pathetic, a virtual groveling. Charlie read the telegram to the reporters: "Am feeling fine. Will be

fully recovered in two or three days. Don't worry. Regards." Grange
was under Pyle's spell, of course, but he was controlled by something even bigger: football's silent-suffering culture. Everyone got
hurt playing the game; the true test of the man was how he endured
the pain. Every man who played the game contemplated injury and
death. Every man who had strapped on a leather helmet knew that
blows to the head would produce a haze of dizziness. The risk was
worth it. There were not many places in the world to test one's mettle. Complaining went against the very ethos of why a player stood
on the field. In Red's mind he faced the truth: "I was bone tired.
It seemed like every inch of my body was covered with bumps and
bruises." But bellyaching publicly or taking himself out of a game
was impossible. It went against the team. It went against the code.

The Bears limped home to Chicago, where they would play the
Giants the next day. Red wanted to play and he worried that he was
letting everyone down. He had already gone above and beyond, and
he was suffering from a wrecked shoulder. His doctors said he had
to sit or he might never play again. He reluctantly sat out, nursing his injury and forlornly staring at the sooty Chicago sky. Despite
being banged up, he wanted to be out there. It would hit the papers that he wanted to play and people saw him as brave and pos-
sessing a manly vulnerability. The bedraggled Bears lost 0–9. After
another examination Dr. Cooley told Red he shouldn't suit up until Christmas because an x-ray still showed ruptured muscles and
a hemorrhage. His shoulder was a mess and his body on the brink
of falling apart, but he was now a rich man. Grange and Pyle were
splitting, pre-lawsuits, more than $100,000 from the games, and
the endorsement deals were bringing in another $100 grand. Red
and Charlie were far from done. The barnstorming tour was only
half over. There would be more money, and pain, ahead.

11

"Cash 'n' Carry"

RED GRANGE AND C. C. PYLE

THE BEARS WERE EXCHANGING the brutal Midwest winter for palm trees. The second leg, the southern swing, of the barnstorming tour had begun. Thirty players, managers, coaches, trainers, and hangers-on were in the Floridian, escaping a raging snowstorm. Wanting to make amends, Charlie had scheduled fewer games, provided two sets of jerseys, and booked first-class accommodations on the Pullman. Despite the more livable conditions, Red was still ignoring the signs from his most important asset, his body. He convinced himself he was ready to go again; the ten days' rest, along with daily treatments under powerful heat lamps, had softened Red's arm. The warmer climes would cure him, too, he hoped. Realistically, he needed at least three months to heal. No one was discouraging him from playing. Certainly not George Halas, who was actually making money for once and could feel the momentum of the public shift every time Red Grange stepped on the field alongside his Bears. And Charlie guaranteed that the second part of the barnstorming tour would be like a vacation.

And it was in this way, the buzz saw of Red's popularity pushing them, that Red and Charlie went forward.

The first stop would be Coral Gables, Florida, where they would play on December 25, 1925. Charlie had tried to get even more games. They were supposed to have a few contests in the South — Georgia, Alabama, maybe even Cuba — but no one in those states or the island nation could come up with the money. Promoters were always coming to Charlie and promising that they would give him a percentage of the gate, but Charlie wanted his cash up front. He was very particular on this matter. The newspapermen made note of it and started calling Charlie "Cold Cash" Pyle, or "Cash 'n'

Carry" Pyle, a moniker that he loved. "Little do they know," Charlie told *Liberty* magazine, "how they flatter me." Well, the Coral Gables people did come up with some money, so "Red Grange's Chicago Bears" would have a relaxing three-thousand-mile trip south where they would play on Christmas, then go to Tampa and Jacksonville (if those two communities came up with the cold cash), and then swing over to New Orleans, up to Los Angeles, Frisco, Portland, and Seattle. Along with some additional acolytes and Clem, the porter, who would serve the Bears the entire journey, Halas and Pyle signed some more players. They were trying to make the second leg less of a torture fest, and Red's presence was attracting existing pros as well as college stars. They brought in Roy Lyman, Nebraska tackle, who had played with the Cleveland and Philadelphia pro teams; Richard "Dutch" Vick, former Michigan quarterback and more recently a member of the Detroit Panther eleven; and Harold "Swede" Erickson, former Washington and Jefferson back and a dandy passer who starred with the Chicago Cardinals. Michigan's Paul Goebel, a six-foot-five All-American, captain of the 1922 Wolverines, was charged with blowing open the ends for Grange. "He came across as somewhat austere and intimidating but he was a true gentle giant," recalled his granddaughter Meg Goebel. Goebel was an excellent teammate — Michigan great Bennie Oosterbaan said "he always thought twice before doing anything for himself" — and the tall Teuton could buckle the knees of the opposition. In the first leg of the tour, Goebel played for Columbus and he had been so dominant that the Bears avoided his side of the line the entire game. Years later the blue-eyed Paul, who had served in World War I, would reenlist for World War II, earning the Bronze Star.

In Coral Gables, Grange experienced the insanity of the 1920s land rush. "Don't go to Florida," he would later warn friends, "even if you are invited on an excursion with all expenses paid and free money in your pocket." The Midwest seemed to be descending en masse on the Florida swamps. The Bears went to the field where they could smell the bare earth and freshly sawed planks. But where were the stands? Within forty-eight hours, workers constructed the bleachers for twenty-five thousand seats of a makeshift stadium.

Pyle priced 50-yard-line box seats at $19.80, and he had plenty of takers.

The players' heavy boots, once wet from tramping in the mud, were now light and cracking, their uniform sweaters clean. Paul Goebel played his typical he-man game, destroying the opposing end and letting Grange get off his flying runs. The Galloping Ghost's touchdown came in the second period, when, after a 33-yard sprint around end, he was given the ball on the 2-yard line and in two attempts went through center for the score. Grange played three full periods, and in the closing moments he gave the crowd another thriller, racing 45 yards, and had eluded the Coral Gables barrier when Red Barron, former Georgia Tech star, pulled him down. The Bears beat the Coral Gables Collegians 7–0.

Red seemed to be back in form; at least there were moments when people were offered a glimpse of his excellence. But underneath it all his athletic ability wasn't the same. It was an experiment gone wrong. Red always had great vision on the field. He could detect the future movements of all the players. He still had the vision but he wasn't always reacting quite as quickly because he had played eleven pro games in thirty days. Before the barnstorming tour he had played a seven-game college schedule. Red had played eighteen games over a three-month period. He played offense and defense, and he took the brunt of the cheap shots. He still had eight games to go.

On New Year's Day the Bears faced off in Tampa against Jim Thorpe, one of America's greatest athletes. Thorpe, a Sac and Fox Indian, was an Olympic gold medalist in the pentathlon and decathlon, played major league baseball, and starred in college and professional football, perhaps his greatest sport. Thorpe's trainwreck speed once mowed over Dwight Eisenhower, inflicting the future president with a knee injury.

Thorpe was one of the founding fathers of professional football, its first attraction, and the league's inaugural president. He had even been in the Canton Hupmobile showroom in 1920 when the league was formed and helped give the league some credibility. But Thorpe was unfairly tainted. He had violated his amateur status by playing minor league baseball to earn a little pocket money and as a result had to surrender his track medals from the 1912 Olympic

Games. Thorpe was a draw, but he was an Indian and all that that meant to the wider American public, and Thorpe never had a C. C. Pyle in his corner. About Thorpe the *Pittsburgh Dispatch* once reported: "This person Thorpe was a host in himself. Tall and sinewy, as quick as a flash and as powerful as a turbine engine, he appeared to be impervious to injury." Thorpe still had a regal presence from the faraway stands and on the field he was a relentless trash talker — "Let's give 'em a show, let ol' Jim run" — and if a tackler didn't let him by he would drive his hip and shoulder into him, often knocking men cold, once demolishing Knute Rockne in a charity game. But Thorpe was almost forty and on the downside. Age and drink were hobbling him, and he was getting cut from every legitimate team he tried out for. Jim, probably the greatest athlete of all time, was becoming a novelty act. Grange would never have Thorpe's world-class speed and he was tired. But on one of Grange's touchdown runs, he bowled over the cirrhotic Thorpe. It was now Grange's world.

The Bears were scheduled to play the Jacksonville All-Stars on January 2, 1926, but Charlie and the town elders were playing chicken. The Jacksonville fellows had come to Charlie with a proposal. They wanted to hype their town, maybe even start a pro team in their community where the land rush had started to sputter because of a lack of new buyers. (Charles Ponzi, of Ponzi Scheme infamy, had developed a subdivision that he claimed was near the city, even though it was sixty-five miles west and had twenty-three lots to the acre; Red and Charlie would each throw $17 grand into the Florida real estate boom — and lose it.) John S. O'Brien, a Jacksonville booster, persuaded the *Times-Union* to publicize the game and hundreds of athletes showed up for tryouts. They needed a draw so they contacted Ernie Nevers, Stanford University's star fullback, who, reading about the jack Grange was earning, requested $25,000 plus 5 percent of the gross gate receipts. (Among football players Grange was creating exciting opportunities to make money, and players were starting to reconsider the pro game.) The promoters went house to house to raise the funds. The nonstar players would make $200 for playing in the game. The quality of football on the tour was up and down. The Bears were damaged and their opponents were often eager but lacked playing time together. "Nevers, captain, fired the trainer, and ignored the coach," reported *Liberty* magazine, which described other players — not all of whom had the bona fides — jumping on the Grange football bandwagon. "Willie Gruber, who claimed the Oregon Aggies as his alma mater, was rejected forthwith. Mr. Gruber was quite bald and slightly drunk." The Bears won 19–6.

On January 10 the Bears played the All-Southern Stars in New Orleans, the nation's second-largest port city, population 430,000, its riverbanks lined with coffee-roasting plants, the scent of chicory fogging the air. Red spoke at the Young Men's Business Club (a record four hundred young businessmen showed up and Red was given a football made of pink carnations); there was a horserace named the Red Grange Handicap, and the Ghost went to the Boys' Commercial High School, where Grange must have been hung over to give such a lame speech: "There is only one way I know to become an athlete. Get lots of sleep and live a normal regular healthy life. Keep away from the bright lights and eat plain food. Don't eat too much meat. Any vegetable is good. Spinach and potatoes are excellent. Chew the food well. Don't be a loafer on the street." His legs were tired but Red was making a serious run for financial security. He might never have to work again. There was nothing to do but play the games and collect the checks. But sometimes Red's insecurity would escape. He blurted defensively at one reporter that in two years, "I'll have enough so I can say when I'll work and where I'll work and work at what I want," and he added that officers in a Champaign bank were investing his money in Liberty bonds, and that his income from his investments "was several hundred dollars a month."

There was tension. Charlie had a temper and he didn't mind showing it. During the New Orleans game Red went for a long run, which was called back because of a clip. Charlie was on the sideline and he was stomping up and down, screaming at the umpire. The people wanted to see Red do well and it was the referee's job to make sure that happened. *A clip!* Charlie had done this before. He was a hothead. He started screaming and the Bears got riled up. The cheap shots started flying. Trafton's leg was torn from ankle to thigh. Charlie was incensed. (His employees were getting injured, after all.) Halas couldn't control the situation. It was Charlie's team. A brawl started. It intensified to the point that a mounted police-man galloped onto the field to break it up. "Here comes one of the Four Horsemen," Grange cracked. Luckily these types of incidents didn't make it into the nation's papers. The writers didn't like to criticize Red too much. He had become untouchable. A primitive god. In Red's heart he knew it was a long, long way from the real drama and the glory of the college gridiron.

In Los Angeles the January 16 game had been hyped for a month. The tilt would be played at the Coliseum, another stadium built in the 1920s stadium boom.

Charlie had the game, Grange's movie negotiations, and the so-cial calendar booked. In the background were bougainvilleas, the ocean breeze, the brilliant light, the scent of the orange groves, the acacia, the itinerant preachers who seemed to be on every street corner. But the real scenery was the dames. The Bears partied with Douglas Fairbanks, Mary Pickford, and Harold Lloyd and met the Hearst family and the Wrigleys — all the big-time Hollywood play-ers. At one event Trafton wiggled the Black Bottom with the comely actress Priscilla Dean. ("What a sex pot — and I don't mean Pris-cilla," joked one teammate.) The women were just about every-where, in their flowered taffeta skirts ... the stunners made the men step back. The movie colony and its incandescent residents were like nothing else in the country — the late-night beach parties, the air, all redemption, a grown man's playground, too good to be true. Red spent a day visiting movie studios, having a "harder bat-tle to get away from the studio beauties who wanted to pose along-side him than he ever had against Coach Yost's best ends," one pa-per noted. In a sense Grange was replicating what he had done in New York. It was the same type of scene as in the Polo Grounds, just warmer, and the crowd of seventy-five thousand was not so damn hostile, not so in need of escape from tenements and cramped hu-manity. But, of course, Los Angeles can be deceptive. Grange was served with a lawsuit from some crackpot named George Lazo, who sued him for $50,000 and two days later was arrested for her-oin possession. That same night Grange went to the Windsor Tea

Room, where three hundred Illinois alums had gathered for . . . a Bob Zuppke speech. When Grange entered the room, there was an ovation. "The tension of the situation was immediately felt," reported the *Los Angeles Times*.

After making his way through the boosters, the men met. Red Grange, who had the look of a man already, wanted approval from his coach.

"Hello, Red," said Zuppke, who always saw the boy within him. Coach Zuppke wanted Red to repent for blackening the purity of football, Illinois, and Bob Zuppke, but he didn't want to make a scene so he was slyly dismissive. "I wish you lots of luck tomorrow."

"Hello, Coach. Have you got tickets for the game? If not I want you to sit on our bench."

"Thanks just the same but I've sat on enough benches for some time to come."

For the Los Angeles game the Bears played the Tigers, who were led by George "Wildcat" Wilson, a Washington University star, who fancied himself a West Coast Grange.

"That was the first time real [pro] football was ever played in the West," said Grange, who would make $25,000 (some said $50,000). Wilson, who would always complain that he was underpaid, received $5,000; most of the other Bears players made $500 and the Tigers earned $250 apiece.

The game had been built up plenty and the chatty Ed Healey gave the pregame speech. "As a player your whole thrill of the ball game is hitting someone with emphasis," Healey liked to say. "It's more or less controlled warfare." Healey, a Dartmouth grad, should know. He had served in the cavalry and seen action in World War I, and he was a respected leader on the team. Lawrie Walquist would crack that Ed should speak at his funeral. "Can't you just see the pallbearers pick up that coffin, throw it over their shoulders, and run out to the hearse?" The Bears were mercenaries and their brand of football was something to behold. Halas drilled them relentlessly on technique, and they had little tricks, such as looking where a man stood on his feet and pushing him off balance at just the right time. Football aficionados loved watching the line play of Healey and Trafton, who were so smart about conserving their strength until just the right moment. Anyone with eyes couldn't help but admit that Red was soaked by exhaustion and maybe a little too easy to catch from behind. But when the games really counted, Red would undoubtedly turn it around and dominate the suddenly interesting professional game, wouldn't he?

The Bears won the game, 17–7, and it proved so popular that they almost played another one in Los Angeles, but other promoters couldn't stomach Pyle's endless demands so the Bears played a casual practice-like game in San Diego for a small payday before heading north to San Francisco.

The time on the train, the forced togetherness, the slave wages, and the long period of time away from their families and real jobs wore on the team. Even daylong deer-hunting trips, introductions to Luther Burbank, the badminton with society types, walks on San Francisco's Market Street with its freak shows (*Queen of the reptiles! Cages of monkeys! Captain John Leal, nature's miniature gentleman!*), and Chinatown, where Pyle would claim that he was making arrangements to bring the Galloping Ghost to the Far East, couldn't lighten the mood. The strained togetherness came to a head in San Francisco on January 24, 1926. *It was the seventeenth game on the tour.* Someone threatened a reporter, and right before the contest against the San Francisco Tigers — who had players named "Rabbit," "Stew," and "Hobo" — Dutch and the Brute got into a fistfight. Dutch Sternaman had benched George Trafton. You didn't bench the Brute. Trafton took a swing. Then Sternaman pushed Trafton through a window. San Francisco beat the Bears 14–9. It was a testament to Grange's popularity that he could continue to attract attention wherever he appeared. To San Francisco's great embarrassment, it did not rival Los Angeles's enthusiasm, as *only* twenty thousand attended the game, but for a pro matchup it was still astonishing. The Grange and Pyle duo would split $34,000.

The two-month tour was winding down. They had all been through a lot. A birth. And there was something beautiful about Grange's bodily sacrifice, of never a complaint. There was not only legitimacy; there was a cachet to the sport. Sure, Grange and the rest of the players had been knocked around. But no one whined publicly. Red had made his decision. He was now his own man. It had not always been pretty, but Charlie's promotional genius had put professional football into America's consciousness. He had flair. With his exhaustive aggression, he had taught the owners how to sell the sport.

Going to the Pacific Northwest for the farewell games was a homecoming of sorts for Charlie because it had been the center of his vaudeville life. As a younger man, Charlie had joined the Margarita Fischer Stock Company in Silvertown, Oregon; formed C. C. Pyle's Greater Lewis and Clark International Exposition in Moscow, Idaho; and acted in his own theater company, always joking that Brownsville, Oregon, was the only town that egged him. In the second-to-last game of the tour, the Bears played the Portland, Oregon, All-Stars. Chicago won, 54–3 or 60–3 — the different reporters lost track of the score.

At Tacoma's Hotel Winthrop, where the team stopped, the lovelies hounded Grange. As the tour wore on, the female conquests increased but it was Charlie doing most of the conquering. Publicly Red was perceived to be the ladies' man, but it was Charlie who was the real player. "They were more eager than a crowd of the opposite sex at a bargain rush where silk dresses are offered for 39 cents," wrote the *Tacoma News Tribune*, which also made fun of Grange's peculiar sense of fashion. "The Red Head arose to leave the room for a photograph. He wore a very light tan tweed suit, the bottoms of which make a sailor's trousers look like skin-tight trunks. The style is referred to as 'bell bottoms.' Well, Grange's could be called 'Liberty Bell bottoms'. They were inclined to remind one of the old bell in size at least, and they no doubt offered his legs much liberty." The reporters were bringing up names of women connected with Red. Pyle would call the reports nonsense, flick cigarette ashes onto the hotel carpet, and then crack, "Is she good-looking?"

Pyle, the Bears would concede, was the most voracious ladies' man they had ever seen. He had a special affinity for showgirls. While he was married to Effie, Charlie wrote a letter to Valeska Suratt — a film siren with an hourglass figure — that was ostensibly about a stock investment that Charlie had secured for her, but it obviously went beyond a simple business correspondence:

My darling: —

Your check for $1,100 received. Am enclosing receipts. This stock will make you money. You can always have your money back anytime you want it. *Always remember that.* Yours was a sweet letter. Cant write much but honey I am thinking of you. Your a sweet girl I love you very much.

Yours always,
Chas.

Did you get your little piano?

(In 1928 Ms. Suratt, her looks fading, her career on the decline, sued Charlie for two grand. The case was settled out of court.)

No matter the geography, the promotional demands never seemed to dissipate. Red was waylaid and couldn't make one appearance at a sports store. A lot of boys showed up but went away disappointed, one saying, "Aw, gosh, Red ain't comin'. Ain't that a shame? I sure wanted to see him. Didn't you?"

In Spokane, 250 people greeted his train. "Red will play a game of football here next year," shouted Pyle, just as the conductor waved the starting signal. The crowd cheered.

On January 31, the day after the Portland contest, Red Grange and the Bears played their final barnstorming exhibition against George Wilson's Washington All-Stars. At the pregame luncheon honoring the Ghost and Wildcat Wilson, Charlie — tongue firmly in cheek — insisted to Seattle's Young Men's Business Club that he had made no overtures to sign Wilson to a professional contract. The crowd roared. Charlie Pyle, that sly fellow, was up to something. In the waning days of the tour, with his trainload of cash, Pyle could finally execute his next move. He was in a beautiful position, the money and fame creating substantial power. Red and Charlie had signed a three-year exclusive contract. Charlie Pyle didn't need George Halas and the Chicago Bears. Hell, he didn't need the National Football League. In Seattle the Bears won 34–0, with Grange carrying the mail nine times for 99 yards, an average of 11 yards a try. He threw one 30-yard pass, which resulted in a touchdown. He ran for two more, dashing 30 yards for each.

With eighteen touchdowns during the course of the barnstorming campaign, Grange had been spectacular — in spurts — enough to keep the crowds interested. No one, of course, could have played great at that pace, and most people just wanted a glimpse of him. *Sixty-seven days, nineteen games.* Red had also played a college season before the tour, and there hadn't been much sleep between with the rattling trains, the boisterous teammates, the countless luncheons, speeches to business groups, theater outings, the whiskey, the flappers ... America had followed the tour in the sports pages, and when Grange came to town, the papers chronicled his every move. In retrospect the journey had been a thrill, but for Red it had also been a drab, sometimes spooky trip through Chicago, St. Louis, Philadelphia, New York, Boston, Jacksonville, Tampa, New Orleans, Los Angeles, San Francisco, Portland, Seattle, and the little villages in between, the gangly children, the needy eyes, the jealous shouts of "You yellow bum!" any time Red didn't perform well. Red was permanently in their consciousness — a human embodying supernatural gifts — and that aura had become a part of professional football. Hundreds of thousands of people witnessed greatness; millions more had read about Grange's feats. Only a few months earlier pro ball had been seen as a laughingstock, faintly criminal, or just not very interesting. Now it had lore, glamour, and excitement. The sum of him. His reputation wider, but cheaper. Pyle told the press that the trip had been "very successful"; in money terms that meant that Pyle and Grange each, after expenses, made at least $100,000 on the games with a lot more coming in for endorsements, probably $300,000 each in total (or $3.42 million in modern times, according to the Consumer Price Index) in an era when athletes were not highly compensated. A lot of money for a few months' work, and there was more money to come. Grange would soon sign a lucrative movie contract, which would put his image into even more minds and even more cash into his pockets. George Halas had done OK, too. He could probably buy some more extra jerseys, footballs, and even tape, and his team was now the most watched pro gridiron team in the nation.

But it was not all good. With Red's college and barnstorming tour he had experienced at least ten serious concussions and two major shoulder injuries. With the lack of recovery time between games, opposing players' penchant for giving him cheap shots, and the extracurricular activities (broads and booze, mostly), the tour

—he would later confess—had burned him out. The strain had taken away his ability to improvise. "I took on too much," he confessed to *Sport* magazine. "The human frame can't stand 30 football games in 12 weeks, with railroad jumps in between." He would have a nice long off-season, a chance to play solitaire with his checks, a little vacation, some time in glorious Hollywood, and then a return to the gridiron. There was more money to be made. Just one more scheme with Charlie and he would control an entire league. Their secret was out. The news was already leaking that Charlie wanted a piece of the Bears or a New York team or he was going to start his own breakaway league bent on breaking the NFL monopoly. With a growing confidence, and on-the-job training from Charlie, Red was now a different man. Speaking to crowds and handling his fame were never enjoyable, but he handled things with more grace. He had had his doubts about Charlie, and perhaps Pyle had driven him and the rest of the Bears to the brink, but Charlie's ambition had rubbed off on him. Charlie had it all figured out. The tour had established them. They were now a major force with money and power. They *were* pro football.

12

|||||||||||||||||||||||||||||||||||||||

Outlaws

RED GRANGE'S NEW YORK FOOTBALL YANKEES
PLAYED IN YANKEE STADIUM

WHY DON'T YOU QUIT NOW?" Grantland Rice asked Red. "You're fixed for life."

"I've just started."

Red and Charlie wanted to squeeze themselves into the NFL, and Pyle had his designs on the Chicago Bears.

Charlie talked with Halas about a one-third share, if Grange suited up during the regular season.

"No third," said Halas. "Nobody's worth a third of the club."

"Then you play without Red," said Pyle.

"Then we play without Red."

"Do you figure how much you're going to lose at the ticket office?"

"I figure, and I still say no third, nothing."

"I'm going to build my own club, build it around Red."

"They won't let you in the league."

"Then I'll build my own league."

"Go ahead. And close the door behind you, on the way out!"

Halas felt sorry for Red. Pyle, his arm around Grange, was taking him on a wayward path. George Halas wasn't so much older than Red, but he wasn't nearly as naive.

"OK," said Pyle. "That's your last word."

"I told you that in the first place."

Charlie didn't care. It was probably better that George had turned him down. Charlie had seen enough of America to know that the real money was in New York, so he decided that was where they would center their lives. After the barnstorming tour they had secretly signed a five-year lease at Yankee Stadium. Red Grange, who could draw a crowd for tying his shoes, would pull them in, and with Red headlining his own team, the whole league would cash in on the gate receipts. That would be their pitch at the February 6 league meeting in Detroit. Charlie's pushiness grated on some of the owners — "He seemed to think that he was God's Gift to Sport and should be received with joy to Abraham's bosom," opined Dr. Harry March, the Giants' general manager. Charlie, a football carpetbagger, was not the most popular man among the league owners, but his entrance into the NFL seemed like a cinch.

Besides the Grange-Pyle matter, there was some other business, of course — reprimanding the Chicago Cardinals and the Milwaukee team for using high school kids, booting the Milwaukee owner from the league, raising the application fee for a franchise from $500 to $2,500, voting the Chicago Cardinals the 1925 league championship over the Pottsville Maroons, and approving a squad size increase from sixteen to eighteen players. Charlie followed the goings-on at the meeting. Their vision was so limited. They needed a strong commissioner. A man with creativity and an iron fist. Charlie Pyle and Red Grange came to dominate the meeting. The barnstorming tour had created anger among college presidents. The college game had been kneecapped, but the National Football League didn't want to bring down any more wrath so the league adopted the "Grange Rule," which stated that collegiate players cannot participate in professional games until after their class has graduated. And restrictions were placed on the number of games played in a week to two (again, a reaction to Grange's insane barnstorming schedule). But the most pressing issue was Grange's bid for a franchise. Red was modest as he introduced himself to the owners, all of whom had coveted him. Charlie would give the big pitch in the Henry II Room at the Hotel Statler. "I have the biggest star in football and I have the lease on the biggest stadium in the country and I am going into your league," Pyle said with the tenor of threat in his tone. New York Giants owner Tim Mara, Pyle's sworn enemy, was incensed. All of New York was the Giants' protected territory, and no other franchise could play there without the consent of the Giants' management. Yankee Stadium was a thousand yards away from the Polo Grounds — just across the Harlem River — and the season was too short to accommodate two pro teams. "Hell had broken loose," said the Giants' GM, Harry March.

Mara was plenty upset at Pyle and Grange, and any owner who

was willing to abandon him, but he contained himself and offered a compromise. Pyle and Grange could put their franchise in Brooklyn, but never play on the same days as the Giants. There wasn't enough interest in pro football for two teams playing at the same time, and Brooklyn was a safe ten miles away, so Grange's team wouldn't steal the Giants' existing fan base. It seemed like a good, if not wholly generous, compromise. Grange agreed to it. Red wanted to avoid conflict. But it wasn't up to him. Charlie had him under contract. Red told Mara that his future was in Charlie's hands. "Grange could not lead a grand march at an American Legion ball unless Pyle got his bit," said the Giants' March, "couldn't endorse a cigarette or a typewriter unless the cash was first carried to Pyle."

Pyle was not thrilled with the proposal. *Brooklyn!* Charlie wanted to be close to the action. *Brooklyn!* It was insulting. Pyle felt confident that a Grange team would outdraw the Giants. Charlie was in the power position. He wasn't going to make concessions.

There was hatred between the two men but no one wanted to step forward and broker a deal. The other owners decided to stick Mara and Pyle into a room. Let them work out their differences. There was no compromise. There wasn't even much discussion. "Pyle's chin narrowly missed a massaging," said one witness. "The men disliked each other and there was no harmony possible." Charlie wasn't finished.

Cash 'n' Carry decided to end-around Mara and met with the other owners. He pleaded with them. *Red Grange! He had Red Grange! The barnstorming tour had attracted legions of fans. The league needed Red!* Nineteen of the twenty owners, Charlie claimed, actually agreed with him. Red Grange could make them a lot of money. They didn't like Charlie's smug attitude but this was business. They debated the issue but they realized that crossing Mara would be bad for the league, and they couldn't create mistrust among the owners by crippling one of their fellow members. Turning their back on Mara was not a good way to run pro football.

Pyle was flabbergasted, plenty mad, and bent on revenge. *So they wouldn't let him into their pissant old boys' club.* OK, he would start his own damn league and steal some of the disgruntled owners. Four hours later he announced his traitorous plot. He would hold a meeting in Chicago the following Wednesday to create a rival league. There were teams in cities such as Boston, Newark, St. Louis, and Hartford that wanted into professional ball, and he would poach them as well as create new teams. The NFL, Pyle convinced himself, was doomed.

When Tim Mara returned to New York, the reporters wanted his reaction to the Grange-Pyle league. "I haven't a thing in the world against Grange. He is a great football player and a fine fellow personally, and I'd like to have him on the Giants' team, but if he plays any pro football at Yankee Stadium it will be an outlaw league . . . With Pyle still holding the reins I can promise him a fight to the last ditch. I never could warm up to him and this last act of his has soured me against him entirely . . . Pyle practically ignored me during his visit here with Grange. He refused to consult me on certain matters at a time when I was ready and did him every sort of break. Now this latest mix-up has been the final blow . . . He's fired the opening gun. Let me tell you I have a whole arsenal to fire back at him."

The war was on.

Pyle had no problem finding NFL defectors, each of whom put $3,000 per team into the new league's coffers. Rock Island was the first entrant. Then Bob Folwell of the Giants broke away from Mara and started the Philadelphia Quakers. There was a team in Boston, one in Newark, and another in Brooklyn called the Horsemen, which would have one of the Four Horsemen, Harry Stuhldreher, as its featured star. Wildcat Wilson would have a traveling team. Pyle wanted into the football-mad Chicago market so he convinced Bears quarterback Joe Sternaman — Dutch's brother — to join the "Outlaw League." That was a nice little coup that was a slap in the face to the Bears. Little Joey would have the Chicago Bulls franchise.

The only reporter to question the league's viability was the *New York Herald Tribune*'s influential columnist W. O. McGeehan, who once sarcastically wrote, "It is all right to say that Washington never had a hatchet and his father never had a cherry tree, but do not take from us the Ice Man of Wheaton." McGeehan was not much of a believer in pro football, and he thought the Outlaw League so much folly, writing in his "Down the Line" column, "Mr. Grange, astute business man though he seems, may also go bankrupt."

Red was no genius with numbers, and McGeehan had a point. Of course, there was risk, but Charlie had been invincible on the tour and this latest gambit was bound to go according to plan. Red was playing craps with the money he had earned on the barnstorming tour, but it felt like the odds were in the Grange-Pyle corner. He figured they could parlay their barnstorming money and triple it at the very least, and in a few years he would be set for life. Everything they did made money. Red had been an impoverished college player less than a year before. As he ended his college career, he was haunted by his decisions, but he would soon be an owner in his own league. His sudden good fortune was an American success story. Everyone had Charlie Pyle wrong. He had a vision. Red wasn't into the details. He didn't always think it through. That was Charlie's job. Undoubtedly they would make another bucketload. His American Professional Football League, centered in New York, had all of the makings of something great, much greater than the backwater National Football League, whose headquarters were in — er, Columbus, Ohio.

Pyle promised to hire an iron-fisted commissioner who would run the APFL like major league baseball (the weakling NFL would kick teams out of the league, and then turn around and let them sit in and vote at league meetings). The APFL teams would play two games a week; the league would be organized so there would be one champion (the NFL had a disputed champion practically every year). One percent of the gross receipts of all games would go into the league's treasury, half of which would go to the owners of the championship eleven and the other half to the players of the teams finishing among the first four, on the basis of 50 percent for the leader, 25 for second, 15 for third, and 10 for fourth place. Pyle had some innovative ideas for the outlaws and it made so much sense that Red and Charlie had put most of their money into it, borrowing even more cash from their nice banker friend H. E. Mc-Nevin, who seemed to be making a bet on the league with depositors' savings accounts. Red would spend the upcoming football season leading the New York Yankees, getting his name in the papers, and helping to build his new venture, which many simply called "the Grange league." The enterprise had all the makings of being a complete success. The NFL owners had a right to be worried about it. There were local stars, like Paddy Driscoll in Chicago, but Red was the only national hero who could bring in fans wherever he played, and that meant attendance and press attention would follow. There had been games during the barnstorming tour that hadn't been sellouts, but when the games really mattered and Red's body had the proper rest to show off his sublime abilities, the people would come in droves.

Charlie had spent the football off-season in a conquering frenzy. Who could resist him? Only a few, actually. Grantland Rice turned down the $25,000-a-year job to be the league commissioner. So did the former University of Chicago star and the conscience of football Walter Eckersall. And Pyle had trouble finding the right man to run the Yankees franchise. Charlie wanted Ed Healey, the brilliant and talkative Bears tackle. Ed had kept the boys in tow on the barnstorming tour. "Like the others, I, too, enjoyed the frivolity of our travels," said Healey, "but you must have somebody who evidences leadership, who takes charge." Pyle sent for Healey and told him to meet him in Chicago at the Morrison Hotel. When Healey arrived, there was a party going on. Red was there and so was Joie "Chesty" Ray, a runner. In the bedroom with C. C. Pyle was a member of the female sex. The woman, Healey noted, did not answer to the name of Mrs. Pyle.

Charlie told Ed that he wanted him to select, coach, and manage the Yankees playing personnel for a salary of $10,000. "That was more than I was making altogether from Mr. Halas and from another employer, Mr. George A. France of the France Stone Company, which by now employed me in the quarry business in the state of Indiana. And mind you, I had gotten $150 a game for thirty ball games that season, which figures out to $4,500, doesn't it? Furthermore, pro football by this time was a week-long proposition, although Halas would give me a few days off from practice to attend my other job when necessary."

Healey said, "Charlie, I'll give you an answer on that today."

"Oh, you don't have to answer me today," he said.

"Well, this *is* shocking. I've never really been up against anything where I had to make a decision with reference to leaving people I'm established with."

Healey went across the street to the Conway Building, where he met with George and Dutch. "There's the situation, boys. There it is, right in a package. Now what am I to do?"

They couldn't match the offer, but they upped Healey's salary a bit.

Healey walked across the street. "You had better look for someone else."

Ed could have used the raise but he was loyal and suspicious. "I figured that any man that could be married and divorced three times and come up with a broad in another room, I didn't have any business working for him," said Healey. "If I had gone with him to New York, he might have taken care of my situation, and then again, he might not have. I had no reason to regret my decision. In that connection, my thoughts are of poor Ralph Scott. He came from Montana and was a World War I veteran, shot up a bit . . . Well, Ralph Scott was the damn fool that took that job Pyle was offering. Scotty didn't have any more business being in New York than I did. I mean, New York is a fast town. The last I heard, the poor guy shot himself. I don't know whether he killed himself or somebody killed him, but he never came back from New York."*

The league president job fell to "Big" Bill Edwards, a whale-fat (a *Brooklyn Eagle* writer likened him to a galloping mastodon) bureaucrat who had been a Princeton guard in the 1890s. Big Bill was a New York legend because back in 1910 some nut had tried to shoot Mayor Gaynor but Edwards dived, tackling the would-be assassin low and hard, saving Gaynor's life. As payback, Edwards had spent two decades as an IRS bureaucrat and New York's street cleaning commissioner, but taxes and street grime were far from his first love, which was definitely football, his college memories recounted in a 463-page act of tedium called *Football Days*, which was published in 1916. "I have accepted the Presidency because I want to help preserve high-class football as it is played at the colleges. The tradition of our great game is that it is a clean, red-blooded sport — a great character builder — and it must retain these splendid qualities when played professionally." He liked to say, "Football for all and all for football," the slogan of the new league. "Professional football is nothing new; it has been played for over thirty years but the success of professional football, the class of game presented and the demand of the game is new."

---

* Ralph Scott, a Walter Camp All-American from Wisconsin, actually left New York, but on August 15, 1936, in ill health and facing the prospect of losing a leg, he asphyxiated himself in a car outside Billings, Montana.

After a meeting in New York's Hotel Commodore, the nine franchises (two were mostly traveling teams) were rolled out: the New York Yankees (owned by C. C. Pyle, wearing red, white, and blue); the Brooklyn Horsemen (owned by Humbert J. Fugazy, a fight promoter, wearing maroon and black); the Newark Bears (owned by W. J. Coughlin, wearing purple and white); the Boston Bulldogs (owned by Robert K. McKirby; dark blue); the Philadelphia Quakers (owned by L. S. Conway; light blue and gold); the Cleveland Panthers (Gen. C. X. Zimmerman, who had been court-martialed early in his military career for misappropriating funds; brown and gold); the Chicago Bulls (Joe Sternaman, the NFL Benedict Arnold; orange and black); and two traveling clubs, the Rock Island Independents (A. H. Bowlby, a refugee from the NFL; green and white) and George Wilson's Wildcats (light brown). The new league looked formidable: Little Joey Sternaman had secured the rights to Comiskey Park, meaning the football Cardinals were now without a stadium; and the league had legitimate stars in the running back position: Grange, Joey Sternaman, Wildcat Wilson, Eddie Tryon, Harry Stuhldreher, and Pooley Hubert of Alabama. The NFL fought back hard. Pyle tried to steal other franchises, but the owners convinced the always rebellious Pottsville (Pennsylvania) Maroons to stay in the league because rural Pennsylvania and Ohio were pro football mainstays. To pinch Pyle's league, the NFL started new franchises in Hartford and Brooklyn. The western leg of Grange's barnstorming tour had created interest in the West Coast players and fans, so they also brought in the Los Angeles Buccaneers, a road team with many players from the coast.

Both leagues looked stronger with the edge tilting to the Grange league. But the Grange league had its weaknesses. The owners were not proved and they were not loyal to each other. And Pyle was so entranced with playing in Yankee Stadium that he had made a bad deal. He was overlooking a critical point: the football Yankees shared Yankee Stadium with *the* baseball Yankees, and Pyle and Grange were betting that the Babe Ruth–led Yanks wouldn't be in the World Series. They had been horrible the year before and it seemed like Babe Ruth was washed up. It was a big gamble. If the baseball Yankees were in postseason play, Grange's team — the league's primary revenue source — would not be able to play some of its home contests.

13

Amateurs

GRANGE, PYLE, AND TENNIS STAR
SUZANNE LENGLEN ON THE SS *PARIS*

WHILE CHARLIE WAS MAKING all of the league decisions, Red Grange was in Los Angeles enjoying his summer. He lived in the Ambassador Hotel. With its palm trees and gurgling streams, the Ambassador felt like an oasis. Guests of the hotel, which sat on twenty-four acres, complete with rifle and archery ranges, an eighteen-hole pitch 'n' putt, two tennis courts, and an Olympic-sized pool with three diving boards, could wile away their days in relative peace among other celebrities. "There were always important people — movie stars, playwrights, royalty . . ." remembers Carlyn Frank Benjamin, whose father managed the hotel, allowing the family to live in a hotel bungalow from 1921 to 1937. There were always a few gawkers, of course, people who would sit in the cream-colored lobby and lie in wait for celebrities to get off the elevator. There was Joe, the organ grinder, and his ring-tailed monkey, and the photographer who worked the hotel, but he and most of the fans would leave you alone if you didn't want to be pestered. It might be fashionable to have dinner at the Brown Derby, but the Cocoanut Grove nightclub with its bands made it just as easy to doze away all day, and drink and eat all night, in the hotel. "N.C.," the maitre d' would say as Red approached. It was Ambassador-speak for "no cover." The Ambassador took care of its own and kept their secrets. Keeping one's mouth shut was a fine art in Hollywood, and if any unsavory proclivity was exposed the hotel publicist or the studio publicity machine would snuff it out. You had to be a real degenerate, a Fatty Arbuckle, to get your name in the papers.

Red wasn't exactly anonymous (his life, according to the Pacific Mutual Company, was worth $500,000), but he had already become part of the fabric of Hollywood. Many of the directors and ac-

tors, male and female, were football fans — or at least loved the latest and hotsy-totsy thing. As usual, it wasn't the stars or even the
comely groupies who got Red into trouble; it was one of Charlie's
connections. Charlie had some family living in Southern California
and they all wanted to meet Red, of course. Charlie had a cousin,
Charles H. Taylor, who lived in Beverly Hills, not far from the Ambassador. On June 8, 1926, Charles Taylor, his wife, Clarice, Red,
and a group of friends went for a drive on Wilshire Boulevard, a
major Los Angeles thoroughfare that goes from downtown to the
palisades overlooking the Pacific. The feeling in the car wasn't exactly tensionless because Clarice and Charles had spent the past
five years in very public fights, some of them physical brawls, and
the couple had even temporarily separated in May 1921. In September 1925 Clarice and Charles were living in Miami when Clarice had had an affair with one Robert Snowdon; Charles had become so upset by the relationship that he confronted Snowdon
and a fistfight broke out, resulting in Charles being arrested. Clarice and Charles seemed to dislike each other in about every way.
Charles described Clarice as a nicotine addict ("persistently smoked
cigarettes"); a slut ("she believed in free love and that she thought
it was a woman's right to do as she pleased in such matters"); and
violent ("kicked [Charles] so severely in his legs and/or groin that
he was rendered unconscious"). As for Charles, Clarice said he was
a two-timer ("keeping another woman") and violent ("choked, beat,
pushed and shoved" her). During their time in Miami the quarrel-
ing Taylors had crossed paths with Red and the Bears on the barnstorming tour. One evening Clarice had asked Red to dance, but he
had refused. Since that rebuff, however, she had developed an infat-
uation for him, baiting her husband by saying that Red was "wonderful," a real man.

Now, driving underneath the palm trees lining Wilshire Boulevard, the three of them were squeezed together in a crowded car;
Clarice was flirtatiously plopped down on Red's lap and, according to witnesses, kissing him. Soon afterward she called Red at the
Ambassador Hotel and arranged to meet him there. That kind of
thing was hardly unusual for a fellow in Red's position. Red did
not refuse the come-on and Clarice soon visited his room. Once
there, Red carried her around the suite and then, after an hour of

drinking bootlegged liquor and performing other acts, the football player drove her home to 121 North Clark Avenue, a few miles
away. Red dropped off the woman and was greeted by Mr. Taylor,
whose wife kept taunting, chirping that Red was a "wonderful boy."
Red went back to the hotel. Soon after this encounter, the Taylors
went through divorce proceedings and Charles couldn't resist putting Red into his deposition. Of course, it hit the papers, but the
reporters — bless their souls — left out the parts about the Ambassador Hotel and the drinking and carrying on because they were
writing for family papers after all, and everyone knew the morals
were looser in Hollywood.

That summer in Hollywood, 1926, Red developed a reputation
in the movie colony as a lady-killer. The first rumors emerged about
his relationship with his pretty costar, Mary McAllister. Milky skin.
Heart-shaped lips. A swimmer. Blond, brown eyes. Eighteen years
old. It was when her lipstick was taken off, when she didn't have the
popular bee-sting style, that she was particularly alluring. (Years
later when Red tried unsuccessfully to get his life story on film, one
Hollywood player wrote about the screenplay, which made Red
into a bland goody-two-shoes and described in scene after ponder-
ous scene what a great husband he was: "He still bears the scars of
Mary McAllister — and, need I add? — others." To the reporters who
visited him later in life, after he waited for his wife, Muggs, to leave
the room, he would whisper and wink: *The women . . .*" But he also
made them promise not to mention it in their stories.) Mary, whom
everyone called Billie, was an acting veteran, one of the first child
stars. She had done her time in New York, Chicago, and San Francisco and was educated at Hollywood High School; she said that
her ambition was to be "versatile." The five-foot-two, 110-pound dynamo had migrated to adult roles with ease, becoming one of the
more popular sirens of the time.

Despite Hollywood's tendency to create egos, Grange held on to
his natural humility. He enjoyed meeting the stars, but his friend
and roommate Beans DeWolf said, "People were more anxious to
meet him than he was to meet the people." While they were living
at the Ambassador, Grange lost a wristwatch, which had been given
to him at Illinois. It was valued at $700. "If it's gone, it's gone," said
Grange, casual about losing the sentimental timepiece. Later Beans

found it in a shirt in the dirty linen. Red gave the one he'd bought
for himself to Beans and took his Illinois watch back. It was a telling moment for Beans, who watched so many of Red's games and
knew him privately as well. "I think that's what made him such a
great player," Beans said. "He never worried, and he just figured he
would do his best."

The silent film era was coming to a close, but was not yet over,
which was probably good news for someone lacking vocal talent.
Making the movie bored Red. There was a lot of sitting around.
Beans was one of the players in the flick and so was Wildcat Wilson.
A lot of it was filmed at Pomona College, the climax calling for an
"autumn day football game in the Midwest," but it was summer and
hot as Hades in Southern California. Of course, Pyle came up with
an idea. He took out an ad in the papers promising that anyone who
wanted could watch Red Grange for free if they wore an overcoat.
With his cake makeup, his lips smeared with lipstick, eyes dramati-
cally darkened, he looked like a gothic doll. On the screen the effect was a football version of Valentino. Instead of the pained scowl
staring out from the photographs and the newsreels, which was so
wonderfully counterintuitive to the pop-and-fizzle 1920s, Red was
now showing up in all the papers with a smile on his mug and a
pithy quote underneath his happy-go-lucky image. After shooting
the film, Red would return to Wheaton by train. He went to the Los
Angeles train station dressed in a pith helmet with a sky-blue band
and a pastel-colored tweed suit. Mary "Billie" McAllister accompanied him. Responding to a reporter's question about his love life,
Red laughed. "Not me, I'm no love pirate. I'm in the ice business
myself." Just a regular fella. "I had a great time in the movies. Movie
work was hard at first but when I got used to it I found it easier
than football. And I met a lot of very nice people. Naw — no girls."

Charlie — in his hotel room with H. E. McNevin — was getting
his share of ink, too. He had a stack of close-ups that he was showing to McNevin and the reporters.

"That Grange is a real actor. He is taking the city of Hollywood
by storm," he said, trying to sound convincing. "Why, all the critics
thought that he would not be much on the screen, but he is making
a tremendous success. It is unbelievable. He dominates every scene
in which he plays. It is the story of a college football hero who wins

a game in the last quarter. It is a fine story, and will go over big. The story was made for Grange and it fits him."

"What is the low down on this story of his proposed marriage to Vivienne Segal, the actress?" he was asked.

Charlie snorted. "It's the bunk, pure and simple. It was merely the product of her efficient press agent. Grange only saw her for a minute, when he was introduced to her. That is all there is to it."

As planned, Charlie was operating a budding sports empire. He was creating his new football league around Red. But Charlie wasn't about to stop with football. His mind was churning new ideas. He was looking for other stars. Turning amateur athletes into pro stars was a good angle. It automatically generated publicity.

One day in February 1926, Pyle met with Damon Runyon, who told him he should sign Suzanne Lenglen, the French tennis star. "People hate her," someone in the room said, dismissing the notion.

"People will pay to see anybody they hate," replied Charlie, who excitedly went to work. He asked around and soon found out that Suzanne wouldn't be as compliant as Red. Suzanne — the brandy-drinking, short-skirt-wearing amateur tennis star — was definitely the ideal candidate to turn tennis, the most snobbish and amateur of sports, on its head.

Charlie immediately started telling people that he would bring Lenglen to America. He bragged that he knew her. He claimed that she was willing to give up her amateur status.

"Will Suzanne Lenglen come to America this fall to play tennis, as reported?" a reporter asked Pyle one day.

"Certainly. Everything is ready, contracts are signed and I will sail from New York July 15 for France, where final arrangements will be made. The itinerary for her tour is only tentatively arranged. It will be announced as soon as it is ready."

In reality Suzanne thought the whole matter absurd. She had yet to even meet Charlie Pyle. To Charlie, actually meeting Suzanne and signing her to a contract were mere formalities. Later that summer he traveled to Paris, and he planned to return with Suzanne for an exhibition tour September 1. She would play only in special exhibition matches and would retain her amateur standing, the papers reported dutifully, even though it didn't make a lick of sense. Everything Charlie was claiming was a lie, but he knew he could make it happen.

"We are bringing her to America because the American people are desirous of seeing her," declared Pyle, who liked to portray himself as the agent for egalitarianism. "I am in the business of promoting such enterprises for the people, and I want to give the people what they want."

With his varied, and far-flung, enterprises, Pyle could be a bit distracted. Instead of paying as close attention to the new football league as he should have, he spent the off-season on the French Riviera, trying to persuade Suzanne Lenglen, the six-time Wimbledon champ, to give up amateur tennis. Suzanne was Charlie's type of girl. She could drink, smoke, enjoy dirty jokes and men. "Suzanne is a prima donna," wrote *Time* magazine. "Every stroke, to her, is an emergency which she must meet in some sensational manner. Mlle. Lenglen likes bandeaux and silks and flounces; the little brown moons under her eyes suggest that she has come to the court without sleep after a night of carnival." In a legendary 1926 marathon against Helen "The American Girl" Wills, Lenglen had needed smelling salts and brandy to get through the sets. "One-time King Manuel of Portugal, Grand Duke Michael of Russia, ex-King George of Greece, the Rajah of Pudukkottia, watched the amber glass tilt up and up," wrote the *Time* writer, "the linesmen, the umpires and 4,000 of the smartest women and the richest men in Europe counted her rapid swallows." Author James Thurber called it "a match that transcended statistics." She won the match, which was still being talked about among the Cannes crowd. Suzanne was *très dramatique* but she also was an expert technician — her brilliant shot making had been drilled into her by her overbearing father, who put handkerchiefs on the court and made her hit the silk squares during daily multihour practice sessions; he also, going against convention, had her practice with men, which helped her speed and power. Lenglen had done everything she could in the amateur ranks, and she would never return to Wimbledon after accidentally, or so Suzanne claimed, keeping Queen Mary waiting in the Royal Box.

Despite Lenglen's anti-elite elite attitude, Pyle had a difficult chore in persuading her to join his fantasy of professional tennis. To begin the negotiating process, he had sent his front man, William Pickens, to France. In Paris, Pickens stopped to speak with Victor Breyer, editor of *L'Echo des Sports,* who was shocked by Pickens's

temerity. "I looked temerity up that night in my vest pocket diction-
ary," said Pickens, a well-known auto racing promoter known for
putting up barriers at his races . . . *for the cars to run into.* "It meant
gall, which made me a millionaire in the temerity business." Pickens
went to Nice and started the negotiations, which were rocky at best;
once Papa Lenglen held up a fistful of newspaper clippings about
Suzanne turning professional and insisted that he had never heard
of Charlie Pyle or Red Grange! Now, *that* was temerity. Lenglen was
making a handsome living on the French Riviera: she had a limou-
sine to take her here and there. Perhaps her reputation would be
ruined by taking the money Pyle was promising.

When Pickens was finally able to get past her father and have a
meeting with Suzanne, he was impressed with what he witnessed.
"She was dressed in negligee, reclining on a chaise lounge and holding a Pomeranian in her arms. I could see that she was no schoolgirl
tennis star who could be salved with one of those what-you-owe-
the-sport arguments." Despite her effect on men, she was hardly
pretty. In his book *Covering the Court*, Al Laney described her as
"far from beautiful. In fact, her face was homely in repose . . . it was
a face on which hardly anything was right. And yet, in a drawing
room this homely girl could dominate everything."

In 1921 Lenglen had lost to Molla Bjurstedt Mallory in a one-
setter at Forest Hills, and the defeat, and the poor reception from
New York's country club set, soured her on the good ol' U.S. of A.
Pickens tried to counter her negative American experience by
claiming that the American *vox populi* adored her. His boss, C. C.
Pyle, was no snooty New Yorker. He was a *real* American and a gentleman of the first order. Mr. Pyle would serve as her protector and
confidant, and he would ensure that Mademoiselle wouldn't lose
her amateur status (an out-and-out lie); Pyle would get her a movie
deal (another stretch) and even put her in a traveling musical com-
edy show (unequivocally absurd). Lenglen, flattered, said that her
features "were not suited for such work." Pickens told her that den-
tists could work wonders.

To finish up the deal, Pyle had gone to France accompanied
by his legal counsel, Col. William Hayward, who was practically a
French citizen. To help him juggle his growing enterprise, Charlie
had been on a hiring binge, bringing advance men such as Pick-

ens into his fold and offering big contracts to the APFL executives. Hayward was one of his first, and probably cleverest, hires. New Yorkers, circa 1926, knew the Colonel. It had not been so long ago that Hayward led his charges, a Negro regiment, on Fifth Avenue for a victory parade after the Great War. From 23rd Street and Fifth Avenue to 145th Street and Lenox Avenue, the crowd — numbering in the hundreds of thousands and including William Randolph Hearst, Secretary of State Francis Hugo, Helen Astor, and Governor Al Smith — clapped as jazz legend and soldier James Europe conducted the regiment's ragtime military band.

Everyone knew the story of the 369th United States Infantry, which had been organized and led into battle under Colonel Hayward, a wealthy white Republican adviser to New York's governor. With his Noel Coward looks, Colonel Hayward seemed the least likely person to lead men, much less Negro men, into battle. And yet in the enduring mystery that separates good men from great ones, Colonel Hayward had resigned a comfortable governmental post to join the army and lead the all-black 369th. The regiment had been drilled in Lafayette Hall on 132nd Street and Seventh Avenue, made its way to South Carolina for more training, where it was greeted with racist vitriol, and then went on to Europe where the 369th became known as "Harlem's Hell Fighters" for the men's incredible bravery. On June 6, 1918, in Belleau Wood, the 369th came under heavy attack and a French general ordered the regiment to retire. Hayward tore the eagles off his own insignia, grabbed a gun, and went ahead of the company. "Retire! Retire!" the general roared. Hayward's helmet had been knocked off. He ran back toward the general. "My men never retire," he shouted. "They go forward, or they die." Colonel Hayward and the 369th received the Croix de Guerre for "gallant conduct." Hayward earned the rank of Officer of the Legion of Honor and from the United States the Distinguished Service Medal. All in all, the 369th spent 191 days in the trenches, longer than any other American unit in the war; some of the time there was nothing between the German army and Paris but the 369th. These men had experienced the cruelest of times, what John Dos Passos called "the reek of chloride of lime and the dead." When the regiment left New York in December 1917 it had not been allowed to participate in the New York National Guard's

"Rainbow Division" farewell parade. Colonel Hayward was told that "black is not a color in the Rainbow." Colonel Hayward, who had many political connections, made sure that his men had a victory parade on their return. "Their rows of bayonets glancing in the sun, dull-painted steel basins on their heads, they made a spectacle that might justify pity for the Germans and explain why the boches gave them the title of the 'Blutdurstig schwarze manner,' or 'Bloodthirsty black men,'" was how the *New York Times* described the scene. The admiring throngs threw cigarettes, chocolate, and silver coins. "I love them, every one, good, bad and indifferent," Colonel Hayward said.

For a while there was talk of the war hero becoming the next New York governor. Hayward had been the secretary of the Republican National Committee. He had the endorsement of his old boss, former governor Charles Whitman. But Hayward decided to settle into private life. At the Plaza Hotel he married a financier's widow (Mrs. Hayward was paid $2 million a year from her dead husband's estate), relaxed by going to the Nile (on one trip he bagged seven lions and three rhinos and brought back eighty-nine heads of twenty-three different species) and the Arctic (he brought four polar bears back to the American Museum of Natural History), set up a private law practice, and lived in a limestone mansion at 1051 Fifth Avenue, which had palm trees in the foyer, a study lined with leather books, and a billiard room and was packed with eighteenth-century paintings and tapestries. The home was the envy of many and had been featured in *Good Housekeeping*, *House and Garden*, *Vogue*, and *Town and Country*.

For Pyle, Hayward was a perfect choice because of his New York connections and the help he could lend with the Lenglen signing. Suzanne's primary concern was social position, and Hayward's patrician air couldn't have hurt. "Money never hurt anyone's social standing," Pyle would tell her cheerfully. "Ten years from now if you go into a smart hotel and order an elaborate luncheon, you won't be able to pay for it by reminding the head waiter that in 1926 you were an amateur tennis star." Charlie gave her some cash as an advance on the $150,000 he promised her. Suzanne signed the contract. As Pyle's partner, their finances entangled, Red had a stake in it, too.

The tennis tour kept Charlie's name in the papers. He was fighting battles on two fronts: one against the National Football League, the other against the tennis stiffs. Charlie didn't seem too concerned, choosing instead to chat about Suzanne's dental work. "We'll have to get those teeth" — which Pyle said protruded "unhandsomely" — "fixed up for the movies, you know," he told the reporters. He was having a tougher time getting other players to join the tennis circus. René Lacoste had already turned him down. Pyle offered $50,000 to Bill Tilden to play six months of pro tennis. Tilden rejected him. "Mr. Tilden, I think you are a damned fool," said Charlie.

"Mr. Pyle," Tilden returned, "I think you are right."

When Suzanne came over on the *Paris* — Pyle had fresh flowers and Champagne delivered every day to her first-class cabin, and he promised that he would show her America from the seat of a Chandler automobile (a marketing stunt) — the newsreels were there when she arrived and so were Grange and Pyle, to publicize "Mademoiselle Lenglen's Tour." The millions who watched International Newsreel would see President Coolidge signing something with a feather pen ... balloons straight out of *The Wizard of Oz* ... different angles of the wondrous Niagara Falls ... American generals reviewing marching troops ... and then Pyle, aboard the *Paris*, bow-tied and dapper, hands in his suit pockets, very sure of himself, smoothing his little mustache, his eyes dancing, making people around him laugh. Red looked smashing, too — bow tie, a V-shaped suit jacket, a vest, and an overcoat — chitchatting with Lenglen. (After all, without Red, why would most Americans care about a snooty Frenchwoman tennis player?) Lenglen, with her powdered face, dark lips, and pulled-back dark hair, wore a fox shawl, pearls, and two tassels on the front of her light-colored dress, which fell just below her knees. She did have a sense of style. And she wore her clothes well, walked with the self-assurance that athletes possess. She was not a bad-looking woman, but her jagged teeth were "unhandsome." There were even hints that Suzanne and Red would make a wonderful couple.

Suzanne remained in the docked ship for several days. One night Pyle hosted a party for two hundred friends and reporters. Pyle stood up, held up his hand for silence, and blinked his blue eyes. And then Vincent Richards, the tennis golden boy, who at age fifteen had won the U.S. doubles championship with Bill Tilden, walked into the room. Richards was twenty-three and about to be awarded the number-one U.S. ranking, so it was shocking that Pyle had captured him. The crowd was silent for a moment as this idea sunk in, then cheered. Charlie was brilliant! As the crowd buzzed, they settled in and watched the players go at each other in a good-natured Ping-Pong match.

Charlie was at the top of his game. The Charlie and Red empire looked unstoppable. The first tennis match would be on October 9, 1926, in Madison Square Garden, and thirteen thousand people (including Governor Al Smith) — an unbelievable number for a tennis match — were on hand to watch Charlie's show, which included the players being announced as if they were boxers as they trotted onto the court, clowns who performed between matches, Charlie — clad in a tuxedo — enticing Bill Tilden to say a few words over the loudspeaker, and 25¢ programs with a section in which Pyle discussed his so-called philosophy of professionalism.

Emulating Grange's barnstorming adventure, Suzanne would headline the tour, playing thirty-eight matches against Mary K. Brown. Suzanne, who traveled with a personal maid, an Irish masseuse, and her own publicist, Anne Kinsolving Brown, would win them all. Grange would often sit in the stands. The tour was hardly flawless with such a temperamental star. In the middle of one match, Lenglen told Charlie that she was menstruating and couldn't continue. Pyle, earthy as ever, replied that all the women he'd ever known complained when they did *not* have their periods. Lenglen busted out laughing and continued the match. The troupe was on the road for four months, but Charlie spent only a few weeks traveling with them. At the Coronado Beach Hotel, Charlie saw Vincent Richards near the billiards room.

"Shoot a game?" Charlie asked.

They began playing Manhattan pool at $2 a shot. In a few minutes it ran up to $400. A reception was about to start and a group had gathered around the table, telling them to hurry up and finish.

"Shoot you eight hundred or nothing," said Pyle.

They shot. Richards won.

The next morning Pyle approached Richards: "I'll shoot you sixteen hundred dollars to nothing."

Again Richards won. They started playing at two o'clock for $200 a shot. At one point Richards had him $2,100 down. At dinnertime Pyle had the meal delivered and the men ate as they played. Two hundred people, including the golfer Walter Hagen, had gathered to watch. At midnight a watchman came in. "Gotta close up," he said.

Pyle threw him a fifty and the man went home. By three in the morning Richards was so tired he could barely stand. At six in the morning Richards owed Pyle $3,000.

"I've had my fun," said Pyle. "All bets are off. Let's turn in."

The tour brought tennis to many people who would never be able to step inside a country club, meaning Charlie had singlehandedly ruined the sport for many tennis fuddy-duddies. Charlie was on such a winning streak that he decided to bring his daughter, Kathrine, to New York. He had hoped Red would date her but it didn't click. He paid, or at least promised to pay, Suzanne Hetherford, who had worked in his theater business, $1,000 a month to watch over his daughter, a fledgling actress. Pyle also promised to buy Hetherford a house back in Illinois. But there were cracks forming — Lenglen, who would make $25,000 from the tour (far below what she expected) and who by 1930 would be selling sports clothes in a Paris retail store — had taken up with a playboy, who was married, named Baldwin Baldwin, AKA The Sheik, who wanted to cut out Pyle. Charlie simply disbanded the tour in February. And yet Charlie was far from done; he had another idea stewing in his head: *A cross-country running race! Los Angeles to New York! An American spectacle!*

While Charlie was creating the Pyle-Grange sports enterprise during the summer of 1926, Red was resting his body for the upcoming season and enjoying the fruits of his fortune. Red had wrapped up his movie earlier in the summer, and now he was back in Wheaton, overseeing the construction of a new house. It was not far from the Grange apartment on Front Street but far enough that the trains shunting back and forth were quieter now and it smelled — *ahhh, the cleanliness, the newness of resin and polish.* Red had built the house for his father, Lyle. It was a triumphant moment of happiness and redemption. Pa selected the furniture — bird's-eye maple bedroom suites, overstuffed furnishings for den and living room, tapestry-upholstered easy chairs, a nine-foot grandfather clock, hand-carved cabinets, walnut and mahogany tables, and even padded velvet carpets. Red's trophies rested upon the fireplace mantel. Upstairs Red built a billiard and recreation room with a regulation pool table and puzzles, board games, and a Victrola. The front porch was screened in so Pa could go outside and wile away his day in comfort. This was a man's house. Red put in a working three-car garage so Red, Lyle, and Red's little brother, Garland, could work on their new cars.

The Granges had never known such comforts. They had been three men in an apartment, quiet as if they had silencers in their throats. Just listening to the train outside at all hours. Dutifully working and not really getting by. Resigned to what life had given them. The house told the town, and the Grange family, that they were now a part of the dream.

Red knew Pa hadn't really wanted him to leave the university, and Pa didn't say it really but Red knew that he didn't like Charlie Pyle. But Red was free of the old life. He told Pa that the house was his. Lyle Grange, lumberjack turned cop, owned a mansion. Pa wasn't much on tears, but he couldn't really talk when Red told him, just saying in a choked-up way, "You didn't have to do it, son."

While in Wheaton, Red promised Mr. Thompson that he would work the ice route later in the summer to get ready for football season. Red had already outgrown the town but he wouldn't admit it. He was trying to re-create it, the way it should have been. Mr. Thompson, a jokester with a gravelly voice, eyed Red's new Packard Cabriolet with the white upholstery: "Grange, see here, you better drive that car around behind. I can't tell who's hiring whom!"

Then, one day in late July, they took the new automobile — *If Ma had such a machine . . .* — for a family vacation to Forksville, Pennsylvania, where Red had been born, where his mother had passed on. They would visit family and friends, stay with Dr. John R. Davies, who attended Red's birth — and who had been at the Penn game to boot. Not far from Wheaton some jerk-off motorcycle cop gave Red a speeding ticket for going forty-five miles per hour through a town, which chapped Pa who was storming about professional courtesy. When asked his occupation, Grange told the judge

"Iceman." The magistrate descended from the bench and shook his hand, letting Red go for a $25 cash bond, and then they continued east to the ancestral home and Ma's final resting place.

When they hit Williamsport, Pennsylvania, they duplicated her final journey, made eighteen years earlier to Forksville, when she had hemorrhaged after a pulled tooth, the event that had set everything in motion — the forced bachelorhood, the womanless upbringing. Red made his way through the ravines, between the hills, which his father — the former lumberjack — had once conquered with logs in tow. Once they arrived in the little town, Pa would show him the white clapboard church and the red covered bridge. They would pay their respects at his mother's grave in nearby Warburton, a little holler that yields on its backside to the Endless Mountains. Standing in the ferny mist, he would catch some trout in the Loyalsock River, just steps from his boyhood house, the one he wished to buy as a retreat. The vacation would give him some time with Pa, a chance to rest his shredded body, and most of all time away from the relentless and consuming attention, but when Red and Lyle wheeled into town the locals held a banner; in red letters it said, "WELCOME HOME RED GRANGE." In their backcountry gaudiness they cheered him. There was nowhere to hide.

14

|||||||||||||||||||||||||||||||||||||

New York, New York, 1926–27

OPENING NIGHT OF *ONE MINUTE TO PLAY*

T HIS, IT SEEMED, would be the year that made Red into a financial mogul, bigger than football, bigger than his raging popularity, if that was possible. Theaters were full of his movie trailer, the first part of which felt like an occult ritual, as white-garbed collegiate band members marched frantically around a giant bonfire.

New! New!
The Screen's Newest and Most Sensational Sports and Star Surprise

The Star —
Hailed as a Great Screen Star by the stars themselves —
Including Gloria Swanson

The Story —
Acclaimed by the Foremost Critics as the Greatest Sports Story
Byron Morgan
Ever wrote!

The Picture —
Cheered by Big Bill Edwards Bob Sherwood Grantland Rice
And every leading sports celebrity as the Finest Football Picture
Ever Made

See Red Grange come crashing through —
Ripping-Tearing-Crashing-Plunging
At Sixty-thrills-a-second speed
in
"One Minute to Play"

An airplane dropped little footballs on New York as a promotional stunt before the movie opened on September 19 at the Colony Theatre on Broadway. Ushers wore football sweaters. Red was at the premiere, and the Red Grange Quartet played a little ditty to introduce him as Red gave a little speech about how it felt to put greasepaint on his lips.

Red, cast as "Red Wade," actually softened it up. He was shown running the ball, the swiveling hips like an Oriental dancer's, nervously acting like a college boy in his collegiate clothes and bow tie, and then in his football uniform sidling up to Billie as she melted into his vigorous clutches.

They drenched the papers with applesauce.

A Barrymore in Moleskins (Under Management of C. C. Pyle)
    Mightiest Star of the Ages! Galloping Colossus of the Sport World! Supreme and Unchallenged — The Greatest Individual Box-Office Attraction in the History of World Amusements! Joseph P. Kennedy presents (By special arrangement with C. C. Pyle) The One and Only Red Grange.

The reviews, actually, glowed. "Grange Scores Touchdown in First Film," declared the *Los Angeles Times*. The *Variety* reviewer showed uncommon generosity: "This far-famed redhead may be a screen bet. His first release carries a wallop. Grange has a clean-cut appearance on the screen. A vein of awkwardness runs through his work, but the surprise is that it's so thin." Pyle had been unintentionally correct: the boy *could* act! The miraculous transformation (perhaps greater than any gridiron miracle), the creation, masterminded by Pyle was almost complete. People were flocking to the showings during the first weekend and the movie would gross $750,000 (it took $100,000 to make), but then — of all the rotten luck! — Rudolph Valentino had to go and die and there was a rush for Valentino movies, as women went to the theaters and blubbered into their hankies. The Rudy retrospectives just killed the *One Minute to Play* box office, but Joseph Kennedy, who liked to brag to Grange about his own kids' athletic abilities, was impressed enough with the numbers and Grange's abilities that he gave Red another contract. Since Red liked driving fast and had a growing collection of speeding tickets, they started developing an automobile flick to shoot the following summer. They would call it *Racing Romeo*.

Red, who had celebrated his twenty-third birthday that summer, was bigger than anyone in the country.

The Hollywood stuff and the league were amazing financial opportunities, but Red was anxious to get back on the field. Football was what he was. As he had done every autumn his entire life, Red prepared for the upcoming season. Because the Yankees couldn't train at Yankee Stadium, Red took his team to Aurora, Illinois, on September 20, 1926, for a preseason tune-up against the Illinois All-Stars. Red's New York Yankees won 20–0 before an impressive crowd of eighteen thousand, the largest attendance ever at a football tilt in northern Illinois outside of Chicago. Red had gathered an all-star squad, among them Paul Goebel, the brilliant blocker from Michigan; Pooley Hubert, the Alabama back who had a great arm; Bullet Baker, a USC star whose speed matched his name; and August "Iron Mike" Michalske of Penn State, who was one of football's best guards, a grueling position — he had to block the biggest linemen and pull from the line to lead the interference; on the other side of the ball, the offense would run the ball straight at him. Ralph Scott, the troubled All-American from Wisconsin, who had accompanied Red on the barnstorming tour and who was Pyle's second choice to manage the team (Ed Healey being the first), would play a bit and coach.

Pyle had been forced to put the Yankees on the road because the New York baseball Yankees had made it to the World Series. Pyle was gambling that the weather would be OK at the end of the season when Grange returned to New York City.

The forecast looked very good.

Twenty-two thousand fans watched Grange in his first official outlaw game, which was in Cleveland against the Panthers, a team made up of many NFL veterans. The Yankees lost 10–0, and Red did not get loose for any big runs. The Yankees played Rock Island in Illinois for the next game, and a good crowd showed, but there was a problem. The other teams, without Grange as a draw, were attracting minuscule gate receipts. But even his star-laden team was struggling on the field, and Red had responsibilities beyond football. In addition, Ralph Scott was sort of coaching the Yanks but everyone looked to Red for the lineup and the plays. In Chicago for the next game, the Bulls beat the Yanks 14–0. Luckily, Red would finally be playing in Yankee Stadium for a long home stand. The stadium was not the best place to see a football game because it was a baseball park — the configuration was all goofy with one of the end zones having another end zone of blank grass behind it — but Grange's Yankees would provide a nice Sunday diversion for New Yorkers. *Go to Yankee Stadium on a nice fall day and watch the superhuman Red Grange . . .*

And then soot-covered raindrops started hitting Gotham. It rained. And rained.

The baseball Yankees had finished their season by losing in the World Series to the Cardinals, a series Charlie, who was now a part of the fabric of New York sporting circles, had attended with Suzanne Lenglen, who called baseball "so interesting but complicated." Because of the baseball Yankees' championship bid, the New York papers essentially ignored Grange's team when the two sports overlapped, reducing Grange to two-inch stories on page three of the sports section. Often the New York football Giants and the Outlaw League game stories were combined into one brief piece; the teams were literally diluting each other. On Halloween the sky just unloaded on the East Coast. The rain was so torrential that the Brooklyn Horsemen — a team, the *Brooklyn Eagle* complained, that had only one of Notre Dame's infamous Horsemen, Harry Stuhldreher — were rained out for the second time at Ebbets Field. The field was soaked; fans couldn't read the outfield sign, "Ever-Ready Shaving Brushes Can't Yank 'em Out," or the "Betting or Soliciting Bets Prohibited" sign in right field. The Newark Bears quit the league, and after the first week in November the Cleveland Panthers were gone, too. Then the Horsemen, featuring Stuhldreher and Red's pal Earl Britton, played against the Yankees on November 7; but after its Grange payday the Horsemen combined with the Brooklyn Lions of the NFL.

The Grange league had turned into an out-and-out disaster. Grange and Pyle's money was dwindling. They and just about everyone else blamed the weather, but a large part of the problem was Red Grange. Eddie Tryon, his teammate, was getting most of the yards and the headlines ("Eddie Outshines Grange," read the *Brooklyn Eagle*). Though the reporters tended to treat Red with generosity, dismissive remarks were creeping into game stories. "Grange Again in Background as Team Wins" was a typical one. Charlie had pushed Red so hard that he was no longer the same player. Some of his speed and agility had leached out of his body. Still people came to glimpse him; they wanted to see him perform magic. It wasn't enough.

But the outlaws' bad luck *was* a boon to the NFL, strengthening the league because more skilled professional players were now available, making the NFL game fundamentally faster and better played. And although professional sports leagues need time to get established, Pyle had shown NFL owners that they couldn't just put a team on the field and expect people to show up. Teams needed stars, and Pyle provided a blueprint for box office success. It was all entertainment. Red Grange was an entertainer. Pyle, the ol' vaudeville man, understood that. He was the first one to push the point, and, unfortunately, it was to Red's detriment. The owners were not dumb. The owners had to make the game interesting for fans by creating characters; hence, the next season the NFL promoted the hell out of Benny Friedman, the great quarterback. Red hadn't played spectacularly well since college, but people came to see him because he was Red Grange. For the casual fan (and most pro football fans were not particularly loyal) it was enough. But something was missing, something was not quite right. The games just didn't have the embedded rivalries of the college game, the moments for Grange to capture the public's imagination. He couldn't live up to the expectations he had created. He was popular and he scored touchdowns, but his runs had not been as electric. Red couldn't sustain an entire league. But the Ghost didn't evaluate the numbers too closely, and he figured Pyle would get them out of the financial mire. Other than the house, some land in Santa Rosa, California, that Pyle convinced him to purchase, and some cars, Red had all of his money tied up in the league. Red never felt like he deserved his riches. He had become more comfortable as a star, but by temperament he wanted to be just another player.

On November 14, 1926, Westbrook Pegler — whom the renowned literary editor Maxwell Perkins so admired that he wanted him to give up the newspaper racket and write a full-fledged book — was at it again, observing the unraveling, going with one of his beautifully snarky story leads: "Red Grange and his associates in the football business entertained a quiet Sabbath crowd of about 18,000 this afternoon with a substantial victory over Herb Treat's Boston club, known as the Bulldogs, 24 to 0. Grange made three touchdowns and kicked one of the ensuing points. Charlie Pyle, guardian of Grange's career and of the box office, sat on the bench among his athletes, impersonating Bob Zuppke and large Will Edwards, the ancient Princeton center, who is president of the league, honored the home club by sitting with the boys throughout the game."

The old-line Midwest football owners never displayed much showmanship in promoting their teams, but Charlie didn't scrimp on fun. In what is probably the first mention of professional cheerleaders, Pegler wrote: "Two lady cheerleaders, who Pyle said were society girls, recently lured from amateur cheerleading at one of the exclusive seminaries, flounced along the low wall in front of a certain section of the bleachers which seemed to be populated by the home club's regular following and evoked periodic yelps of applause for Grange."

But for all Charlie's déclassé fun, the league could be seen as more a burlesque show than a serious football enterprise. Again Pegler, who was an everyday visitor in Charlie's Astor Hotel suite, writing about the same game:

"An unforeseen ethical point arose during the progress of the game and it required a snap ruling from President Large Will Edwards, sitting en banc as the Supreme Court of professional football, to save the situation. After Mr. Coglizer's goal from the field, the football valued at nine dollars wholesale, went on into the bleachers and somebody tempted to steal the same in accordance with the rule of finders keepers. They had only one football . . . Mr. Edwards ruled that the customer who got the new football would have to give it back."

Apart from the crumbling league, the Yanks were facing the indignity of coming in second to the Philadelphia Quakers. The squads played against each other on Thanksgiving Day in Yankee Stadium. Twenty-two thousand fans watched Philadelphia win and Grange get his hip hurt. Two days later the teams faced off in Shibe

Park with twenty thousand watching Grange sit on the bench. The Quakers won and secured the title.

"So far most of the promoters have had a good look at the hole in the doughnut, but they haven't seen much more," Big Bill Edwards told the *Brooklyn Eagle*. The season, and the league, ended on December 12, 1926, in Chicago, when ten thousand people came out to watch Red play against the Bulls on a slippery field of ice. Not that it mattered much, but the Yankees won 7–3. "It was a fitting conclusion for any campaign," wrote the *Decatur (IL) Review*, "and certainly brought down the curtain on the American Professional Football League in admirable fashion."

"The American League — which is what Pyle called his 'Outlaw' organization — never had one winning day for all nine of his teams," said a gleeful Dr. Harry March of the Giants. "The losses must have been enormous. Many players never were paid in full. It was a three-month losing streak for Cash and Carry." The NFL owners had shown solidarity with Tim Mara and the Giants and it had paid off. They broke Pyle's Outlaw League quickly and without remorse. Charlie and Red had bet it all. *Poof.* The money was all but gone.

Red Grange was broke.

15

An Athlete's Death

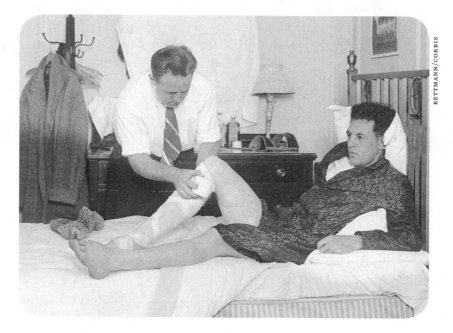

GRANGE OUT OF ACTION

1927 NEW YORK FOOTBALL YANKEES

Red Badgro, E

Bullet Baker, TB

John Bayley, T

Bob Beattie, T

Mush Crawford, T

Jug Earp, T

Ray Flaherty, E

Wes Fry, FB

Red Grange, TB

Dick Hall, T

Norm Harvey, T

Wild Bill Kelly, BB

Louis Kolls, C

Fritz Kramer, G

Jim Lawson, E

Verne Lewellen, WB

Red Maloney, E

Larry Marks, WB

Jack McArthur, C

Mike Michalske, G

Bo Molenda, FB

Bill Oliver, G

Forrest Olson, G

Ralph Scott, T

Ray Stephens, C

Charlie Pyle and Red Grange were knocked down but they were staggering to their feet. The Outlaw League had gone under, but Charlie knew that the National Football League would forgive Red Grange because he was a valuable commodity. He wasn't dashing for yards as he had done in college, and he was looking a little chubby with an extra fifteen pounds over his regular playing weight, but his name still resonated with fans. Charlie and Red, who still had another year on their contract together, were broke and desperate to start recouping their losses. Charlie had made the mistakes and he planned on getting them out of the mess. Just a financial hiccup, Charlie would say.

The first step would be humbling. Charlie went to Tim Mara and admitted defeat, asked forgiveness. Mara could have exacted some revenge. He had lost $40,000 competing against Grange's Yankees.

But the owners had stayed together when Mara needed it, and now Mara would do the right thing for the league. He wasn't a vengeful man and he liked Grange, so Mara, a Catholic, granted Pyle his forgiveness, and the league added some pittance. They would let Pyle and Grange keep their franchise — Red Grange's New York Yankees — but they would relegate the team to traveling status, which would give the teams hosting the Yankees better gate receipts because Grange always brought in the ticket buyers. They did let the Yankees play in New York when the Giants were not in town. Despite being on the road all of the time, with four future Pro Hall of Famers (Red Badgro, Ray Flaherty, Mike Michalske, and Red Grange) and a future College Hall of Famer (Wild Bill Kelly), the 1927 squad looked like a certain contender. Besides Grange's star chops, the quick and shifty Montana boy Kelly, who was popular enough to have a Lucky Strike ad, was a good box office draw, too, and maybe he would take the pressure off Red.

Before the football season began, there was evidence of some dissent within Grange's entourage. Beans DeWolf, Red's childhood friend and traveling secretary, wasn't so fond of Charlie. He thought Pyle's constant wrangling with studio heads was killing Red's film career. Pyle just didn't sit right with him. Beans couldn't really get his best friend's ear and, anyway, he was spending the summer falling in love with Loretta Young's sister, a woman who, in the end, broke Beans's heart and led him to a life of bachelorhood.

The laid-back Los Angeles summer was a critical one for Red. He really needed the movie money to recoup his failed sports investments. Even the $17,000 he had borrowed from the Illinois Trust & Savings Bank was gone. He had the Yankees, which would pay off for him eventually, he hoped against hope; and if *Racing Romeo* was a big hit more movie roles would come. He needed everything to work out because Pa had quit the police force, so Red was supporting him and his baby brother, paying off a mortgage, furniture bills, cars, and clothes, and the taxman had already come calling. Red would bounce back. He just needed to stay healthy.

The season began. All road games: Dayton, Detroit, Cleveland, and Buffalo. The one that everyone was excited about would be in Chicago on October 16, 1927, against the Bears. Red Grange had abandoned the Bears and George Halas for C. C. Pyle. Outsiders imagined tension between Halas and Grange, but George hadn't passed judgment on Red. He never blamed the Ghost. They had both been duped — and helped — by Charlie Pyle. The controversy was good for the box office, however. Red would return to battle the Bears and their new headliner, Paddy Driscoll.

There was always something about coming back to Chicago, the wide streets and the river slicing through it; a city built for architecture because — unlike the cramped grid of New York — the layout gives it the breadth for people to appreciate its manly buildings. Within this masculine masterpiece of a city, the sharp midwestern autumn defined, and will always define, what would become known as football weather, and Red, All-American, exemplified the human frailty and glamour of the game for its more arduous fans. On the field the players and the owners, all the men who understood football, loved him for a different reason. They couldn't pick up a paper or go to a movie without seeing him quoted, advertised, or weaving through helpless defenders, but Red never bragged, never wanted acclaim, and every last man came away awed by his humility. He was one of them, another working-class kid. Sunday would hold a battle between two Chicago area legends — Red versus Paddy.

Paddy Driscoll, slight but impressive, lived at 1316 Winona Street in Chicago's middle-class Andersonville neighborhood. His house, a two-story affair with a butterscotch cut-stone front, was less than ten years old. Andersonville was an area in transition. As late as the Great War it had been an industrial area, but the scatterings of older frame houses and vacant lots were being replaced by two-flats and small apartment buildings. Young saplings lined the streets.

On Sundays Paddy could take the Clark Street streetcar line to Wrigley Field, a twelve-minute ride on a scarlet-colored car moving past the walls of St. Bonifacius and Graceland cemeteries, and listen to the deep clang of the streetcar gong, the grinding gears, and the *dink-dink* of the conductor's bell cord; the air-operated folding doors opening for passengers to step aboard the rear platform; the smell of the other passengers' seldom-cleaned coats and scarves, of coal smoke hanging over the city.

During the week Paddy had a regular job at St. Mel High School.

Since it was growing colder, he would put on a full-length overcoat and felt fedora, drive south on the newly widened Ashland Avenue into a district of small factories, gas holders, and coal yards, then take Logan and Humboldt boulevards, across the North Branch of the river, past the posh Logan Square homes, head south through Humboldt and Garfield parks. Soon enough ice skaters would be on the Humboldt Park lagoon and cinders would be sprinkled on the packed snow. Paddy coached the St. Mel High School sports teams. In 1926 the St. Mel basketball team had won the National Interscholastic title. Paddy spent most of his time in the gym, or outside the four-story red-brick building — with Indiana limestone trim around the windows and doors — on the enormous field, a weedy vacant lot two blocks long. The kids were always begging him: "Drop-kick one for us, Paddy!" And he would boom one 50 yards and the kids would all open their mouths. Everyone said Paddy had the smallest feet of any grown man on earth. He had been a scrawny boy and he was not a very stout adult, and to see him kick was simply an astonishment. As a kid he had developed his kicking ability by playing soccer with Scots immigrants. The ten-year-old campus was a collection of brick buildings at Kildare and Madison streets, the dividing line between Chicago's North and South sides, a retail district filled with department stores (Madigan's) and theaters (the Marbro and the Senate), which could be a little sleepy on a Sunday morning. There was an occasional horse-drawn wagon going down the street, and some Model Ts, and the wealthier merchants — and mobsters — were replacing them with more stylish cars from the new companies, like Cadillac. Everyone knew the St. Mel boys. They were working-class kids from the neighborhood. The parish priest sponsored many of them to attend the school. These were Paddy's people.

Paddy, born on January 11, 1895, was the son of a railroad laborer from Cork, Ireland. As a freckle-faced boy he beat up kids from the local private school and played football with a stocking cap filled with rags. He was not much more than a street urchin, watching his first football game (University of Chicago versus Northwestern, 1904) by climbing a tree near the stadium. His mother forced the reluctant boy into high school, saying, "You'll be backwards all your life if you don't get some real education." As a 148-pound high schooler he combined speed with a surprising toughness that bordered on brutality. Buoyed by an athletic reputation, two years later he entered Northwestern and was named captain of the team in 1916. He scored 9 of Northwestern's 10 points in the Wildcats' victory over the University of Chicago, the team's first win over the powerful Chicago team in fifteen years. Northwestern lost only one game that year.

During World War I Paddy had been stationed at the Great Lakes Naval Training Station, and he was a standout on Great Lakes' fabled football team. The squad had so many talented players that they played — and beat — Illinois, Purdue, and Iowa. Notre Dame's coach Knute Rockne said it was the greatest football team he had ever seen. When his navy team played against All-American Paul Robeson's Rutgers eleven in Ebbets Field, Paddy took a punt 80 yards for a touchdown. He added four more scores, and he personally kicked the extra points, meaning he scored 35 points. The same team, the Bluejackets, went to the 1919 Rose Bowl. Driscoll kicked a 30-yarder and passed one to George Halas, his current employer, for a score. Final tally: 17–9. After his discharge from the navy, Driscoll went to the baseball Cubs; Halas went to the Yankees. Both had short-term baseball careers. They were football men. In 1925 Paddy drop-kicked a 50-yarder, and in Grange's professional debut he punted away from the Galloping Ghost twenty-three times, almost causing a riot. (As he left the field, he told his wife, "They sure are booing Grange." His wife replied, "They're booing *you*.")

Paddy had come a long way but never really departed. St. Mel teachers were known for tough discipline — good knuckle thwackings were common, and the four hundred or so students lived in fear of the principal, who was named Brother William Francis but was known as "The Bear." The Bear — who was short but built like Bronko Nagurski — would roam the halls, and if a student got in trouble he would be sent to stand outside the classroom and Brother Francis would grab him by the scruff of the neck and say, "What are you doing here?" But the students did not consider it a cruel place. The brothers dedicated their lives to educating the poor, following John Baptist de la Salle, a seventeenth-century French Catholic cleric. The teachers wore black habits, long robes with rabat collars straight out of *The Three Musketeers*.

At the church down the street, Monsignor Purcell would say in-

vocation, the Christian Brothers bowing, the altar boys trying to remain still, the congregation settling within the Romanesque church.
Everyone knew Paddy. The boys admired him as a man's man, a fellow who despite being on the front of the sports pages — "the idol
of every boy," wrote the sportswriters — would always put his arm
around you and say, "Hello, lad"; eighty years later they would weep
at the memory. (When he left the school in 1937, at the height of
the Depression, they would give Paddy a new Dodge, even pulled it
up to the fourth-floor auditorium to surprise him, hundreds of kids
and Christian Brothers packing the place, clapping.)

Let us recall that we are in the Holy Presence of God.

Paddy was not a nervous type. He was not the kind of man
who looked backward. He looked at life as a series of contests, and
Paddy had won many of them. The congregation knew Paddy was
a tremendous athlete — he downplayed it so much that some did
not understand his accomplishments — but he would be tested today against Grange and his Yankees. Paddy, the local kid who never
left, versus Grange, the rural Illinois kid they watched on the Pathé
newsreels at the Marbro and the Senate. Some of the more fortunate students had Grange-endorsed football equipment — like the
$2.79 "Red" Grange Helmet made with stiff leather and lined with
white felt, including an autographed picture — from Sears, Roebuck and Company of Chicago. Some of them went to sleep at
night clutching the Grange Scholastic Football. Still, the congregation could not help but cheer for Paddy. The Bears did not capture
Chicagoans' imagination like the Alonzo Stagg–coached University of Chicago teams; the great Stagg, who coached the Maroons
for thirty-five years, to his death despised professional football, but
in two short years after Grange went pro more All-Americans were
following his path. In Chicago, so dedicated to football and its local
legends, a Grange-Paddy matchup was irresistible for football aficionados.

St. John Baptist de la Salle.

The congregation said, "Pray for us."

Live, Jesus, in our hearts.

The congregation said, "Forever."

After the St. Mel Mass, Paddy's supporters — like thousands of
other Chicagoans — made their way to Wrigley. Despite now weigh-

ing 165 pounds on a five-foot-eleven frame, he was still a bony man who could have easily been lost in the crowd. Paddy was not much of a dresser. He would never have been mistaken for Red Grange. A decade or so younger and Paddy could have been one of the newsie boys hawking papers, screaming about the game today. Whether or not they realized it, many of the people had watched Paddy grow up, and grow old, but most people, new to the pro game, had missed it. As a young player, when he was creating his reputation as a Chicago legend, Paddy cut his hair short on the sides but kept a tangle of hair on top, swept back, making him look like he always wore a helmet. His face was a Milky Way of freckles. He was a different-looking man now. Despite his enormous skills, Paddy had never reached Grange-like status. George Halas paid Paddy $10,000 a season, more than most players, but he was not a national figure, hawking underwear and soft drinks. Paddy was a high school coach.

Bobby Dorr treated Wrigley Field like a mother decorating an expectant baby's room. Dorr had been Wrigley's head groundskeeper and superintendent for nine years. When William Wrigley Jr. decided to redesign the park in 1923, he promised Dorr that he would never have to pay rent again while in his employ, so Dorr literally lived at the ballpark in a six-room apartment, adjacent to the left-field corner gate. Dorr took his job seriously. He wanted to preserve the park's appearance, make the fans sit back in awe of its beauty. Charley Weegham, a clean freak who made a fortune in the lunch counter business, had built Wrigley thirteen years earlier, and his ideas about customer service remained. Food sellers moved throughout the place, and there were permanent kiosks (the first of their kind) within the stadium. At a time when stadiums were dusty and cramped with surly vendors and the stench of humanity, Weegham aimed at respite. Dorr had worked in Baltimore and in Rochester, from where he was recruited. Dorr — a fastidious man who favored driving caps — painted the stadium constantly, making it gleam. He always wanted the stadium to look brand-new on opening day, so much so that he usually painted the cream and red trim and the green seats up to the last minute. Opening-day customers knew that the Irish green paint, glossy and somewhat sticky, might even rub off on their clothes. (In 1937 Dorr would plant two hundred Boston ivy plants to give Wrigley its signature element on the outfield brick.) There was always something to do, something to look out for, something to kill. Dorr monitored different strains of weeds and worms, tested the soil for lime, lined the field with pulverized chalk, dressed new grass with mulch, leveled the field with subsoil and top pit soil, raked and brushed new turf with a broom, and hand mowed and leveled, and — oh! — it was endless. Dorr found baseball groundskeeping easier with its loping players and rainouts. He struggled during football season.

Only several weeks before the Yankees-Bears game, Dorr had used fifteen hundred yards of sod to cover the infield so there was no trace of dirt. Well, not dirt exactly; Dorr had his own mixture on the infield: three shovelfuls of selected loam to one shovelful of bank sand. The bank sand was obtained from riverbanks, flood residue that contains no pebbles. It took him and his staff of sixteen men six days to make the change for football season. They would use the back of a wooden rake, spike rolling it into the ground so it would enter the soil. In the outfield, and on the football grounds, Dorr used topsoil and peat moss, as well as Kentucky bluegrass. The players would soon tear it to shreds.

Out on the grounds, Red Grange warmed up on Dorr's grass, which the groundskeeper liked to keep wet, sprinkling it with water sometimes for forty-eight hours straight. With its eighty-five thousand feet of land tile under the field, Wrigley, Dorr said, had the best drainage of any stadium. It also made the sod yield — sometimes unpredictably — to sharp cuts, which were Grange's specialty.

Red looked toward the assembling crowd. As a kid he used to hop on the train and come to Chicago and cheer for Shoeless Joe and the Sox at Comiskey Park. The shy Grange would sit, taking it all in, unable to afford any food or drinks, just a kid watching a game ("bled for them," he said), maybe even catching a glimpse of Jackson entering the stadium in his pink silk shirt and patent-leather shoes (he was self-conscious about his nickname), and gazing around Comiskey at the "No Betting Allowed In This Park" signs, the men clutching their crotches as they made their way to the bathrooms, the scorecard types scribbling away at every at bat, the newly arrived immigrants searching for their seats, and the aged, nearly extinct, Civil War survivors wondering how it had all come to this.

Different sport, different stadium, different decade, but today was not so much different. Grange had walked into Wrigley's concrete hallways with the scurrying fans. There had even been some young women, dressed as if they devoured *Screenland, Picture-Play*, and the other movie magazines. They had recognized him and tried to catch his attention. With their moist brows, they were Chicago versions of Mary McAllister (and the other actresses he now knew so well), trying to follow the latest Hollywood fashions, but they were not quite as polished, as witty, as unchaste. Mostly the crowd was filled with rowdies, men with betting slips jammed into their inside suit pockets, right next to silver flasks. Bootleggers were getting busted every day. The area around Wrigley was rife with them, but the police were not winning the drinking game. Not by a long shot. Chicago was a city of drinkers, and they seemed particularly thirsty at sporting events, even ones played on Sunday. Still, on the field it felt pastoral, calm, normal. The WGN radio guy, Quin Ryan, would do the play-by-play; Quin had started his broadcasting day at 11:00 a.m. on his hourlong "Uncle Quin" show, during which he retold news stories and read the comics from the *Chicago Tribune;* Quin bore witness on Grange's college career, too, providing the play-by-play and creating an image in the mind's eye, as he described *the Autumnal splendor of the scene . . .*

"I would rather beat the Bears than any team in the circuit and I know they would rather hang it onto me with the same compliment," Grange told the *Chicago American*. Someone said something about the crowd, which would make Halas happy. They would pay the Cubs 15 percent of the gate plus the concession, but the Bears would reap the rest.

The Bears had Paddy. For the most part Halas felt fortunate to have him. Halas had played with, and against, Paddy many times. Up until the previous season, Paddy had been with the crosstown Chicago Cardinals, but Halas had needed a star after Red's rude defection. Halas must have looked at Paddy and seen a damn good player, a local hero, but an aging one. The crowd had really come to see Grange. Halas told the papers "in the future the pro promoters will endeavor to sell their customers experienced football players rather than big names." But it must have worried Halas a bit that

Grange's New York Yankees were the real draw. Paddy's red hair was practically gone. Creases were forming around his hazel eyes. His freckles were disappearing. Paddy had always liked to sing "The Minstrel Boy," and perhaps, in the confines of the locker room, away from the crowd, he sang it as he put on his uniform, Halas knowing the song, realizing it was not such a popular ditty anymore.

So many people wanted to see the game, to see Grange. Twenty-five thousand tickets were sold, but another five thousand people rushed Wrigley Field's center-field bleacher gates, breaking them, climbing the fences, and crowded the sidelines, on the low-cut Kentucky bluegrass, where they were close enough to see the Ghost's breath after a long run. The players could smell the fans' cigars; when players were pushed beyond the sideline, they would bump into the people standing wingtip to wingtip, fedora to fedora. It felt just like the way the crowd would stand on the sideline back at Wheaton's orchard, where Red played as a kid. There was no escape — the very definition of a crowd. The fans were not exactly where they were supposed to be, and Halas was furious about the people storming the place and cheating him. The grandstands, in the process of reconstruction, were jammed, thousands standing on the forms for new cement foundations for the upper deck.

The tickets said New York Yankees versus the Chicago Bears. Both teams were undefeated. New York was a hated rival city, and Red had left the Bears for her. But it was bittersweet. The mob could not cheer against Grange. Despite New York's cavalier attitude toward the Yankees, and increasingly about Grange, in Chicago he was one of them. Grange always stepped onto the field with high expectations, and it was the same on this blustery Sunday, at 2:30 p.m., atop the moist grass. According to the stats, Grange was not even the best player on the football Yankees. Eddie Tryon, an All-American at Colgate University, had been the league's leading scorer during the previous year's ridiculous charade. It did not matter. The crowd understood. They had bought their tickets to see Grange, even if he was wearing the red, white, and blue uniform of the Yankees. Like museum goers or ballet aficionados, sports fans want to see something they have never seen; they want to be transported somewhere. When Red played there was always a chance to experience the unexpected.

Grange always liked the crowd, the hometown atmosphere. The team had spent October in Dayton (attendance: 6,000); Detroit, against Benny Friedman's Cleveland Bulldogs (20,000); and Buffalo (3,500), where Grange had sustained a serious leg contusion. The pro game was not at all like the collegiate one with its dedication and school pride. The people would come to watch Red but they thirsted for a battle, Red against someone. Today, it was Red against Paddy. That is what people paid and gambled their hard-earned wages for.

The game started and, teeth clenched, hands thrust deep into his overcoat pockets, George Halas followed the ball up and down the field, bellowing at his players, badgering officials, coaching from the sideline. As a kid George had sneaked into Cubs games, fighting — and running away from — the 14th Street Gang, listening to and repeating the ethnic slurs of the neighborhood, which he would use today with frequency. He would study his current star, Paddy, knifing through the Yankees line inside of Dick Hall at right tackle and sprinting 30 yards down the center of the field. Bill Senn made 30 yards at right end. Little Joey Sternaman, another NFL traitor who had been let back into Halas's fold after going against the NFL family, picked up 2 more. They were driving. Bill Senn planted the oval on New York's 1-yard line for a first down. Then Driscoll went in for the touchdown on the next play. After the score Driscoll drop-kicked the pigskin, but it was wide and it went into the crowd, and someone stole the ball. Halas did not like freeloaders. Balls weren't cheap. So there was a delay in the game because Halas wanted the Yankees to replace the ball. Everyone looked to Scotty, the Yankees coach, who never seemed to have many answers. An oval was finally placed on the field. And as the rules allowed, the Yankees chose to kick off and the ball went to Driscoll, who ran, knees high, dodging and twisting, stiff-arming Wild Bill Kelly, making his escape toward the end zone.

Across the field came Red. Leg contusion or not, burnout or not, statistics or not, the way Red ran was beautiful to behold. The gentle stride had so much harmony and then the turn of speed (a "soundless rocket," Zup had called him) instantly made everyone else look slow. *Huh-huh-huh-poosh*. He was gone. Paddy was running for a TD. He was sure to make a touchdown. Paddy was fast. But even as beaten down as Red had become there were moments when he could amaze. Out of the corners of their eyes they could see a figure gaining on Paddy with remarkable speed. It was Grange. *Huh-huh-huh-poosh.* Grange chased him down all right. Red slammed Paddy to the ground at the 11, near the south wall where sometimes, after a score, players would spill into the first-base dugout. With a whoosh, the crowd cheered the 80-yard run, and Grange. The fans looked at each other. They had witnessed the great Red Grange. The two men whom they had paid to see, of whom they expected so much, for playing a game, had taken each other head-on. What was said between them, if anything, remains a secret, but it was the last time the Galloping Ghost ran free, ran, really ran, in that quiet way.

Other events, the little filler of life, progressed. Bill Senn, an agile runner who had gone to tiny Knox College, carried the ball twice and scored. Senn was called the "Knox Red Grange," one of the lightest players on the field, but his fellow players considered him one of the toughest. (He would do a screen test in Hollywood for the movie role of Tarzan, but he was rejected because he was too small.) After Senn's touchdown, Paddy went for the extra point, but to the amazement of the crowd, the always reliable Driscoll missed another drop kick and the score was 12–0.

In the second half the Yankees attempted a comeback, and they even made it to Chicago's 2-yard line, but they were held back. Grange, carrying too much weight and nursing his bruised leg, rested for most of the third quarter, but he knew he couldn't stay out too long. He had to play. He was the star. They came to watch him, not the Bears or the Yankees. Him. Jeers and boos were much worse than bruises and concussions. Red had obligations, too. If he started taking himself out of games the people would stop paying to watch him. They wouldn't come to his movies. He had to play through it. With a little help from Charlie Pyle, he had put himself into a financial morass and he had to work himself out of it. It was his job to endure pain and try to summon as much of the old luster as he could. Except for catching Paddy on that long run, which was a hollow moment for Red, Grange was struggling to give the crowd a show. He put himself back into the game right before the fourth quarter and carried the ball six times. *Uh-uh-uh-phew.* No gain. *Uh-uh-uh-phew.* No gain. *Uh-uh-uh-phew.* No gain. Three times he failed to get any yards. The other three efforts netted a positive 13 yards. Red didn't have the consistency that he had had in college. And for the more cynical, Charlie had turned him into a mere circus act.

The clock ticked down. There was no time left in the game, that witching hour when players worry about dumb injuries. In the final half minute Grange and George Trafton, old teammates and barnstorming roommates, went up for a pass. George was Red's best friend with the Bears. George and Red had spent many an off-hour together, going to haberdasheries, to shows, George always cracking up Red, Red always deflecting attention, George seeking it. Buffalo-haired, with nine fingers and a smashed-up face, Trafton scrambled for the ball. The shapes, all blurs, number 77 colliding with number 13 — and then suddenly they stopped. There was a muddy spot on the field. Grange: "We both went up in the air. Coming down I caught my cleat in the sod. Trafton fell over my leg and it twisted." Grange could not get up.

Athletic injuries are often described as "freak." It seems unimaginable that men blessed with balletic control over their bodies can get hurt. To watch them at practice, hitting tackling dummies made from five-by-six-foot gym mats rolled tightly on their long axes and sewed in a double canvas sack, made the game feel peaceful, as if the *uh-uh-poof-poof-poof* had no consequences. On game day they were not hitting canvas; men collided in flashes with only leather and wool and sponges sewed into their pants to protect tendons, bones, and flesh.

The Brute carried the Ghost off the field, like a fainted bride. Grange was stricken with fear. As much out of honor as apprehension from Trafton's withering gaze, lines formed to let them pass. The people whispered worriedly as Grange was brought to the cramped dressing room, but the word was that he had strained a calf tendon. The Brute loved the Redhead, as he always called him. Trafton consoled Red in his agony and witless bafflement. Inside, because that is where Grange really lived, he thought he would never play football again. Grange's knee swelled into a wretched sphere. He could not stand on his right leg or bend it without dazzling pain.

·   ·   ·

In 1923 Royal Whitman, M.D., M.R.C.S., F.A.C.S., wrote a book — *A Treatise on Orthopaedic Surgery* — that became the textbook of its time for the study of orthopedics. Regarding knee injuries he wrote: "Severe wrenches of the knee may cause rupture of the lateral ligaments, rupture of the crucial ligaments, usually the anterior and avulsion of the tibial spine or its anterior tubercle." To repair such an injury, Whitman — the surgeon to the Hospital for the Ruptured and Crippled — recommended replacing the anterior ligament — that most often ruptured — with a strip of the iliotibial band about eight inches in length, which, attached below the tibia, is "passed through a hole bored in the external condyle then through another, beginning just in front of the tibial spine and ending externally just over the prominent part of the internal tuberosity of the tibia."

By modern standards Whitman's recommendations were sound. But the chance for successful knee surgery was not a good gamble. There were not many physicians trained in the technique, and the hole Dr. Whitman proposed drilling in the external condyle needed to be accurate to the micromillimeter. Miss the exact area and the knee would collapse sooner rather than later. Acute arthritis was also a side effect. At the very least, Red Grange needed to rest the knee, perhaps hope that he would not damage it more.

However clever, maddening, and strange, Pyle understood human nature better than most people, but he was not so insightful when it came to the human knee. If he had read *A Treatise on Orthopedic Surgery,* he would have told Grange not to play. Or maybe he would have. Hell, people would pay to watch Grange *crawl* into the line. And the two men needed the money. Pyle was still making headlines. Along with the football league, C. C. had Grange put some of his football salary into a hockey league. They were taking more wild bets to get out of their financial hole. In March, Charlie had taken over Los Angeles's Winter Garden Palace with the intent of staging big-league ice hockey with four teams in Los Angeles, Hollywood, San Francisco, and Oakland, and then Pyle, in his entertaining hubris, announced "C. C. Pyle's International Transcontinental Footrace & Follies," a Los Angeles–to–New York race with $25,000 for the winner. The "Bunion Derby" was already being ridiculed in the papers, but Pyle said he was not worried, even if he had no chance of paying the runners — or even feeding them — on their cross-country trek. They had the Illinois Trust & Savings Bank, which was loaning them money even as it failed. H. E. McNevin was betting, and betting the savings of the working-class folks of Champaign, that C. C. Pyle and Red Grange would hit a big score.

Grange went to his hotel room. He did not feel so good. When a reporter asked him about the injury, the once Galloping Ghost infused his statement with obfuscation: "I thought it was my knee until we got to the hotel but I think treatment will bring it around all right." Give him a week's rest and he would be able to play against Green Bay next Sunday, he said. Newspaper readers, and football ticket buyers, would be reassured. He had to say it. Otherwise no one would go to the games — *to see Colgate's Eddie Tryon!* — and the Yankees, like the league the year before, might go completely under. Secretly Red and Charlie hoped Grange would be able to go against Benny Friedman's Bulldogs on Thanksgiving.

The papers did not know it, but Grange was plenty concerned. Babe Ruth's guy, "Doc" Woods, was called in. Doc had made his popular reputation by keeping Babe Ruth's gimpy legs (and hungover body) in the lineup while also doing personal favors for the Bambino: signing autographs, going through his mail for checks and "letters from broads." Doc wore whites, head to toe, and a bow tie. He had a gold five-sided pocket watch with an engraved baseball scene and inscription — *Yankees World's Champions 1923* — in his pocket, and (metaphorically speaking) $4,276 of bonus money from the latest World Series pennant, won on October 8, 1927, eight days previously. During the off-season Doc was a knee wrap for hire. He had an office in New York City and treated people afflicted with "Sciatic, Muscular, and Inflammatory Rheumatism." His specialty was "Corrective Manipulations," and he advertised himself as a "Trainer of Big League Baseball Clubs for twenty-three years. For the past six years and present Trainer of the New York Yankees." Along with sinusoidal wave, static, and diathermy machines, a Bristow coil, baking lamps, ultraviolet generators, different types of wraps and bandages, and bicarbonate of soda (Babe drank it by the barrel full), Doc always brought his poodle with him, which was now on a diet because Lou Gehrig and the rest of Murderers' Row had been feeding it scraps from the Yankees' dining car.

When Doc examined Grange's knee he must have known it

was bad. There were protocols. For the ligament to "heal itself," it needed rest. But he did not want the Ghost's legs to atrophy, so he called for nearly constant massage of the Ghost's quadriceps and hamstrings and "patellar setting" exercises, which meant Grange exercised his leg muscles by contracting and relaxing them, a workout that makes the leg feel exhaustingly weak. When he was not getting massage or doing his exercises, the Ghost stabilized his leg, no pressure exerted. Doc put long felt strips on the patella and a wider strip behind the knee. And then he put a bandage around the knee. The Ghost would need to walk around on crutches, or at the very least with a cane. "For years I longed to carry a cane," Red told a reporter, "but I was too shy. Now I can carry one, but I'm not so keen about the condition which makes it necessary."

He went to Wheaton to recover. He stayed in Pa's house, which the Ghost had bought after the barnstorming tour, but the bank still owned it — there was a $12,000 mortgage on a house valued at $40,000. Pa had quit his job as the chief of police the previous year. "I've got him fixed now," said Red as the house was finished. "He'll never have to worry." Would Grange's injury mean that his aging father would have to find work again? The money had a positive flow back then; buying a house or a new car had not seemed like a problem. Red wanted to make his father proud and prove him wrong. Lyle had been skeptical of Charlie Pyle. It was not easy to go against the old man, but it had all turned out OK until now.

The athlete's life span is short. It had been eighteen years since Red had defied him, coming home, standing at the dinner table with two misplaced vertebrae. Since that solemn night, with his father's apprehensive approval, his life had been defined by football. Now here he was, a man with a major knee injury. Not much difference. Same bad luck, only the burden had shifted. It is easy to see through your child. Red could not have hidden his pain, his thoughts about the inevitable, the future. Red needed a knee specialist. He needed rest. Whatever Mr. Pyle recommended would undoubtedly be based on shadowy greed, not his son's welfare. But even if Red could not make it as a football player, he was bigger than football, *right?* He could make movies, have his own vaudeville show . . . or something.

· · ·

The next week, in Green Bay, knee wrapped, muscles sore from rubdowns, Grange dressed in his uniform. Eleven thousand fans, the most people to ever watch a pro game in Wisconsin, had bought tickets to see him. Pyle had promised them the Galloping Ghost, even sent a telegram to A. B. Turnbull, president of the Green Bay Football Corporation, stating: "Grange not hurt as badly as reported. Will be in condition for next week's game." With his cane, Red dragged himself into the middle of the field for the coin flip. The people cheered him, but it was all for show. The Ghost could not play. The Yankees lost 13–0. They returned to Chicago the following Sunday for a contest against the Chicago Cardinals. The ticket buyers had been promised Red Grange and fifteen thousand people showed up, so Red went out there. Soon he was hobbling out of the game. Bullet Baker went down, too — three broken ribs as well as two fractures of his left hand. Bullet was sent to the hospital. Grange sat next to his cane, trying not to listen to the screams. Men who admired the Ghost through news stories would bring their boys to the games. Professional football — the game he single-handedly legitimized — was played in large cities but it was also played in Portsmouth, Ohio; Green Bay, Wisconsin; Pottsville, Pennsylvania. These were towns like Wheaton, and Grange knew these people. Here was their hero, whom they had never seen except in newsreels. The newsreels had given everyone false expectations of speed. The cameras were hand cranked and averaged sixteen to twenty frames per second. The cameramen used the hand crank like music tempo; a man running with the football should look fast so they spun it faster. More dramatic that way. The people were oblivious. They hungered for him. Grange, squinting into the stands, spitting on the saturated soil, must have thought of his father, the "toughest man he had ever known." The crowd, a sea of men like Pa, with their boys in tow. Many had read, some could even recite, Grantland Rice's Grange-inspired, but already dated, poetry:

> *A streak of fire, a breath of flame,*
> *Eluding all who reach and clutch;*
> *A gray ghost thrown into the game*
> *That rival hands may never touch . . .*

Was the Galloping Ghost mortal after all? Three weeks after the injury, Red was back in New York, getting ready for a game against the Bears. Doc would wrap steaming woolen blankets over his right knee and the Ghost would tell reporters that he would be playing "a few years or more." He needed the money. He didn't want to lose his house, or the Yankees. He had to play. Grange hobbled into the arena. Limping badly, he willed himself to play defense. The ten thousand fans applauded the effort, but on offense when he was handed the ball, he could not make it past the line. So he started passing the ball just to be a part of the action. Pyle kept telling the papers that Grange would be fine; Grange said it, too. So people paid money and went through the turnstiles, not quite comprehending why they had paid money to see Red play defense, limping around the field, and, mostly, the back of his coonskin coat. Grange could not perform, the havoc of *What would I have done differently?* replaying in his mind but never expressed. His knee grew worse. So he sat on the sideline, shielded by animal fur, a shadow with thousands of bright, and then increasingly angry, eyes upon him.

This was the kind of thing Grange's college coach, Bob Zuppke, had predicted. The longer it went on, the smarter Zup seemed to get. Here was Grange, in the longish moments playing cards in a hotel bed, knee a tremorish mess of ligaments, Charlie telling him it would be all right and to rest the thing for next season. Charlie was not really able to sell his membrane of a sales pitch anymore. Red could now see the looks on the faces of the hangers-on, the pretend smiles reaching toward shame, the creeping malaise. He played, sure, showing up to throw the ball, maybe even plunging for a couple of yards here and there. He was due to play in Philadelphia in mid-December against his old friend Earl Britton. Britt, who could barely pay his bills playing pro ball, was slaving for the Frankford team now. He was a journeyman.

"My leg is about right now," said Grange in a long-distance talk with Yellow Jacket officials, reported Philadelphia's *Evening Public Ledger,* which headlined the article "GRANGE IN SHAPE FOR JACKET TEST." "I won't have to favor it as in previous games." If only it had been true. On December 11, 1927, the New York Yankees squared off against the New York Giants at Yankee Stadium. Red couldn't really play in what one writer described as "a sea of

mud." Preceding the game Ford Motorcars had him drive in its latest roadster around the soggy track inside the Polo Grounds. "Expert eyes said there were 2,500 people in the stands, and there may
have been at that," wrote the *New York Daily Mirror* scribe. "But
they were so scattered through the vast stadium that they looked
like a mere handful." The story turned into an epitaph. "Mr. Grange,
while a great carrier among the college gridders, is a good deal less
than with the boys who play for dough." The Yankees were through.
Grange was through.

Charlie's time was ticking away. In late December, George Mc-
Comb would pay Red a visit, to see if he could repay the $17,000
he owed the Illinois Trust & Savings Bank, which had gone under
because of mismanagement and defaults on loans. Red couldn't
manage it. Charlie, the P. T. Barnum of sports, whose immense talent was never meant for the long haul, would move on to another
mark and put his energy into the Bunion Derby. Coach Zuppke had
known something all right. What had he said at that football dinner? "The Grange we know . . . is a myth. As time goes by those runs
of his will grow in length with the telling. And soon they will be forgotten . . . Grange will pass on. He will be forgotten."

A Year to Be Forgotten

RED GRANGE IN CHICAGO

O N OCTOBER 25, 1928, Helen Flozek sat in a Chicago court-room. Flozek, nineteen, whose grandparents had emigrated from Ireland, had a round face, large eyes, a slender waist, curvaceous legs, and black hair tucked under a snug brown hat. Her pursed lips were brush-stroked with vivid red lipstick. In her arms she held a restless and rather tubby baby.

"What's its name?" asked a woman.

"Princess Haroldine."

Harold E. Grange's name was called to appear for a 240096 — fathering an illegitimate child.

"I met him at the Morrison Hotel," declared Helen.

"*Harold Grange?*" the clerk repeated.

The judge wasn't happy about the no-show. "You know that it is the order of this court that defendants appear in person," he said. "I will not make an exception in this case."

Grange's lawyer, Congressman John J. Gorman, answered for the football star: "He didn't know about it, your honor. The officers that served him didn't tell him it was called for today. It was only by inquiry I found that out myself."

"You will have to get him here this morning."

Congressman Gorman left the room to fetch Red Grange, who was supposed to talk on the radio that night on behalf of the Republican National Committee, but given the illegitimate child hullaba-loo Red's speech was in the process of being unceremoniously canceled. It was not difficult to find Grange, who was rehearsing for his vaudeville show at the Oriental, a theater with gaudy Cambodian Chimeras, Indian elephants, and Thai temples. Red was performing with Paul Ash, a redheaded emcee, whose act consisted of sitting on a throne, singing pop songs, throwing out jokes, and introducing, and bantering with, a fat comic, colored singers who belted it out while moving images of trains whizzed behind them, a French juggler, a Swiss girl enticingly moving her hips as she sang a ditty and flirted with Ash, the leggy Gould Girls dancing themselves silly . . . and, during this engagement, Red Grange, doing a collegiate act (*Wasn't he getting a bit old?*) called "Come on, Red." One critic said the "show lacks speed, pep, hurrah, and probably a good many other minor essentials." As for Grange, he "makes a well formed impression on general conduct, while not scoring any touchdowns with his talk and a few light steps with a girl."

As Red stood there, a bit wobbly on his ruined knee, a large screen showed a highlight reel of Red scoring touchdown after touchdown after touchdown . . .

Red was just trying to scratch out a living, but it smacked of desperation when he wrote a note to the University of Illinois, hoping for some publicity. "Football season's here — and so am I — in person, not a moving picture this time. No kidding, I'll be at the Missouri theater the week of November 24th in a collegiate stage show I'm sure you'll like . . . P.S. No. 77 — remember me?"

After retrieving Red from rehearsal on the ol' boards, the congressman brought his client toward the courthouse, which was becoming a bustling mob scene of beggars, criminals, court workers, and cops. They all wanted to get a look at their hero. *Was the golden boy a philanderer?* An hour and a half had passed. The courtroom was filled now with a panting crowd who murmured as Red, favoring one leg, wearing a tan suit, walked onto the stage of public opinion. He grinned at the onlookers, many of whom stood on their chairs.

"And now pretending he don't know me," Helen hissed to the social worker by her side. "All that time not answering my letters when I was telling him what was happening, and now saying he never saw me. Why, last Saturday I came up to him at the theater and he recognized me all right, he says, 'Hello, kid, how's Wheaton?' Then he says it was in June we met and not in April. *Well, he remembers me all right.*"

Assistant State's Attorney Otto B. Steiskal, the prosecutor, was starstruck, according to Meyer Levin of the *Chicago Daily News*. He pumped Red's hand over and over. Helen, it seemed, didn't have a chance. She was just a hat check girl at the Morrison Hotel, a place favored by showbiz types and mobsters, where Red practically lived when he was in town. Just a girl whose life was crashing all around her. She had been sixteen, maybe seventeen, when she had her first kid, Leo Jr., who was now three. She had been married to her son's father, Leo Flozek, a truck driver, on April 4, 1924, but he had deserted her after a month and had refused to pay the $1 a day she needed to take care of the little boy. She was living with her family now; her dad, a building laborer, one brother driving cattle at the stockyards, eight of them in all under one roof at 10360 South Spaulding Avenue, and they were gossiping about Helen in her neighborhood — *And hadn't she just asked for it naming the little girl Haroldine Grange, fer Christ's sake?* — and now the whole city, the whole country, knew. Helen's public aid lawyer had come to Red with a settlement offer a few days earlier. If Red paid her $800 they would call the whole thing off, but Red had refused. Usually the threats were never acted upon, or Charlie (*Where was he?*) had taken care of all the legal stuff.

Now, in court, Red turned to Charlie's associate, Frank Zambreno, and quipped: "Put your hat on or they'll get your bald head into the picture . . . Aw, they tried the same stuff on Babe Ruth. Remember — a year ago, wasn't it?"

Helen and Red stood before the judge. They did not look at each other. The baby was now asleep.

"I would like to have a continuance until after the election, as I am busy campaigning, and want to have time to make some investigations in this case," said Congressman Gorman. The motion was granted.

Just four years removed from the Michigan game and all the American grandeur that followed, and now Red was sucked into the panting crowd, someone saying, "Hey, say something yourself. Say something about girls that send mash letters." Red wanted to keep it clean: "I'll talk about football, but not about women. Expect to get in a few games yet this season. The old knee is getting back in shape." The eager crowd followed Red out of the courtroom, asking for autographs. "Sure; got a pencil?"

Frank Zambreno handed out a prepared statement: ". . . there is nothing in this case except attempted blackmail, and I instructed my attorneys to proceed to trial at once . . ."

For anyone leaving the courtroom that day, there was one un-
mistakable characteristic of the chubby little baby named Haroldine Grange. She had red hair.

Where *was* Charlie?

Over the summer Red had starred in *Racing Romeo*, filmed out
in California at the Ventura fairgrounds. Money troubles never
worried Charlie, who had rented a ten-room house with a house-
boy and cook. They would make the money back. Maybe Charlie
could still snake his way into the NFL. "Pyle is like a skyrocket before it goes off — full of explosives," said Vincent Richards, the tennis player who knew Cash 'n' Carry. "These are his dreams. They are
the most dangerous things about him. They will either shoot him
out of sight or let him fall to the ground and fizzle out. He would be
the last person to worry about his future. Apparently all the inspira-
tion he ever needed to make money was to be completely broke."

Red had his entourage — Charlie, Beans, and Ralph Scott — with
him as he made the movie. That summer Pyle still had him thinking they would be OK. It was stupid for them to make Red into a
racecar driver, of course. He should have been doing another of the
increasingly popular football films. Even Fielding Yost was in town
as an adviser on *The Quarterback*. At night Red and his friends had
a regular poker game going with Walter Hiers (who was always trying to get Red on the vaudeville stage), Adolphe Menjou, Lloyd
Hamilton, Al Green, and Mark Kelly, a sportswriter. Every Sunday
they would go to Tom Gallery's house where he and his wife, Zasu
Pitts, would put on a party.

Those were pretty good times, but the movie seemed to be jin-
xed. One day Red was in the cramped confines of his racecar with
Walter "Fat" Hiers when Red hit a hornet's nest and the insects got
into the automobile; Fat was so big that the two men couldn't get
out and they were badly stung. Tragically one of the racecar driv-
ers was killed during moviemaking. And Charlie was squabbling
with Joseph Kennedy over the *One Minute to Play* profits. The arguments grew so bitter that Kennedy hustled *Racing Romeo* into
the theaters and left Red out of most of the publicity campaign,
but Red took the brunt of it in the papers: "The ways of producers
are strange indeed. At the Hippodrome this week they permit Red

Grange to destroy his ready-made movie popularity by appearing in a feeble film . . . a witless racing yarn." Pyle had pissed off so many people in Hollywood he ruined Red's big-screen future.

It was obvious that the football league had been a failure, his star client could barely walk, and Red's Hollywood career was failing, but Charlie had a big score planned to recoup the money. His cross-country race, about which he had been noodling for a while, had gone off earlier in the year. Runners from all over the world — "Orientals, Poles, Anzacs, and Aztecs," Charlie claimed — descended on Los Angeles on March 4 to begin the Bunion Derby. Charlie figured to make a haul. He had planned to sign promotion deals with shoe, beverage, mattress, liniment, and food companies, among others. He figured twenty million people would watch the race, which would go on the new Route 66, and the towns along the highway would be fighting to reap the publicity, so he would play them against each other. "A promoter of sports, to my mind, is nothing more nor less than a servant of the public," said Charlie on a rainy day in his Los Angeles Gramercy Place residence, "and what the public demands, he must provide. Consequently, the thousands of persons drawn into the towns and cities through which the noted runners pass, through each city advertising the event 100 miles in each direction, must be provided with amusement and entertainment while awaiting the arrival of the runners."

One reporter wondered if the race didn't just sound like a fantastical dream.

"Sure it does. But I'm the gent who makes dreams come true."

When the runners set off from Los Angeles, Charlie peered into the newsreel cameras and, eyes dancing, said, "We have runners from all over the world, and they will all walk or run, but myself? I'll ride." To watch and organize the race, Charlie needed a car, but he did not want just any car; he wanted something he could live in. So he designed a shiny white $25,000 bus with a blue mohair interior, decked out with a writing desk, phonograph and radio receiving set, bed, radio, shower bath, and electric refrigeration. At the rear of the luxury vehicle, which Pyle had dubbed *America*, was an observation platform. So Pyle would bring his own circus, which would be of the caliber of John Ringling, he bragged. There were belly dancers, a five-legged pig, and Piu, an obese snake charmer who performed in drag and drove one of Pyle's trucks during the day. The feature act was a "two-headed chicken," which had the unfortunate habit of scratching off the fake head Pyle had attached to it. "We used insect powder on that chicken at the rate of about a bushel a week, but still it would haul off and scratch itself," a laughing Pyle said privately. "There were some times when I thought I should perish of embarrassment."

Red had helped with some of the publicity when the race started in Los Angeles, and Charlie had hired a couple of the New York Yankees, Bullet Baker and Ray Flaherty, as a security detail and to keep Red company. Red rode aboard the bus, acting as the "assistant race director," mostly fielding complaints. The crowds that came to see the derby couldn't help but marvel at the freak show of bedraggled runners. The runners soon started moaning that Pyle wasn't giving them any water or food and was putting them up in chicken coops and stables. "Our blankets got so dirty that in one town they made us burn them," said one runner. And the contestants, who had given Charlie a $100 entry fee and management rights, were worrying whether there would be a payday for the top finishers when they crossed the finish line at Madison Square Garden. The low point came in Joliet, Illinois, when Charlie's bus was repossessed.

Almost a decade earlier, Charlie had thought up the Virginia Theatre, which had given him Red Grange; but now the entire con — and yes, that is what it was being called in court papers — had come home to roost. Many people, mostly downstate farmers, were caught in the web, which had started with the shady financing of the Virginia "with the fraudulent and malicious intent to wrongfully, wickedly and unlawfully obtain from the Illinois Trust & Savings Bank of Champaign . . . a large amount of its money, of the value to wit, the sum of $75,000, by means and by use of the confidence game." Building his sports empire — Red, Suzanne, the Outlaw League, and the C. C. Pyle Transcontinental Footrace — had cost hundreds of thousands, and Charlie was behind on a stack of bills. Through his banker friend H. E. McNevin, Charlie had expanded his relationship with the lending institution, taken out more and more money, and, according to the people whose life savings were held in the bank, stolen the money out of their accounts. Almon Stoolman, the Champaign contractor who had once been one of the leading construction men in the country, and whose desperate persistence had built the theater and who had sold bonds that he now needed to repay, would never return to his former glory. The money he spent on the theater had put him behind, and the Wall Street crash, and all the misery it would bring, was less than a year away. Almon would survive — he owned some apartments in Champaign — but Charlie had, in effect, ruined his business. The Illinois Trust & Savings Bank in Chicago went under in December 1927, and Charlie, and in turn Red, were being served papers for their part in its downfall. The white bus was seized to satisfy one $21,502 note, which Charlie owed. But in the end Charlie argued successfully that he didn't own the bus, and against all odds he was able to get the first ever recreational vehicle out of Illinois's jurisdiction.

When the runners neared New York, Westbrook Pegler described them as "looking like escaped lunatics, in frayed and faded underwear, with faded numerals painted on their chests and backs and with wild whiskers masking gaunt faces." Andy Payne, an Oklahoma Cherokee, won the race, and Pyle, everyone was reporting, had lost $60,000, and a series of lawsuits had been filed with the New York attorney — by the Bunion Derby's advance man, a Suzanne Lenglen manager, and the assistant timer for the Yankees — for money owed. The woman whom Pyle had hired to take care of his daughter was also hounding him because she was paying for the girl's schooling and housing. She would eventually sue him, too. Pyle told everyone not to worry.

In mid-November the Haroldine Grange problem went away in judge's chambers. Helen Flozek brought Haroldine with her; Red agreed to pay Helen $900 and be done with it. Maybe she was his child. Or maybe he had a vaudeville show to do and he didn't need the bad publicity. As for Helen, she went to court a month later to divorce her husband, Leo, and get some child support from him — a case that would go on for a year, culminating in Leo being arrested and dragged into court. Haroldine Grange, the redheaded baby, would eventually change her given name and surname. The actual lawsuit against Red was somehow, and curiously, lost, as was yet another suit on December 11 against Red for $15,000 in damages from an automobile accident. "Thomas Meritt, Negro, filed suit, alleging he was injured when the football star's automobile, driven by his brother, Garland Grange, collided with a taxi cab," reported the Associated Press.

Whether he had fathered Haroldine Grange or not, Red spent his life never mentioning it. The Ghost would remain (allegedly) childless. As if to confirm his conviction and innocence, he never left anything for the girl in his Last Will and Testament, and Red, everyone would tell you, was a standup guy. With his rather dismal vaudeville run coming to an end, *Racing Romeo* a critical and box office dud, his crippled condition, and no employable skills, Red's financial future was bleak. He could coach, maybe, but he did not like being a leader, and a $4,000-a-year coaching salary wouldn't pay his mortgage or debts. What if his leg somehow healed? Throughout his travels that year, he would visit specialist after specialist about his bum knee, and some were recommending a risky operation, others to rest it. Red worried that he might be limping his entire life. "With a knee operation then you were taking a chance of coming out with a stiff leg," Grange would recall. "I thought a lot about surgery but although I came close, never made the decision. One doctor put a cast on the knee. Another told me to put my leg in a barrel of ice. But 90 percent agreed that I should keep off the leg." Finally, in Los Angeles, Grange met a doctor who told him bluntly he would never walk again — let alone run — unless he began using the leg. "He told me to start playing golf. I was amazed, but decided to try it." Red was out there on his crutches, hobbling around the course. It was not easy to watch.

Furthering the problems, although problem solving many of them, Red and Charlie were splitsville. Their contract was up and Red Grange's Yankees without Red Grange were done for; Charlie, obviously desperate, offered Tim Mara of the Giants a winner-take-all game for the gate receipts at the end of the season. Mara declined. Even the gray blob behind Charlie's shining eyes could not concoct something to keep Grange. "We parted friends," said the Ghost. "We were friends until he died." Red and Charlie were forever linked, but their partnership, the partnership that had changed sports forever, toward gross commercialism, the folding of popular entertainment into the sporting life, a path followed by sports stars even today, was now over. When the two parted in 1928, the *Chi-*

cago Tribune's Don Maxwell wrote that Pyle "exploited Grange with daring and brilliance. He took a chance in professional football and lifted it from the inside pages to the front . . . Grange has played the minor role; Pyle has played the lead.

"'I'm not sure what Charlie plans next,'" said Red. "'He's not broke but he's taken a lot of punishment. He talks now of promoting dance marathons in London and Paris.'" Maxwell would close his Pyle-Grange breakup story by writing, "It may seem a bit sentimental and maybe it isn't deserved, but you can't help wishing that the breakup between Grange and Charlie Pyle could have come before the fall."

There was still a comeback story to be written.

George Halas was clear-eyed. In contrast to Charlie Pyle, he was a man who would always be there for Red. Both men were raised by football and its code of brotherhood. Later in life Papa Bear would write "the golden lad" letters of encouragement and praise, like a loving father. Halas, notoriously cheap, at least by popular reputation, always had a soft spot for Red, volunteering to pay the Ghost's various expenses (as well as secretly slipping money to other players from the twenties) throughout Red's life. There was this notion that Red was loaded, but George knew differently because he had been served the garnishment papers on Red's various debts: the notes from the Illinois Trust & Savings, the unpaid-for train tickets to Southern Pacific, and more. But in the decay Halas realized there was some mutual benefit to be gained. The league, especially the Bears, needed Red. In 1928 the Bears' campaign was the team's worst season to date; they lost five games, going 7–5–1, and were doing just OK at the turnstiles. Although the Grange league had confused the public by muddying the pro football waters, Pyle's promotional fantasia had created actual interest in pro ball and secured it in the public's consciousness. Perhaps more important, Grange's entrance had given it legitimacy for college players.

But now the owners — dull football men without Charlie's brilliant showmanship — were blowing it; they were back to the usual blandness. In some regards the league was stronger. Thanks to Red's Outlaw League, the NFL started on the road toward becoming an eastern, big-city league, and the owners had decided to eliminate the financially weak teams, too, so there were only ten teams in 1928, making the on-the-field product incredibly competitive. But the league, and the Midwest Bears, needed a draw or they would once again fade into anonymity. Halas needed a name, and there was no one bigger than Red, even if he couldn't run. Halas called. Grange wasn't too much on charity. Even as his knee got a little better, he didn't think he would be one-third the player and he told Halas as much. The golfing was helping him, and he started jogging a bit, but he couldn't cut, could not accelerate. How could his flesh be so weak? It had always been his body, wickedly responsive and resilient, that had carried him — battering and flying — across the fields of glory, as the world, and probably even Ma, watched his glittering frame, intoxicated with the unstoppable, quiet beauty of it.

And now his purpose would be less, much, much, less, prophetic. His no longer defined muscles would block, play a little defense, but he would mostly become a sort of circus sideshow, the kind that populated the World's Fair, the Century of Progress, and Times Square, an attraction called Myth. *The Galloping Ghost. What a player . . .* Ticket buyers would come just to show their kids the back of Red's neck, or to see him decelerate into the darkness of the line. Red would just fall into the shadows, subject himself to the scrubs, become a sometime blocker for Bronko Nagurski, the half-man, half-granite back whom Grange would generously call the greatest player he had ever seen. Still, the spectators, and worse, the other players, would see Red lingering out there and they couldn't help but be reminded of his past beauty, and the younger guys couldn't help but question the hype. The 77 stretched across the creases of his flabby middle, which was all balancing on that damn gimpy knee. Iodine would wrap his leg up like a goddamn mummy just to stabilize him and get him on the grass for a few plays. Somehow, it was not pathetic. It was holy. No one in the locker room would go against the manly code and express such treacle, but what else was so real, what else so American? Grange had always talked about the team, the importance of blockers, men like Earl Britton who sacrificed for the greater good, but now Red put his own values to the test. Halas gave the boy redemption, a way out, but it took Red to swallow it, and that was bigger than anything he had ever done on the field.

A Ghost

GRANGE RETIRES

I.

THE GALLOPING GHOST LIVED ON.

After his comeback in 1929, Red Grange soldiered on bravely, playing at a third of his ability. Concentrating on seemingly more pedestrian skills like blocking and tackling, he was even able to summon the occasional brilliant play out of his flogged body. (Coach Zuppke said the Ghost was one of the best tacklers he had ever coached.) During the 1932 season Grange told a reporter, "This is my last year. Fourteen years of football is enough. You know, when a fellow gets around 30, he can't take it. The spirit is willing but the flesh is weak. I'd rather quit, feeling that I could still go out there and play good ball, than keep on playing until I am slow, and crippled, and replaced by some young fellow just out of college whose legs are full of spring. Football is just like any other professional sport. When the legs begin to go bad you are through. But football is worse than most sports. For the old underpinnings are bound to go bad sooner when you have a 200 pound tackle tossing all of that 200 pounds at the legs a dozen, two dozen times, every Sunday."

But Grange didn't quit. Couldn't. It didn't even make it into the newspapers but the Bears were playing Green Bay early in the season and big Cal Hubbard hit Red hard. Hurt like hell. More than anything he had endured before. It was an inside kind of pain, the kind that feels like someone is in there carving your innards with a razor blade. But he kept playing even though his bladder had been lacerated. Had to. Red was also nursing another shoulder dislocation, but he helped guide the Bears to the first NFL championship game. The numb-nuts owners had finally realized that not having an outright champion hurt the league, so they instituted a play-off matchup to decide the champion. In 1932 the two best teams were the Bears and the Portsmouth (Ohio) Spartans. The game was scheduled for Wrigley on December 18, but waist-deep snow made the field unplayable, forcing the game indoors to Chicago Stadium. The setting was intimate with 11,198 fans; people sitting in the front rows could hear what was said on the field; the floor was concrete, made softer by a layer of dirt and elephant shit from a Salvation Army circus. The field was too short, so each time a team crossed midfield, it was penalized 20 yards, making the field 100 yards long, and no field goals were allowed. The teams also didn't want to run into the walls, which were about two feet from the side of the stadium, so they agreed to bring the ball in 15 yards; it was the birth of the hash marks. Chicago looked like a shoo-in to win the game because of its strong D, and because the Spartans' best player and league scoring leader had left the team for his off-season job as a basketball coach. Red was knocked silly in the first quarter, but he returned late in the game. The Bears had the ball on the Spartans' 2, but they couldn't seem to score until Bronko Nagurski acted as if he would run, then backpedaled, throwing a pass to Red, who had fallen down in the end zone. Red, always clutch, caught the pass for the win.

In 1933 the Bears were once again in the championship game, one that Halas would call "one of the greatest ever."

"Marshal your adjectives. Bring out all the superlatives and shift them as you would juggle a jigsaw puzzle. All will fit in a description of the championship battle," wrote the *Chicago Tribune*, which led the story, saying that the twenty-one thousand spectators were "the largest crowd to see a professional game in Chicago since that Thanksgiving game eight years ago when Red Grange, now captain of the world's champions, made his debut on the same gridiron." At the end of the back-and-forth battle with the New York Giants, the Bears were winning, 23–21. The game had gone through six lead changes, and with the seconds ticking down, the Giants' Dale Burnett caught a pass and streaked down the sideline. He was looking to lateral, and almost did, but Red, playing defensive back, tackled the ball and pinned Burnett's arms so he was unable to pitch it to a trailing runner. The game ended on Grange's game-saving tackle, which many, Halas included, were saying was the smartest play they had ever seen.

Despite his timely heroics, Grange was no longer a great everyday player but he needed the game; Halas was cutting salaries by one-third because of the Depression, but he paid Red $8,000 per, a lot of money for such hard times. (The league awarded the Bears $210 each for their championship victory.) Red was still mopping up from his Charlie Pyle losses and money was not so easy to come by. Pa and son were living together in Oak Park because Red's losses had forced them to sell his Wheaton dream house. In 1930 the Chicago circuit court had filed a judgment to garnish Grange's wages on the $20,278.82 note originally given by the defunct Illinois Trust & Savings Bank of Champaign. Red would spend off-season time in Los Angeles trying to get the Hollywood people to take notice, but no one was paying much attention anymore. Red settled for a down-market serial, his last Hollywood job. He needed to pay his debts so he became a glad-hander in a Culver City, California, nightclub, shaking hands and kidding the customers. Red called himself a master of ceremonies. The editorial writers were implying that he was a clown in a restaurant. He told the International News Service correspondent that "a fellow has to think fast when he grabs for something interesting to say about noted people who walk into a night club. It is like broken field running in a football game, only you do it with your bean instead of your legs." The hardest thing was the hours — nine until three in the morning — and standing on the dais telling a couple of stories and a couple of dumb jokes as the boys in the colored jazz band played some spiffy tunes behind him. The dancing girls, wearing shorts with striped football socks pulled to their knees, would kick their legs high into the air, like punters, smiling through their cake makeup and saying, *"Ahhhhh, Red,"* after a particularly bad joke.

Back in Chicago he started a North Side nightclub called the 77 Club, where Red showed off his memorabilia and served Pabst Blue Ribbon beer. ("Think of it! A 7-course delicious dinner and an ALL-STAR FLOOR SHOW for $2.50 per person.") Early in the club's history the club manager, who packed a pistol, accidentally shot Red's secretary. She survived; the 77 Club didn't. It just never caught on, not like Dempsey's joint in New York. When Red quit the club biz, he said, "I can't run a night club and try to play football too, and I'd rather play football." In 1934 Red hosted a CBS radio show doing interviews and training-table gossip; his football knowledge and nice-guy personality played well to audiences, and it turned into a nice sideline career.

Red's gridiron days came to an end on January 28, 1935, in Hollywood. It was the midst of the Depression. There were no career retrospectives, no tributes, not even a mention — not a single line — in the *Los Angeles Times*'s pregame stories. It was an exhibition giggler, a far cry from his Illinois football glory. Red had threatened to quit three or four times, and Halas kept convincing him to hang in there, but Red's body, particularly the bladder laceration, was hurting him too much. No one was crying for Red because, hell, there were Hoovervilles in Central Park, fer Christ's sake, but it wasn't much of a swan song.

Red spent the afternoon of his last game ever on the sideline, sitting on the bench next to the pretty redheaded actress Myrna Kennedy. Myrna had slept with Charlie Chaplin, according to gossipers. Red and Myrna were chatting and laughing. Red's only football today had been during warm-ups, but Halas told him to get in the game. The Bears were winning, 21–0 late in the fourth.

"That's awright," Grange replied.

George smiled. "Get in the game."

Red knew the fix was in. He trotted out there.

Clip, clop.

Clip, clop.

Red Grange's uniform no longer fit like a V. He went out there for the play. Everyone knew they were supposed to let Red run one, give the crowd a thrill. The Associated Press writer wrote, "They massed interference in front of him and shook the ghost of yesteryear into the open from their own twenty.

"Running on legs that no longer had the speed or reception they once possessed, it appeared for a moment he was away when a red-shirted Giant with No. 13 on his jersey, Elvin Richards, broke through. He was the last man between Grange and a touchdown, but Carl Brumbaugh blocked him out.

"Fate, however, ruled against a glorious ending of a great career as Richards got his hands on Grange and he stumbled to the sod, after a 41 yard gallop, the longest of the day."

In the showers Grange, who was figuring that he had played 270 games since starting his high school career, said, "I'm earnest about it. I'm through, definitely through, this time. The legs haven't got it any more. I'm getting out of the game before I get killed. If I had scored on that run, I would have grounded the ball behind the goal posts and walked off the field. I'm leaving the game with many regrets, but my failure to score on that run probably will remain the greatest."

The Associated Press added: "Grange is taking away little of the hundreds of thousands of dollars the game gave him. Most of it was made early in his career, and lost early."

No shameless tears were recorded, just manly resignation.

It had been a shame that Pyle prematurely aged him, that Red was injured so early, and that the films of his greatest runs were already starting to decay, but his image lived on within a generation of men. In 1958 W. C. Heinz wrote a profile of Grange entitled "The Ghost of the Gridiron":

"When I was ten years old I paid ten cents to see Red Grange run with a football. That was the year when, one afternoon a week, after school was out for the day, they used to show us movies in the auditorium, and we would all troop up there clutching our dimes, nickels or pennies in our fists.

"The movies were, I suppose, carefully selected for their educational value. They must have shown us, as the weeks went by, films of the Everglades, of Yosemite, of the Gettysburg battlefield, of Washington, D.C., but I remember only the one about Grange.

"I remember, in fact, only one shot. Grange, the football cradled in one arm, started down the field toward us. As we sat there in the dim, flickering light of the movie projector, he grew larger and larger. I can still see the rows and rows of us, with our thin little necks and bony heads, all looking up at the screen and Grange, enormous now, rushing right at us, and I shall never forget it. That was thirty-three years ago."

But men like Heinz were dying away and taking their flickering memories of the Galloping Ghost with them.

II.

EARL BRITTON, Grange's best friend and primary blocker at Illinois, would end his pro career after a few years because the money was so lousy. He had knocked around, playing for the Bears, Brooklyn Horsemen, Frankford Yellow Jackets, Dayton Triangles, and Chicago Cardinals. After retiring, Britt, who would be called the "Ghost's Shadow," could have been a big hero in his native Elgin, Illinois, but he did not want to live off of his fame, so he moved to Detroit and became an industrial salesman. Throughout his life, Britt spearheaded any and every effort to honor Coach Zuppke, the man who had mercilessly ridiculed him throughout his college career. To the end, Britt was just a big kid, regaling his nephews (he was married but childless) with stories, teaching them how to throw and kick a ball, a man who would go to a tavern, sip bourbon, and make friends with just about everyone in the joint. Earl never made much money, but he had risen in life — his father had been a sharecropper, after all. During the Depression Britton gave his wife a Christmas card: "Dear Jo, This is good for one suede jacket. Not over $15. Not less than $5. Britt." Big Britt always presented himself as a gentlemen's gentleman, from his bow tie to his spit-shined shoes. He continued his love of football, especially the Big Ten, by attending Illini games. Red would always invite him to banquets and say a few kind words about his friend. The Ghost wanted Britt to remember that he mattered.

Earl Britton would retire to Elgin, his hometown, but he died soon afterward in 1973.

Robert C. Zuppke and Red Grange would eventually patch things up. Grange wrote, or at least put his name on the cover of, a biography (*Zuppke of Illinois*) about his old coach, and Zuppke wrote a chapter in Red's autobiography, *The Red Grange Story*. Zuppke, not as successful anymore, threatened to quit in 1935, and Grange sent him a telegram: "Forget this talk about quitting football. Stop. You are still the greatest coach in football." When the new Illinois athletic director, Wendell Wilson, wanted to fire Zup and make himself the coach with Grange as the assistant, Grange was livid that his name was being thrown around to depose his old coach, and Red threatened to sue. Hundreds of letters flooded into Champaign from ex-players who talked about how Zup had made them into men. Red and Zup had become close again. When Zup was given a German shepherd, he named the puppy Red Grange.

Coach Zuppke was eventually fired in 1941, spending some of his retirement in Cuba with his former high school player Ernest Hemingway, a man, in the coaching lexicon, he simply called "Hemingway." Even in Cuba Zup couldn't get away from the football itch, coaching the game at Havana University.

Robert Zuppke continued to live humbly at his apartment in town, exchanging letters with ex-players. He would always believe in the purity of college athletics. In 1947 Grange would telegraph Zuppke asking him to attend a scholarship award luncheon put on by the Illini Club. The curt reply: "I do not believe in athletic scholarships. Your friend, Bob Zuppke." At a 1949 testimonial dinner representatives from every one of his twenty-nine Illini teams showed. Red was there with Harry Hall, Wally McIlwain, and Britt. His ideas, based on athletics and academics, seemed like relics, but his boys held on to the teachings of the great coach, even the ones who had wandered, betraying his ideals.

After the death of his first wife, Fannie, Zup would marry for the second time in 1956, to Leona May, his former housekeeper. But the marriage was short-lived. Zuppke died in 1957 at age seventy-eight. His players, including Halas, the Sternamans, Britton, and others flowed into Champaign, where they listened to a preacher eulogize: "Bob Zuppke created men, but to him the man was always bigger than the game." Grange wired, "I feel I have lost my closest friend and football has lost its greatest genius." In 1966 Memorial's field would be christened Zuppke Field in honor of the coach, who is buried in the boneyard across the street, perpendicular to the 50-yard line.

Fielding Yost's driving personality, energy, and football smarts laid the foundation for an athletic dynasty that goes on even today at the University of Michigan.

Along with Knute Rockne, Stagg, and Zuppke, Yost was one of the greatest coaches of the early era of football. The United Press called him "an epoch in the development of football, and all college sports." Not only did Hurry Up tally an enviable record of 165–29–10; he spearheaded the construction of Michigan Stadium, the largest football stadium in America, with 111,000 seats. His athletic vision still lives on. Just go to Ann Arbor on a football Saturday in the autumn.

Yost retired in 1941 after forty years as either coach or athletic director. He died, quietly, in his home near campus, on August 20, 1946. He was seventy-five.

Reaching the University of Chicago's mandatory retirement age of seventy, Amos Alonzo Stagg refused to retire from coaching, moving to Stockton, California, and leading the College of the Pacific football program from 1933 until 1947. Pacific forced him to retire also, so he co-coached Susquehanna University with his son. A. A. Stagg's wife, Stella, was the scout; once before a game in 1947 she gave him a forty-page scouting report, including a play that won the game. The Grand Old Man of the Gridiron coached football for seventy years, always holding true to his belief that professional football was a "menace" and "evil." Stagg continued to preach clean living and did not smoke or drink; former players were known to grind out cigarettes in their hands rather than let the Old Man know they smoked. Stagg, who had been on Walter Camp's first All-American team, stopped coaching at age ninety-eight when failing eyesight forced him out of the game. "I felt specially called to preach," Stagg, who studied at Yale Divinity School, said weeks before his hundredth birthday, "but I decided to do it on the football field." On March 17, 1965, Stagg passed away. He was one hundred and two.

At the time of Stagg's death, his son, Amos Alonzo Jr., told a reporter that Stagg would never name a favorite player. "He had a real affection for them and considered each as a son. I never thought of myself as an oldest actual son, but one of the many men for whom he had deepest affection."

George Halas always watched over Red, whom he called "the eternal flame of professional football," and on September 7, 1963, when it came time to open the Professional Football Hall of Fame, the two men traveled together to Canton, past the midwestern homes with their dizzying arrays of television aerials; rode in the open-roofed luxury cars, waving at fans; and were enshrined together. Halas's love of the sport and Grange's incomparable talent had set NFL football on course to be America's game.

George loved the Hall of Fame, and so did Red, who would leave $5,000 (Grange did not die a wealthy man) in his will for the institution.

Up on the dais, Papa Bear talked about the beginning of the league and how the first owners met in a Canton automobile showroom and had to sit on the running board of a car. "That prompted my nine-year-old grandson to say, 'What is a running board, Grandpa?'" Before Halas could answer the question, his fourteen-year-old grandson said running boards are "those things that you see on funny, old cars in that television series known as *The Untouchables*." Halas continued, "That little incident demonstrated to me how things can change or disappear until a remark or a question — a child's question — stirs your memory."

Halas, enduring pain because of his bum hip, retired as coach in 1968 with six NFL championships and eight division titles. He coached twenty Hall of Famers, including Grange, Trafton, Ed Healey, and Paddy Driscoll.

Red and George, the two old warriors, would exchange occasional cards and phone calls until Halas's end.

"If anyone asked me who my best friend was, I'd say George Halas," Red said. "We haven't agreed on everything, but tomorrow if I need fifty or a hundred thousand dollars, I could go to George, and I'd have it in ten minutes, and he wouldn't even ask me what I wanted it for." For those who were forgetting Red's place in the game's history, Halas would say, "Grange was to us then what television is to the modern era." George Halas died in 1983 at age eighty-eight. At the time of his death the Chicago Bears were worth $40 million. He was the last surviving founder of the National Football League.

Westbrook Pegler, who wrote so brilliantly about Grange and other sports figures of the 1920s, moved away from the sports desk in 1933 and "plunged into the broad stream of American life." Pegler described himself as a "Sears Roebuck thinker" capable of thinking in enormous volumes on an amazing variety of subjects. Writing for the *New York World-Telegram*, Pegler won a Pulitzer Prize in 1941 for "his articles on scandals in the ranks of organized labor, which led to the exposure and conviction of George Scalise, a labor racketeer." Pegler was whip-smart with a gimlet eye, but he tended to use his typewriter as a weapon, cruelly berating people, sometimes justly, like Mr. Scalise, but too often senselessly. He described Eleanor Roosevelt in his February 10, 1941, "Fair Enough" column as "masquerading as a rather naïve but always well-meaning amateur fuss-budget"; and he wrote about Heywood Broun, his *friend* who had passed away, as a "notorious liar. He was a dirty fighter. Broun was a nudist during one phase of his soiled existence." Pegler later became a supporter of Joseph McCarthy and his House Un-American Activities Committee.

Paddy Driscoll, the best drop kicker the game has ever seen, was a Chicago sports and NFL legend of the early era. He played in two significant games in Red's career: Grange's first pro game and his knee injury game. Apart from Jim Thorpe, Paddy was the first big star of the league. After his stint at St. Mel High School and playing for the Cardinals and Bears, Paddy would go on to coach Marquette University and the Bears. In 1942 Paddy underwent an operation at the Mayo Clinic for an old football injury, the removal of a bone growth on his hip. In 1965 he was enshrined into the Pro Football Hall of Fame. On that September day in Canton, he remarked, "It's inconceivable that a fellow like myself, weighing 128 pounds playing fullback in high school, would come up here to get these high honors. I've had many great days on the football field both at Northwestern and with the Bears and the Cardinals. But, this is my greatest honor, and we'll have to move the furniture around to find a good place for that bust. Thank you."

Paddy died in 1968 at the age of seventy-three.

For a time George Trafton owned Trafton Gym — on 180 Randolph Street across from Chicago's City Hall — where Joe Louis trained, was the line coach for the Green Bay Packers under Curly Lambeau, and was a position coach for the Rams; but he eventually settled in Los Angeles, where he dabbled in the real estate game. The Brute would spend his later years in Los Angeles, limping around with his cane and wearing a blue blazer with a Pro Football Hall of Fame patch on it, telling whomever he could that he had played for the Bears and alongside Grange.

In a bitter letter written just a year after Trafton had been inducted into the Professional Football Hall of Fame, the Brute — who was disillusioned by how George Halas was supposedly ignoring the old-timers while reaping the benefits of the modern league — wrote that Halas "sacrificed that poor kid" on the barnstorming tour. The Brute had a tendency to shoot off his mouth. Several years after his induction ceremony, Trafton needed a hip operation and Papa Bear paid for it out of his own pocket. Not long after the procedure, Trafton — in the Los Angeles convalescent home where he was recovering, still wearing his blue blazer with the Hall of Fame patch, ensconced in a bathrobe — insisted that his biographer come and explain to the other patients who he was.

When George was inducted in 1964, the Brute would give one of Canton's most tender speeches: ". . . then may we say at life's close, I have fought the good fights . . . Today, I am the luckiest man in the world, I have reached the climax of my entire career. The panoramas of God's gifts have unfolded before me, and this is the final reward of my athletic life. I accept this honor with humbleness and pride. Thank God for the thoughtful people who have made this honor possible, who let a small light of happiness into each of our fading lives. Thank you." George Trafton died on September 5, 1971. He was seventy-four.

Haroldine Grange, who changed her name, lives in Chicago. Her mother, Helen Flozek, the woman who accused Red of fathering Haroldine, died in 1982. Although Grange makes no mention of Haroldine or her family in his Last Will and Testament, the former Haroldine Grange contends, to this day, that Red is her father.

And what of Charlie Pyle, one of the most influential, yet overlooked, characters in American sports history?

At the time that Red and Charlie split, the *Chicago Tribune*'s Don Maxwell wrote: "It is rather ironic now that the only public comment upon the dissolution should come from the one who while occupying the limelight was in truth the puppet. Pyle the flamboyant, Pyle the talkative, Pyle the publicity expert, leaves the stage to Grange." Indeed.

For a while Charlie was hounded by the law. An arrest warrant was issued because Pyle, who owed $60,000 from his second Bunion Derby, "didn't have a thin dime," according to Los Angeles's labor commissioner, who was seeking money from Charlie because entertainers and city cops hadn't been paid by the promoter.

After Charlie's second Bunion Derby, he tried to organize a swimming race from St. Paul to New Orleans, but he didn't find much interest and so he would leave the sports promotion biz forever. By 1930 Charlie had started a radio transcription company with offices in Chicago and Los Angeles. He claimed to be leasing transcription programs to more than one hundred radio stations in the country. Always thinking up new angles, Pyle wanted to create English programs to distribute to China. But the radio transcription business, though supposedly successful, was not very exciting for a man like Cash 'n' Carry. In 1933 he went to the Century of Progress, promoting "Professor Pyle's Astounding and Astonishing Aggregation of Educational Oddities," featuring the "Ossified Man." In 1935 Charlie rented a booth at Chicago's Century of Progress Exposition. Pyle was putting on another freak show and Giants owner and one-time adversary Tim Mara happened by it. "He had lined up a bunch of freaks from all parts of the world, and it was typical of him that it was the freakiest freak show ever presented by anybody anywhere," said Mara. "One of his freaks was a guy with a cast iron stomach. He could swallow anything. No kidding. I saw him swallow a watch, a fountain pen, a toothbrush and an electric light globe. Just to prove he wasn't faking he illuminated the globe after he had swallowed it.

"I was around the place several days. On one of these days I found old Cash and Carry in a fierce lather. His human goat was bedridden with a splitting headache and refused to go on.

"'The guy's got me stopped,' moaned old Cash and Carry. 'All day long he eats glass and iron and rock and when he gets a headache I go to him with an aspirin tablet, and what do you suppose he tells me? He cries: "Take it away. I can't swallow it."'"

Charlie would continue in the freak show racket, but he was slowed by a stroke and for more than four months was unable to walk. Grange paid him a visit. "He was very, very badly crippled," said Red. "He couldn't talk and his whole right side was useless." Charlie rented a cottage in northern Wisconsin where he set up some pulleys lined up in a tree. He hired some local kids to tie the rope around his bad arm and pull the rope. He did it for ten months. Physical therapy like this was not common for stroke victims in this era. Yet again, Pyle — *Remember his dream of a large indoor stadium with a retractable roof?* — was ahead of his time.

Charlie actually made a comeback, as spry as ever, according to

Grange. In 1937 he married Elvia Allman, a radio personality: he was fifty-five; she was thirty-two. Two years later he planned to take his freak show to the New York World's Fair, making a splashy promotional comeback. But on February 3, 1939, Cash 'n' Carry, who had lived so colorfully, succumbed to a cerebral thrombosis. He was fifty-six.

The obituaries described his exploits, and the *Chicago Daily News*, seemingly astonished that all his debts were paid, headlined, "Death of Pyle Finds Him All Square Again."

To the *Chicago Tribune* Red would proclaim Charlie "the greatest promoter of all time. The greatest promoter — but not the greatest business man. He had more ideas than any man I ever knew. He was always completely honest with me."

III.

IN OCTOBER 1941 Red married Margaret Hazelberg, a United Airlines stewardess, in a Crown Point, Indiana, courthouse. Back in 1926 Red had described his dream girl: "Pretty? Gosh! Yes! She must be a good dancer, a good sport, and intelligent, but not intellectual." Muggs, as everyone called her, fit the bill. She was a red-headed Wisconsin girl, a registered nurse, who was known as a sweet, tomboyish woman with a lot of common sense. She helped Red with his money management and he never had any financial woes again. The couple never had any children.

Along with his radio *Red Grange Show* ("Yes, fans, it's time to step into the huddle again ... and here he is, Mr. Football himself, Red Grange!"), Red would spend the 1940s giving after-dinner speeches, one year clocking 130. Red had some real beauts: "I can remember one time that Britt (I believe I was a sophomore or junior) inveighed [sic] me to go to Elgin with him and talk out at the insane asylum. [LAUGHTER] We had a few people that were all right, mostly. We had kind of a sporting element there. I was talking, and someone kept jumping out in the middle of the audience hollering 'You're nuts!' [LAUGHTER] And I don't care how callous ya are, it kind of shakes ya up a little bit. [LAUGHTER] And, finally, the thing ... the dinner finished and Britt and I walked out. And the superintendent came over and apologized, and he said he's sorry it happened. He said, 'Those are the first sane words that guy has said in twenty years!'" [LAUGHTER]

Red would talk about the old days with his football stump speech.

He would tell the one about his high school coach:

"He always lettered the two tallest guys and told 'em to carry him off the field at the end of the game. The fans would say, 'Not much of a coach but the kids sure love him.'" [LAUGHTER]

And about the player who was having academic problems and showed his report card to his coach:

"'What am I doing wrong? One D and three Fs.' The coach replied, 'It's obvious. You're putting too much emphasis on one subject.'" [LAUGHTER]

And he always told people about his friend Bronko Nagurski: "One day he was looking out a window, watching two ladies walk down the street. Bronk fell out the window two stories. Policemen ran over and brushed him off and said, 'What happened?' and Bronk said, 'I don't know, I just got here myself, ya know.'" [LAUGHTER]

Red Grange was a winner. Grown men would melt in front of him, even other football players. At one dinner Bears great Sid Luckman said: "Ladies and gentlemen, I tell you this from the depth of my heart, he has always been my hero . . . Try to emulate this human being, who always carried himself with dignity and respect. Love is the most beautiful thing in the world and that is what Red Grange has always emulated."

Red was friends with the other gods of the Golden Age of Sports, but he was more interested in them as men, rather than in their athletic accomplishments.

"Bobby Jones is a real fine gentleman. One of the things I'll never forget is a big dinner I attended where many of the nation's top athletes were in attendance, and I watched Jack Dempsey pick Bobby Jones out of his wheelchair and carry him in his arms to have their picture together." Grange admired valor. "And I always admired Ty Cobb. Ty and I were very good friends and I would frequently sit on the bench and watch Ty play ball." Red admired iconoclasts, even calling Joe Namath "a high-class kid." As his heroes he named his father, because "he simply didn't know fear," and the lonely gunslinger Wyatt Earp, whom he researched, even visiting the Arizona poolroom where the sheriff was murdered. He also liked underdogs: "I've always admired men like Ty Cobb and Babe Ruth and Jack Dempsey. These were guys who came from nothing, from no place, from poverty — same way I did, and nobody was ever poorer than Grange when he was a kid."

The games of his youth fed and clothed him into adulthood: from the job with the mineral water company (the president of the company was such a Grange freak that he had the company self-publish a hardcover biography entitled 77), to Falstaff beer, to the insurance business, the commentary jobs, and the speaking engagements. Red worked hard in the insurance business and claimed he was prouder of his success in business than of his success on the field because he did it himself. But he could never get away from football even if he wanted to. Jim Thorpe would come to his office twice a week and they would sit around and bullshit about the old days all day, and on the streets and in taverns people would stop him and want to chat. It wasn't so bad. "I wouldn't do anything different," he would say. "I'm pretty well fixed for the rest of my days thanks to football."

After his playing career, Red did not lead a completely innocuous life. In 1950 someone nominated him to run as a Republican candidate for a University of Illinois trusteeship, and soon afterward he succumbed to the pull of politics. Red didn't campaign, didn't even want it, he said, but he received more votes than anyone else in the state that election, including (he would brag) Adlai Stevenson. Red didn't really do anything significant; in fact the *Chicago Sun-Times* tabbed him a "synthetic alumnus" who had been nominated to rid the school of its president, George D. Stoddard, a liberal intellectual who was a member of the U.S. National Commission for UNESCO. In a regrettable move, probably fueled by political ambitions — or maybe he was simply a pawn, as some argued — Grange went after Stoddard, who was accused of being a Communist sympathizer. Stoddard's major crime seemed to be having the audacity to recruit Ivy League professors to Champaign-Urbana. Red did the dirty work and had the man fired, but soon afterward Red had a heart attack and got out of politics, vowing to retire to Florida. He never seemed proud, at least publicly, of the

Stoddard incident; when people brought up his time as a trustee he would change the subject. He would always support conservative politicians, particularly Richard Nixon, who wrote him various letters: "As one of your long-time admirers . . . P.S. I thoroughly enjoyed your anecdote about your introduction to President Coolidge back in 1925!" In his private time Red would clip articles favoring his brand of politics. In the margins he scribbled, "The clippings, in this book, were selected by me. In general, they reflect my thinking. Tue., June 13th, 1978 — Florida, Harold 'Red' Grange." The articles were mostly anti–big government ("Operate a private business like we operate the U.S. government and the shareholders would laugh you right off the exchange floor"), anti-Democrats ("Once again, through chicanery and political intrigue, elements of the Democratic Party have duped the American people"), anti-UN ("The U.N. is becoming a society of the highest paid bureaucrats in the world"), and fearful of Communists ("There are more Communist agents operating in the U.S. than there are Shriners at a national convention").

But no one really wants to hear about Red Grange's political beliefs — it ruins the mythology. So Red just kept to his football stories and Americans were happy. The Galloping Ghost spent the rest of his life reliving four years of his life. "Red, tell us how you ran for all those TDs against Michigan." "Red, can you tell us the story about the Penn game?" "The barnstorming tour?" Red would oblige and even wonder why the questioners were so interested, but he always complied with superficial anecdotes. He settled into retirement in Indian Lake Estates — a modest central Florida development of cinder-block homes near Lake Weohyakapka, bordering an ancient scrub forest, moss hanging from the tree limbs, the lightning in the area — the most active on the planet — setting off regular fires, the low-slung, sea-driven Florida clouds going on for infinity. It was a place far enough away not to be bothered. Red was genial enough but he always dreamed of isolation. The calls and letters were not so frequent and glimpses of the Ghost grew infrequent. Still, in 1969, on college football's hundredth anniversary, the Football Writers Association made Red Grange the lone unanimous choice for its all-time All-American team. His big yardage totals behind poor teams; his versatility as a runner, passer, and defender; and especially his clutch performances against the best teams would forever mark him as the best college football player ever. Letters would come to his house at 12 North Amaryllis Drive. He would always write back with charm — "Nice of you to remember me." One letter came from Joseph P. Wilson, the captain of the Penn team, who was now a senior district judge. Wilson kept a photo of the two of them shaking hands before the Penn game in his chambers. "Now the younger people look at it and inquire: "Who are those guys?" wrote Wilson. "The sad thing is that over half the players on my team have passed away." A *Cincinnati Enquirer* reporter paid Red a visit in 1969 and described him thus: "Red's face has lost some of its slim-cheeked muscle of his playing days ... Dressed in a soft blue sweater, casual blue sports shirt, plum-colored slacks and loafers, Red looked like the president of the local bank or chairman of the board of the country club ... Red loves to follow the Reds and Red Sox in spring training in Florida and attends about 20 games, he said. Other than that his only work is making speeches throughout the U.S. during football season for Falstaff beer. Or he may take time out to count the truck loads of oranges from a 40-acre grove he owns near his home."

He had stopped watching much football. "There is absolutely no new football," he would say; "there isn't anything you can do with the football that hasn't been done a thousand times with a football since the forward pass came around in 1906."

He returned to the University of Illinois one last time.

Red! Red!

It was 1974, the fiftieth anniversary of his great game against Michigan. There was a standing ovation as he entered Memorial. At halftime, the crowd chanted, "We want Red!" There were people present who had witnessed his athletic greatness. Red Grange had etched his grace into their memories. The fans, especially the Greatest Generation among them, idolized his stoic humility.

Red! Red!

"I take no credit," he told them. "I just carried the ball."

With his snowy white hair, his rheumy eyes watching the gray sandhill cranes in the lake near his house, Red had become grandfatherly. (He supposedly had no children.) His favorite activity was puttering around in his yard and mowing his grass. "I am kind of a loner . . . I like to be alone," he said. His hometown finally honored him in 1978 after years of self-imposed exile (Red had resisted returning because Wheaton had not given his dad a pension — Pa, the one-man police force who was on call 24/7, risking his life for the town). The Wheaton Iceman returned. After the ceremony, where Grange was touched by the outpouring of generosity, he left Wheaton with one memento, a letter from a little girl that said, "I love you, Red."

One day Muggs drove him into town. She couldn't manage him anymore. He had Parkinson's, the disease of athletic sacrifice. They went through the longleaf pines and the lush wiregrass, the kids riding in the back of pickups, the burning leaves, the bait shops, the red dirt, the honey vendors (Struthers Honey "Since 1935"), the memorial peddlers and RV parks, the buffets. They put him on the second floor of the Lake Wales Hospital Extended Care Facility with its handful of rooms adjoining a small community hospital. There wasn't much to look at, just a Catholic church and State Highway 60. When Muggs got there she told the administrator that there was one rule: you have to protect him, meaning no visitors, no autographs. Red was there to get better and come home. He would be OK, but then he just wasn't there. Muggs would drive in every morning. They brought in a La-Z-Boy for her. She would stay all day in Room 208, just taking a little break once in a while to go to the Catholic church and pray.

The staff loved Red. He insisted on wearing his shorts and polo shirt. No hospital gown, he insisted. "I am not dying, I don't want to go to the hospital." And they could tell he was special — "the way he moved, the grace, you could still see it," said one of his caretakers. Red Barber, the old sportswriter, was on National Public Radio and he encouraged people to send get-well wishes to Red. Although the new generation knew the name, they didn't quite understand the fascination. Something was changing; Red, the last man standing from the Golden Era of Sports, was almost gone. The older folks remembered Red and there was a landslide of cards and letters, and their grandkids made giant paper footballs for the Galloping Ghost. Muggs wallpapered his room with the stuff. It was not unlike the end of the 1923 season when he was just a twenty-year-old kid, feted by his hometown because of his great season down at Illinois, the kids drawing pictures of his likeness, celebrating the glory of his speed. Even now, almost seventy years later, a generation of men remembered him, cherished him for his toughness and beautiful running, his actions creating their childhood memories, defining what a man could be.

Muggs returned every day, and every day Red got worse. He wasn't the man she knew; he was a ghost. Red had trouble walking; he wasn't really talking.

Years earlier, when he was of sound mind, he had said, "I've been kicked, pummeled, spat on, cursed at, and generally abused on some of the good days I had running the ball. But somehow all this individual attention I got from the opposition made me feel kind of proud — proud that they'd singled me out as 'the guy to get.'

"Why do we play at anything? To win. Maybe it's different in other countries, but playing to win is an ingrained part of the American scheme of things.

"I have never had occasion to regret the many years I spent playing football. What would have happened to me if I had never showed up for the grid squad back at Wheaton High School? I don't know — but I doubt that it would have been anything better than the life I have known . . . or even as good. It has been a wonderful ride for me, and my one regret is that it all passed so quickly."

Harold E. "Red" Grange died, at age eighty-seven, on January 28, 1991.

He died quietly, as he had once run.

ACKNOWLEDGMENTS

"With the kind of blocking I had," Red Grange would say, "my Aunt Mathilde could have run for a touchdown."

The blocking analogy can also apply to writing this book.

There are many people to thank.

Researchers: Greg Bensinger (New York), Edwin B. Buggage (New Orleans), Arran Gimba (Portland), Kris Lipkowski (Chicago), John Polacsek (Detroit), Janine Sing (Seattle), Joyce C. Wicks (Champaign). Krista Reynen, a Chicago-based researcher and contributor to the *Encyclopedia of Chicago*, was particularly helpful with court research.

Interviewees: Many ninety-year-olds wrote me letters in shaky handwriting, telling me about their experiences seeing Grange, or talking about specific events detailed in the book. John Whitehead, a former *Los Angeles Times* writer, was collaborating with George Trafton on a biography before the Brute's death and gave me unique insight into the man. Carlyn Frank Benjamin kindly shared her scrapbook of the Ambassador Hotel. Meg Goebel was generous with mementos from the life of her grandfather and Grange teammate, Paul. Lorin F. Pardoe Jr. kindly aided my Grange research in the book's early stages. Robert Julian told me about his grandfather, A. W. Stoolman. Lynn Schwartz and Linda Eder generously made copies of letters and photographs relating to Earl Britton. Thank you to Harold Gardner, who invited me into his home, where he rummaged through old letters and clippings, loaned me videotapes, and then toured me around Forksville, taking me to gravesites, Grange's birthplace, and other significant spots that I would never have found. In the early stages of the book, Brother Tom Hetland, Joe Storto, Jack Crowder, and Larry Hartlaub were particularly generous, recounting stories of St. Mel High School and Paddy

Driscoll. And, finally, Delmar DeWolf, a cousin of Grange's buddy Beans, was constantly sending me copies of letters and e-mails with large — but immensely useful — attachments of photographs and other documents. Mr. DeWolf did not live to see the book's completion.

Librarians, historians, archivists, scholars, and other supporters: Bob Sweeney (Sullivan County historian), Carolyn Adams and Rosemary Raeske (Champaign County Historical Archives), Carol Holliger (Ohio Wesleyan University), Bruce Abrams (New York County Clerk's Office), Robert Rich (Los Angeles County Law Library), Jameel T. Jones (Virginia Theatre), Becki White (Pottsville Free Public Library), Jack Eckert (Harvard University's Francis A. Countway Library of Medicine), Joe Farley (Producers Library), Matt Smith (WPA Film Library), Dennis McClendon (Chicago CartoGraphics), Jory Kruspe and Craig Hooper (Analogue), Jennifer Miller (University of California, Los Angeles, Film and Television Archive), Sergeant Laura Stratton (Columbus Police Department's archives), Julie A. Satzik (Archdiocese of Chicago's Joseph Cardinal Bernardin Archives and Records Center), Mark S. Young II (International Tennis Hall of Fame), Thomas J. Wood (University of Illinois, Springfield), Steve Nielsen (Minnesota Historical Society), Mark Frazier Lloyd (University of Pennsylvania), Robert Allen (Danville Public Library), Kevin B. Leonard (Northwestern University), Tara C. Craig (Columbia University), Kelly McAnnaney (New-York Historical Society), Tamar Chute (Ohio State University), Sandra Stelts (Pennsylvania State University), Diane Donham (Library of Michigan), and Kenneth Fine, M.D. (George Washington University School of Medicine). Special thanks to Alberta Adamson of the Wheaton Historic Preservation Council, who showed me around Wheaton; David Smith of the New York Public Library, who made my visit one of archival bliss — sitting in the Rose Main Reading Room and going through the *New York Sun* morgue files gave me particular joy; Matt Waechter of the Professional Football Hall of Fame, who looked after me during my week in Canton; Kent Stephens of the College Football Hall of Fame, who opened the archival vaults; Roxy Dunn of the University of Illinois at Urbana-Champaign, who dug up important pages from the Zuppke Papers; the University of Illinois's Chris Prom, who went beyond the call in finding materials. Special thanks go to Wheaton College's Keith Call, who stayed late one day so I could finish some research, patiently listened to my Grange ramblings — *and* took me to lunch. Also, kudos to Wheaton's David Malone, who meticulously organized the Red Grange collection.

Sports information: Karrie C. Heartlein (Knox College); John Steinmiller (Marquette University); Dave Hilbert (University of Chicago), who walked me around campus and helped bring alive the ghosts of Chicago football; Bruce M. Madej (University of Michigan); and Steve Snapp (Ohio State University), who fielded my many questions regarding stadium minutiae for a Grange-related story for the *New York Times*. Special thanks to Kent Brown (University of Illinois at Urbana-Champaign), who toured me around the boneyard and Illinois athletic facilities, opened the athletic department's archives for me, and dug up some Grange artifacts, like his jersey and football shoes.

Readers: With her narrative sensibilities, Shoba Narayan was a perfect reader for this book; her suggestions were unparalleled. Samuel G. Freedman read some early pages, and his encouragement gave me confidence to continue; but like all great professors, Sam's teachings live within his students. Even twenty-eight hundred miles away I couldn't get his voice out of my head (a good thing) as his virtual pestering pushed me to dig a little deeper and write a little better.

Other people to thank: Kirsten Coyne, Ed Saxon, Len Saxon, Vickie Macias, Emma Rosales, Mitch Lynch, Patricia Greenwell, and Joseph Suppo.

My agent, Michelle Tessler, a true pro, was an early believer. The book would never have happened without her.

Thanks to the Houghton team: Will Vincent, Elizabeth Lee, Larry Cooper, Barbara Wood, Melissa Lotfy, and Megan Wilson.

I will always be grateful to Susan Canavan, my editor at Houghton Mifflin, who believed in my ambitions for this book, thought about — and commented on — every line, and helped me make the narrative better in innumerable ways.

My parents, Pat and Barney Poole, have been particularly gracious and supportive in infinite ways. My brother, Dave, e-mailed constant encouragement, which really meant a lot to me.

My wife, Leslie, supported me without fail and sometimes beyond reason.

My children, Joe and Rose, have been fountains of joy. Joe, a sweet-natured boy, was born at about the same time as the book started to gestate, so it has been particularly pleasurable to watch him grow through the book's life. In the midst of writing *The Galloping Ghost*, Rose, as is her sweet nature, suggested taking the published book to Grange's grave and leaving it there so he could read it. We will. It's a father-daughter journey we will make together.

APPENDIX A
RED GRANGE'S COLLEGE RECORD

SEASON OF 1923

OPPONENTS	TOUCHDOWNS	MINUTES PLAYED	YARDS GAINED	PASSES COMPLETED
Nebraska	3	39	208	—
Iowa	1	60	175	—
Butler	2	28	142	—
Northwestern	3	19	251	—
Chicago	1	59	160	—
Wisconsin	1	30	140	—
Ohio State	1	60	184	—
TOTAL	12	295	1,260	

SEASON OF 1924

OPPONENTS	TOUCHDOWNS	MINUTES PLAYED	YARDS GAINED	PASSES COMPLETED
Nebraska	0	60	116	6 for 116 yards
Butler	2	16	104	2 for 30 yards
Michigan	5	41	402	6 for 64 yards
DePauw	0	0	0	0
Iowa	2	45	186	3 for 98 yards
Chicago	3	60	300	7 for 177 yards
Minnesota	1	44	56	3 for 39 yards
Ohio State	0	0	0	0
TOTAL	13	266	1,164	27 for 524 yards

SEASON OF 1925

OPPONENTS	TOUCHDOWNS	MINUTES PLAYED	YARDS GAINED	PASSES COMPLETED
Nebraska	0	51	49	1 for 18 yards
Butler	2	41	185	2 for 22 yards
Iowa	1	60	208	2 for 24 yards
Michigan	0	60	122	None completed
Pennsylvania	3	57	363	1 for 13 yards
Chicago	0	60	51	None completed
Wabash	0	5	0	None completed
Ohio State	0	48	235	9 for 42 yards
TOTAL	6	382	1213	15 for 119 yards

GRAND TOTALS

TOUCHDOWNS — Butler, 6; Michigan, 5; Chicago, 4; Iowa, 4; Nebraska, 3; Northwestern, 3; Pennsylvania, 3; Wisconsin, 1; Ohio State, 1; Minnesota, 1.
TOTAL, 31.

YARDS GAINED — Iowa, 569; Michigan, 524; Chicago, 511; Butler, 431; Ohio State, 419; Nebraska, 373; Pennsylvania, 363; Northwestern, 251; Wisconsin, 140; Minnesota, 56. TOTAL, 3,637.

PASSES COMPLETED — Chicago, 7 for 177 yards; Nebraska, 7 for 134 yards; Iowa, 5 for 122 yards; Michigan, 6 for 64 yards; Butler, 4 for 52 yards; Ohio State, 9 for 42 yards; Minnesota, 3 for 39 yards; Pennsylvania, 1 for 13 yards. TOTAL, 42 FOR 643 YARDS.

SINGLE-GAME FEATS

MOST RUSHING TOUCHDOWNS — 5, Michigan, 1924

MOST YARDS GAINED — 402, Michigan, 1924

MOST COMPLETED PASSES — 7 for 177 yards, Chicago, 1924

LEAST YARDS GAINED — 49, Nebraska, 1925

LONGEST RUN — 95 yards, kickoff, Michigan, 1924

SCORELESS GAMES — Nebraska, 1924; Nebraska, 1925; Michigan, 1925; Chicago, 1925; Ohio State, 1925.

(In compiling yards gained, punt and kickoff runbacks have been figured with runs from scrimmage, and losses subtracted. Figures, therefore, are net gains.)

SOURCE: L. M. Tobin, University of Illinois Athletic Association

APPENDIX B
RED GRANGE'S PRO CAREER

CHICAGO BEARS, 1925, 1929–34
NEW YORK YANKEES, 1926–27

YEAR	RUSHING					PASS RECEIVING				SCORING	
	GAMES	ATTEMPTS	YARDS	AVERAGE	TDs	PASS COMPLETIONS	YARDS	AVERAGE	TDs	TDs	POINTS
1925	17	204	1,024	5.0							
1926	16	191	961	5.0							
1927	14	154	762	4.9							
1928	(inactive, injured)					[1925–31 Unofficial]					
1929	14	130	552	4.3							
1930	14	88	382	4.3							
1931	12	72	288	4.0							
1932	9	57	132	2.3	3	11	168	15.3	3	6	36
1933	13	81	277	3.4	1	3	74	24.7	0	1	6
1934	12	32	136	4.3	1	2	46	23.0	2	3	18
PRO TOTALS (1932–34)	34	170	545	3.2	5	16	288	18.0	5	10	60

SOURCE: Professional Football Hall of Fame

NOTES ON SOURCES

Red Grange was covered diligently in 1920s newspapers, whose writers gave wonderfully literary accounts of his games. I did not want to write a book that simply parroted newspaper articles, however, so I set out to dig deeper into his life. Finding inside information was sometimes tricky because many of the players and coaches of the era did not leave many letters and/or diaries, film footage and radio broadcasts are practically nonexistent, and many of the oral histories tended to go by the dictum "what happens in the locker room stays in the locker room." Deducing the facts within the newspaper stories was also a challenge. Charles C. Pyle was a daily fixture in 1920s sports pages, but the writers did not question his often dubious claims; therefore, I spent a great deal of time reconstructing and fact-checking his life. For example, it was reported that Pyle attended Ohio Wesleyan and Ohio State University. At my behest the schools scoured their academic records but could never find that Pyle had even registered at either school. This was one of many incidents that I tried to track down in an effort to find the truth.

To begin the research of this book and create an outline of events, I visited the archives of the College and Professional Football Halls of Fame, the Amateur Athletic Foundation, the University of Illinois, the Margaret Herrick Library, and Wheaton College. (I also had materials sent to me from the University of Pennsylvania, Ohio State University, and Ohio Wesleyan University, among other archives.) Wheaton College, which holds Grange's papers, was particularly fruitful, especially some clipping books called the Newlan Scrapbooks. The scrapbooks were amassed by Joseph Newlan, an Illinois football fan and Grange admirer, and contain over two thousand newspaper clippings; the scrapbooks were invaluable for detailing Grange's college and early pro career. Unfortunately, many of the clippings do not have dates, page numbers, or even the publication from which they were taken, but I was able to deduce the source information from studying the scrapbooks at length.

The forensics of history — and the complications of portraying lives — made me realize that historical research cannot be confined to newspapers, census reports, probate court files, or visits to stadiums; rather the researcher must attempt to understand the context in which the lives were led. To get a better feel for the era — its street language, popular musical tastes, economic fragility, and mores — I soaked in the era's culture: music, movies, advertisements, radio shows, novels like *Studs Lonigan,* the Sears catalog, medical textbooks, *Variety, Photoplay,* photographs, and paintings. I was also lucky enough to meet many descendants of players who were generous with recollections, personal letters, photographs, and documents, and I met and corresponded with people who bore witness — ninety-year-olds who, as kids, had seen Grange play and still remembered his running style with clarity, some looking to their childhood diaries to refresh a memory.

Several books, especially *King Football, Red Grange and the Rise of Modern Football,* and *No Cheering in the Press Box,* were invaluable for learning new facts about events and characters and double-checking old ones. The rich and detailed articles on the Professional Football Researchers Association Web site were also an excellent resource. To give readers a better context for Pyle and Grange's fluctuating fortunes in terms of today's purchasing power, I used estimates from the "How much is that?" site on EH.net (http://eh.net). To better understand the people in this book I visited the significant sites of Grange and Pyle's lives — birth and death places, locker rooms, stadiums, gravesites, and homes. I held and studied Grange's still-muddy college football boots and sweater-jersey, and I made an effort to locate highlight reels — most of which have suffered nitrocellulose decomposition, a term I grew to dread. I did uncover some footage, which can be seen at www.garyandrewpoole.com.

I have made every effort to accurately portray the people and events detailed in the book. Any errors are mine.

NOTES

AUTHOR'S NOTE

ix   *his two false:* Associated Press, "A Quiet 77th Birthday? Not for No. 77," June 14, 1980.
("Park next to the Buick!"): John Wiebusch, author interview.
he wore a burgundy coat: The Super Bowl Today: Super Bowl XII, CBS, January 15, 1978.

FOREWORD

xii   *Every autumn weekend:* Statistics from the Nielsen Company.
xiii *People always asked Bob Zuppke:* Interview, Richfield Reporter and Robert C. Zuppke, December 16, 1934, Robert Zuppke Papers, 28/3/20, University of Illinois.
xiv *Their brains have:* "Wives United by Husbands' Post-N.F.L. Trauma," *New York Times*, March 14, 2007.

1. A BOY

4   *"Of antlered speed":* F. E. H., "'Red' Grange," 1923, Harold E. Grange Papers, 26/20/177, Box 1, University of Illinois.
5   *she had a tooth pulled:* Harold Gardner, author interview.
"It didn't have the beautiful": Harold Grange, *The Red Grange Story: An Autobiography*, as told to Ira Morton (Urbana and Chicago: University of Illinois Press, 1953), 6.
wildly popular, especially in the heartland: Steven A. Riess, "A Social Profile of the Professional Football Player, 1920–82," in *The Business of Professional Sports*, ed. Paul D. Staudohar and James A. Mangan (Chicago and Urbana: University of Illinois Press, 1991), 224.
bored newspaper editors: "Football Brutality," *Decatur (IL) Daily Republican*, November 30, 1895; "Number One," *Sandusky (OH) Star*, October 10, 1899; "Football Death List," *Portsmouth (NH) Herald*, December 9, 1901; "Another Football Death," *Iowa City Citizen*, November 15, 1909; "Blind after Football Fight," *Trenton (NJ) Evening Times*, December 3, 1909; "Boys Decide That Football Must Go," (Elyria, OH) *Evening Telegram*, April 9, 1910; "Football Fatality," *Edwardsville (IL) Intelligencer*, October 1, 1920.
6   *Two vertebrae at the base of his spine:* Michael J. Wayne, "Red Grange's

Comment on His Pro Career and Value of Football to Youth," July 26, 1978, Wheaton College Special Collections.

Lyle grabbed his billy club: Willie Carlson interview, March 12, 1999, Wheaton College Special Collections.

"How do you mean that?": Gene Schoor, *Red Grange: Football's Greatest Halfback* (New York: Julian Messner, 1952), 18.

7   *Puffing after-dinner cigars:* "Grange, Star of Gridiron, Is Banquet Hero"; "'Red' Grange Honored by Home Folks at Big Banquet Thursday Eve"; "Wheaton Honors Grange, All-American Halfback"; Newlan Scrapbook, Wheaton College Special Collections.

8   *"the shattered ends of my ribs [were] chafing my lungs":* "It's Do or Die for Coach, Not School: Grange," *Chicago Sunday Tribune,* December 15, 1929.

   "a beautiful jump and running catch": Walter Eckersall, "Grange Is Illinois 'Punch' That Fells Nebraska, 24 to 7," *Chicago Sunday Tribune,* October 6, 1923.

   But Zup's hand was forced: "Red Grange's Running Again Wins for Illini," *Chicago Sunday Tribune,* October 13, 1923.

   He put Grange into the lineup: "Grange Is Star as Illini Puts Butler to Rout," *Davenport (IA) Democrat and Leader,* October 14, 1923.

   "Grange? Iowa will camp on him": "Illini Plans Iowa Invasion," *Iowa City Press-Citizen,* October 16, 1923.

9   *"Swell tackle, kid. That's the way to hit 'em!":* Grantland Rice, "I Remember a Galloping Ghost," *Sport,* December 1947, 33.

   in the early stages of the contest: "Fisher Hits Them Hard, Yarn about Red Grange Says," *Iowa City Press-Citizen,* October 31, 1923.

   thirty-five thousand people: Joe Godfrey Jr., "Fans Jam Cub Park Despite Bad Weather," *Chicago Journal,* October 27, 1923.

10 *For an hour he stood on the cinder driveway:* Joe Wayer, "Grange's Roommate Tells What Real 'Red' Is Like," *Chicago Evening American,* November 24, 1923.

   Illinois Athletic Director George Huff was barely: "Wisconsin-Illinois Ball War Sets Big Ten Agog," *Appleton (WI) Post-Crescent,* November 3, 1922.

   Wisconsin students were legitimately upset: Associated Press, "Stirs Ire of Badgers," November 8, 1923.

11 *In the second period:* "'Red' Grange Keeps Illini atop Big 10," *Chicago Tribune,* November 10, 1923.

   Despite being half-killed, Grange ran: Red Grange, *Zuppke of Illinois* (Chicago: A. L. Glaser, 1937), 92.

12 *In letters sent from Zup's summer place: Twelve Minutes to Immortality,* WGN-TV, 1974.

2. A GALLOPING GHOST

14 *Britt had nicknamed his friend:* Eddie Jacquin, "Red Grange, $20,000 per Year Businessman, to Author Book," *Champaign News-Gazette,* August 8, 1937.

   Red ignored the boxes of candy, cookies, nuts, and cake: Wayer, "Grange's Roommate Tells What Real 'Red' Is Like."

14   *The men would zoom through Champaign-Urbana:* "Britton, Illini's Human Derrick, Red's Watchdog," *Chicago Tribune,* November 5, 1925.

15   *Some Michigan Zeta Psi brothers:* "Red Grange Off Grid Is a Big Bashful Boy," *Chicago Tribune,* October 20, 1924.

17   *On several plays Grange faked a throw and ran:* Associated Press, "Grange Is Now Full Fledged Triple Threat," October 14, 1924.

19   *read Kant for fun:* Ivan N. Kaye, *Good Clean Violence* (Philadelphia: Lippincott, 1973), 73.
     440-yarder in under 50 seconds: Burton A. Ingwerson Papers, 1967, 28/3/21, Illinois Athletic Association.
     and the 100-yard dash: Robert S. Gallagher, "The Galloping Ghost: An Interview with Harold Grange," *American Heritage,* December 1974, 22.

20   *little green beanies:* Burton A. Ingwerson Papers.
     "I never heard of Grange": "An Evening with Red Grange," Wheaton College, October 28, 1978, Wheaton College Special Collections.

21   *freshmen use nearly every play:* "Zup Shows All of Yost's Great Plays to Illini," *Chicago Tribune,* October 16, 1924.
     Injuries and poor grades: Frank D. Murphy letter to Earl T. Britton, May 28, 1924, Lynn Schwartz Collection.

22   *Yost had really spent a quiet summer:* Gallagher, "The Galloping Ghost," 24.
     away from the chaos: James Crusinberry, "67,000 to See Michigan and Illini Clash," *Chicago Tribune,* October 17, 1924.

23   *During the Great War:* J. Fred Lawton, *Hurry Up Yost in Story and Song* (Ann Arbor: J. W. Edwards, 1947), 27.
     a distinct West Virginia drawl: Edwin Pope, *Football's Greatest Coaches* (Atlanta: Tupper & Love, 1955), 320.
     "Objections to football have been heard in certain quarters": Fielding H. Yost, *For Football and Spectator* (Ann Arbor: University Publishing, 1905), 9.
     At the school he played impromptu: Fielding Yost, "Yost Played First Game He Ever Saw," *Detroit Times,* December 4, 1925.
     Yost joked that each man brought his own bottle: John Behee, *Fielding Yost's Legacy to the University of Michigan* (Ann Arbor: Lithocrafters, 1971), 19.

24   *"Eckersall, Eckersall":* Lawton, *Hurry Up Yost in Story and Song,* 15.
     "Oh Mister Little, Oh Mister Little": Ibid., 34.

26   *what Yost called "sand":* Yost, *For Football and Spectator,* 171.
     "There are eleven good tacklers": Schoor, *Red Grange: Football's Greatest Halfback,* 57.

27   *"What in the hell are you trying to do":* Earl T. Britton letter to Bert Bertine, January 2, 1958, Lynn Schwartz Collection.
     threw out dates: "An Evening with Red Grange," Wheaton College Special Collections.
     "Is there anything in the rule book": "Red Grange Comments on the Michigan and Pennsylvania Games," July 26, 1978, Wheaton College Special Collections.

28   *Grange felt as if the crowd was on top of him: Twelve Minutes to Immortality,* WGN-TV, 1974.
     Yost told his team: "Kick off to Grange": Schoor, *Red Grange: Football's Greatest Halfback,* 59.

29   *"It was my greatest"*: "Giants of the Gridiron: Part I," Box IV B1, Wheaton College Special Collections.

30   *"At Meechigan, we believe that position"*: W. W. Heffelfinger, *This Was Football* (New York: A. S. Barnes & Co., 1954), 65.
     "We make it a fetish to insist that the back run hard, and harder": Robert C. Zuppke, *Coaching Football* (Champaign: Bailey & Himes, 1930), 78.

31   *"On October 18, 1924"*: "Red Grange Comments on the Michigan and Pennsylvania Games," Wheaton College Special Collections; *Twelve Minutes to Immortality*, WGN-TV.

32   *Grange hearing it like a din:* Gallagher, "The Galloping Ghost," 93.
     "I am not going to make you look good again": *Twelve Minutes to Immortality*, WGN-TV.

33   *The son of a jewelry designer: I'm an American!* National Broadcasting Company, WENR, Chicago, Illinois, August 31, 1941.
     From Bowling Green to the Bronx: L. M. Tobin, "Robert C. Zuppke," biographical sketch, 1937, Robert Zuppke Papers, 28/3/20, University of Illinois.

34   *"Scrimmaging against Zup's first team"*: Pope, *Football's Greatest Coaches*, 325.

37   *the people just stood and kept standing:* Seely Johnston interview, Wheaton College Special Collections.
     "Tired, Red?": *Twelve Minutes to Immortality*, WGN-TV.

39   *"ye're a-playin' out there like a wooden Indian"*: Pope, *Football's Greatest Coaches*, 314.
     "The only way to stop him": "Critics Laud Harold Grange," *Detroit Saturday Night*, October 31, 1924.

40   *Little later revealed that at first:* Heffelfinger, *This Was Football*, 66.

41   *"When we win, it's Yost's team"*: Alexander M. Weyand, *Football Immortals* (New York: Macmillan, 1962), 193.
     "I wish you would tell your publicity man": Behee, *Fielding Yost's Legacy to the University of Michigan*, 92.
     It would become an enduring fiction: Gallagher, "The Galloping Ghost," 94; *Bill Stern Show*, September 27, 1946, Wheaton College Special Collections; "Writer Dies at 84," *Champaign-Urbana News-Gazette*, November 22, 1978; Robert Zuppke letter to Allison Danzig, May 15, 1952, Robert Zuppke Papers, 28/3/20, University of Illinois.

3. C. C. PYLE

44   *"There'd be about"*: John M. Carroll, *Red Grange and the Rise of Modern Football* (Urbana and Chicago: University of Illinois Press, 1999), 34.
     Through the front: Author site visit.
     All of the football players were comped: Richard Whittingham, *What a Game They Played* (New York: Harper & Row, 1984), 18.

46   *His second wife:* Geoff Williams, *C. C. Pyle's Amazing Foot Race* (New York: Rodale, 2007), 210.
     Champaign was not far (but far enough): U.S. Bureau of the Census, Fourteenth Census of the United States, 1920.

47   *"A lovely brunette of a Spanish type"*: Theresa L. St. Romain, "An American

Beauty: The Life and Films of Margarita Fischer" (master's thesis, Wichita State University, 2004), 47–48.

47 *threatened to literally tar and feather him:* "Theatre Manager Placed Under Arrest," Margarita Fischer Papers, Department of Special Collections, Wichita State University.

48 *"Two nations of Southern Europe have been drawn":* National Register of Historic Places, Virginia Theatre, 8–86, 25.

49 *the time in Boise City:* Alva Johnston, "Cash and Carry," *New Yorker,* December 8, 1928, 33.
    With his new suit: "Red's Biggest Task Not on the Gridiron," *Detroit News,* November 7, 1925.

4. IS HE DEAD?

52 *the two immense black wooden doors:* Author site visit.
    Stagg — cotton-haired: "Stagg's 54th," *Time,* October 25, 1943; Chicago History Museum's *Chicago Daily News* photographs.

53 *"Did you ever see Grange score without the ball?":* Pope, *Football's Greatest Coaches,* 244.

54 *"Western supremacy in football":* Robin Lester, *Stagg's University: The Rise, Decline, and Fall of Big-Time Football at Chicago* (Urbana and Chicago: University of Illinois Press, 1995), 109.

55 *In 1906, the first year the forward pass was legal:* Ibid., 103.
    He wore several rings on his right hand: Pope, *Football's Greatest Coaches,* 332.

57 *so they couldn't block for Grange:* Associated Press, "Chicago Tries to Stop Illini," November 8, 1924.
    At halftime Walter Camp, sixty-five: "The 'Father of Modern Football,'" *Literary Digest,* March 28, 1925, 72.
    near the pot fires burning on the sidelines: Seely Johnston interview, Wheaton College Special Collections.

58 *The trainers handed out:* Howard J. Savage, *American College Athletics: Bulletin Number Twenty-three* (New York: Carnegie Foundation, 1929), 145.
    a big nose interferes with peripheral vision: "Zupgrams," Robert Zuppke Papers, 28/3/20, University of Illinois.
    "You're playing the Maroons like a piano": Lester, *Stagg's University,* 123.

59 *With Stagg's support Gowdy:* Ibid., 118.
    Concussions were epidemic: Savage, *American College Athletics,* 141.
    back in high school he had been kicked in the head: "It's Do or Die for Coach, Not School: Grange," *Chicago Sunday Tribune,* December 15, 1929.
    unconscious for forty-eight hours: James A. Peterson, *77* (Hinckley & Schmitt, 1956), unpaged.

61 *"Who in the hell":* Earl Britton letter to Bert Bertine, January 2, 1958, Lynn Schwartz Collection.
    many were describing as the most vicious: Joe Godfrey Jr., "Red Grange the Human Meteor of 1924," *All-Sports Magazine,* December 1924.

63 *Short of taking a razor:* "Illinois Squared in Last Work on Home Field," *Minneapolis Daily Star,* November 12, 1924.

64 *"co-ed carnival":* "Gridiron Virus Now Infects All Urbana," *Chicago News,* September 21, 1925.

65 *Bill Spaulding, whose only claim:* Edward G. Walker, "Zuppke to Stand Pat on Lineup That Tied Chicago," *Minneapolis Journal,* November 11, 1924.
Clarence Schutte: "Steals Red's Thunder," *Minneapolis Sunday Tribune,* November 16, 1924.
Ten minutes before kickoff, sorority girls: "Sororities Chosen by Team Captains for Dads' Day Race," *Minnesota Daily,* November 13, 1924.
McIlwain, who was wearing: Earl Britton letter to Bert Bertine, January 2, 1958, Lynn Schwartz Collection.
even toothing his skin: Rice, "I Remember a Galloping Ghost," 33.

5. ICEMAN

70 *Red would arrive at L. C. Thompson's Wheaton icehouse:* "My Days on the Ice Route," January 14, 1997, Wheaton College Special Collections.

71 *would walk around town with a piece of tape:* NBC, *Grange Program,* October 29, 1978, Wheaton College Special Collections.
"It was as though Joe DiMaggio": Ed Fitzgerald, *Sport,* December 1950, 62.
It was the grind: University of Illinois transcript.

72 *Two-hundred-pound blocks would come:* Richard Crabb, "Red Grange's Comment on His Pro Career," July 26, 1978, Wheaton College Special Collections.
if it had been two inches: Gallagher, "The Galloping Ghost," 22.

73 *working himself into 170 pounds of muscle:* "Question of Grange Looms Again on Grid," *Chicago Daily News,* September 1, 1925.

74 *Another opportunist, an auto dealer:* Associated Press, "Grange Accused in Car Ad Deal," *Cleveland Plain Dealer,* November 20, 1925.

75 *North Washington Street in Delaware, Ohio:* State of Ohio, Delaware County, 1900 Census; author site visit.
Anna was a telephone operator: "Death Ends Career of C. C. Pyle Former Delaware Grocery Clerk," *Delaware Gazette,* February 4, 1939.
and crushed his partner's thumb: Vincent Richards, "Pyle, the Audacious," *Personality,* July 18, 1928, 52.

76 The Freshman *could have:* *The Freshman,* directed by Sam Taylor, 1925.

78 *"How would you like to make a hundred thousand dollars?:* Gallagher, "The Galloping Ghost," 94.

79 *"Sounds good," said Grange:* Schoor, *Red Grange: Football's Greatest Halfback,* 88.

80 *they trained at grand Memorial:* "Illini Boast Finest Training Quarters," *Chicago Daily News,* August 27, 1925.
in a stuffy warehouse: Bruce J. Evensen, "Jazz Age Journalism's Battle over Professionalism, Circulation, and the Sports Page," *Journal of Sports History,* Winter 1993, 238.
"On the practice field Red": James Braden, "Gridiron Virus Now Infects All Urbana," *Chicago News,* September 21, 1925.

82 *Britt was having serious academic problems:* "Illini Must Do with Green Line," *Chicago Journal,* September 25, 1925.

84 *Signed as a right fielder:* "Just Like Papa Played," *Time,* December 6, 1963.

86 *"Plan on spending Christmas under the sun":* John Wiebusch, "Barnstorming: The 10,000-Mile Odyssey of Red Grange," *Pro! The Official Magazine of the National Football League,* September 25, 1977, 3C; John Wiebusch, author interview.

He paid *the porters:* Myron Cope, *The Game That Was* (New York and Cleveland: World Publishing Co., 1970), 48.

87 *Garland Grange's shoulder popped:* "Garland Grange Quits Urbana; Injury Cause," *Chicago Daily News,* September 26, 1925.

a doughy-faced 230-pounder: Harold Johnson, "Needs Backfield Man or Two to Fit In with 'Red' Grange," *Chicago American,* September 17, 1925.

One lone bright spot: W. V. Morgenstern, "Zuppke Thinks Forward Wall Poor on Attack," *Chicago Examiner,* September 28, 1925.

But after his team barely beat the frosh team: "Illini Outscore Frosh, 14–2," *Chicago Tribune,* September 26, 1925.

88 *"I'm sorry you came":* Grantland Rice, *The Tumult and the Shouting* (New York: A. S. Barnes & Co., 1954), 196.

Mitterwallner was mixing up the signals: Walter Eckersall, "Grange Held Helpless by Cornhuskers," *Chicago Tribune,* October 3, 1925.

there was plenty of blame: Cy Sherman, "Cornhuskers Vanquish Illini, 14–0," *Lincoln Sunday Star,* October 4, 1925.

"Those pesky Nebraskans, fast chargers": Warren W. Brown, "Grange Stopped in '25 Debut as Captain," *Chicago Examiner,* October 3, 1925.

89 *"The color scheme was all red":* Grantland Rice, "Punts and Passes," *Lincoln Star,* October 6, 1925, 10.

a breather the following week: "'Red' Grange Fit for Butler; 'Zup' Tries New Center," *Chicago American,* October 8, 1925.

Red was back to form: "'Red' Is Himself as Illini Beat Butler, 16 to 13," *Chicago Herald-Examiner,* October 10, 1925.

the crowd clanked cowbells: "Grange, Kutsch Draw Record Crowd to Iowa," *Chicago American,* October 17, 1925.

he ran 65 yards for a touchdown: Phil Creden, "Red Grange Turned Loose on Iowa Today," *Chicago News,* October 17, 1925.

90 *His face couldn't hide:* "Grange Rallies Illini Players," *Chicago Journal,* October 21, 1925.

Bubbles and Red had: "'Red' Plays 'Rosalind,'" *Chicago American,* October 9, 1925.

"seared the heart of the veteran coach": Walter Eckersall, "Yost's Eleven Resolved Red Shan't Repeat," *Chicago Tribune,* October 21, 1925.

Yost hosted the reporters in the lobby: Harold Johnson, "Yost's Crew Set to Blot Out Rout of 1924," *Chicago American,* October 23, 1925.

91 *"Just throw the cantaloupe":* Don Lund, author phone interview.

"cool and deliberate field general": "70,000 to See Duel of Grange-Friedman," *Grand Rapids Herald,* October 23, 1925.

The starting elevens went the entire game: Associated Press, "22 Who Started Illinois Game Finished It; Rare in Big Ten," October 25, 1925.

the New York papers: Walter Eckersall, "East Turns Out to Get First Sight of Red," *Chicago Tribune,* October 30, 1925.

6. AMERICA'S HEARTS AND MINDS

95   *"The East awaits the coming of 'Red' Grange"*: Jimmy Corcoran, "East Shines Up Lamps to Glance at Grange Go against Penn," *Chicago American*, October 27, 1925.

96   *When the writers:* Oliver Pilat, *Pegler: Angry Man of the Press* (Boston: Beacon Press, 1963), 103.
     "It's my fault for putting him in such temptation": Jimmy Breslin, *Damon Runyon: A Life* (New York: Ticknor & Fields, 1991), 219.

97   *"I have taught you all I know"*: Wiley Lee Umphlett, *Creating the Big Game: John W. Heisman and the Invention of American Football* (Westport, CT: Greenwood Press, 1992), 172.

98   *Young had solid ends:* Schoor, *Red Grange: Football's Greatest Halfback*, 76.
     "This is a typical Pennsylvania eleven": Herbert Reed, "Coaches to See Penn-Illini Tilt for New Ideas," Universal Service syndicate, October 30, 1925.
     The ends would go directly: "Penn Eleven on Threshold of Grid Fame," *Detroit Free Press*, October 28, 1925.
     "Grange was a genuine leader": Grange, *Zuppke of Illinois*, 97.

99   *"Santa Claus himself would experience difficulty"*: Warren W. Brown, "Snow Blankets Philly and Also Illini Hopes," *Chicago Examiner*, October 30, 1925.
     forced their way through the crowd: Associated Press, "Snow Greets Illini in East," October 30, 1925.
     "I hope my team doesn't skid tomorrow": Associated Press, "Zuppke Hopes Team Won't Skid like Car That Hits His Auto," October 30, 1925.

100 *the Penn team was in Abescon, New Jersey:* "Penn Varsity Gets Warmed Up with Zuppke's Attack," (Philadelphia) *Public Ledger*, October 29, 1925, 18.
     "We've got to beat Illinois today": James Braden, "Quakers Weakened by Injury of Kreuz, Who May Not Start," *Chicago News*, October 31, 1925.

101 *"We have been licked twice this year"*: H. G. Salsinger, "Yost and Zuppke Hand East Her Worst Setback," *Detroit News*, undated, Newlan Scrapbook, Wheaton College Special Collections.

102 *toughest ticket in the world:* "Grid Marvel from West Holds Eye of East," *Chicago American*, October 31, 1925.
     Among the VIPs: "Illini Rooters to Tour Philadelphia," (Philadelphia) *Public Ledger*, October 31, 1925.
     the English royal family's: "A King's Physician," *Time*, September 1, 1930.
     Up there, in the stands: Leo H. Lassen, "College Football Is Fine, but You Can't Eat Cheers," *Seattle Star*, January, 28, 1926, 1.
     Surrounded by still cameramen: Ed Pollock, "Red Grange Runs Wild as Illinois Hands Penn First Defeat, 24 to 2," (Philadelphia) *Public Ledger*, November 1, 1925.
     "I want you to line up strong either right or left": "Red Grange Comments on the Michigan and Pennsylvania Games," July 26, 1978, Wheaton College Special Collections.

104 *"It's not a bad way to enter a game"*: James Braden, "Illinois' Victory Due Mostly to Red but Partly to Team," *Chicago News*, November 2, 1925.

104 *"weird, mud-bespattered pyramid of gnomes":* Walter Eckersall, "Grange Leads Illini Charge to Victory over Penn by 24 to 2," *Chicago Tribune,* October 31, 1925.

O'Hara had been experiencing a powerful melancholy: Matthew Joseph Bruccoli, *The Selected Letters of John O'Hara* (New York: Random House, 1978), 13.

105 *He was expected to show up at 8:00 a.m.:* Frank MacShane, *The Life of John O'Hara* (New York: Dutton, 1980), 27–29.

named by Zuppke: Raymond F. Dvorak letter to Robert Zuppke, November 24, 1941, Robert Zuppke Papers, 28/3/20, University of Illinois.

Grange, wiping his hands on his pants, was calling the signals: Richard Crabb, "Red Grange Comments on the Michigan and Pennsylvania Games," July 26, 1978, Wheaton College Special Collections.

106 *"It is a good deal like the basketball pivot":* Associated Press, "Grange Writes about Football in Magazine," September 25, 1925.

"It did not seem humanly possible": "Illinois Wins Inter-Sectional Football Game by Score of 24–2," *Pennsylvania Gazette,* November 6, 1925, 136–40.

107 *"Countless columns have been written about Red Grange":* Pollock, "Red Grange Runs Wild."

108 *"Grange went over to the bench":* Stanley Woodward, "Views of Sport: A Grange Vote from O'Hara," *New York Herald Tribune,* January 8, 1944.

109 *"We upheld the honor of the conference":* Warren W. Brown, "Red Stopped? No, Just Resting, Says Zuppke," *Chicago Herald-Examiner,* October 31, 1925.

7. A PASSAGE TO MANHOOD

111 *At every stop that afternoon:* "20,000 Welcome Illini Home; Red Greeted like Emperor," *Chicago Tribune,* November 1, 1925.

"rattled the effete East": Ralph Cannon, "Rain Seen as 'Break' for Staggs," *Chicago Journal,* November 7, 1925.

112 *"We-er-had a fine visit down East":* Associated Press, "Grange Plays Romeo Role for Admirers," November 2, 1925.

Graham Kernwein, Chicago's halfback: Cannon, "Rain Seen as 'Break' for Staggs."

had to close practice: Associated Press, "Chicago Plans to Halt Red Grange," November 4, 1925.

113 *The governor and Senator William McKinley:* Howard G. Mayer, "70,000 Throng Twin Cities to See Grange," *Chicago Evening American,* November 7, 1925.

played jazz on the: "Illini Bang Piano, Sing and Study on Eve of Battle," *Chicago Examiner,* November 6, 1925.

As rain hit the clapboard country club: Howard G. Mayer, "Maroons Yellow? Never! 'Red' Grange Assails U.C. Alumni Tactics," *Chicago Evening American,* November 7, 1925.

114 *At game time the field was a complete mess:* Harold Johnson, "Maroons Step Out to Halt 'Red,'" *Chicago American,* November 7, 1925.

Zup never gave much credit: Harvey Woodruff, "Maroon Line Stops Grange, but Fumbles Cost 'Em Game," *Chicago Tribune,* November 7, 1925.

"Without Britton there never would have been": "It's Do or Die for Coach, Not School: Grange," *Chicago Sunday Tribune,* December 15, 1929.

115 *"I haven't made any plans":* Associated Press, "Grange Passes Up Pro-Grid Inducement," *Chicago Herald-Examiner,* September 30, 1925.

116 *"I'm no more professional":* Schoor, *Red Grange: Football's Greatest Halfback,* 90–91.

The dealer told the press about the shakedown: Associated Press, "Grange Accused in Car Ad Deal," *Cleveland Plain Dealer,* November 20, 1925.

117 *Kinley found the celebrity worship:* David Kinley letter to Robert C. Zuppke, November 18, 1924, President Kinley Correspondence, 1919–30, Series 261, Box 129, University of Illinois.

To the faculty who wanted to condemn: David Kinley letter to Edward Keator, December 16, 1925, President Kinley Correspondence, 1919–30, Series 261, Box 129, University of Illinois.

118 *At season's end 370,000 people would have watched:* Associated Press, "370,000 Watch Grange Play," November 17, 1925.

"I don't like the idea of professional football": "America's Grid Ace Has Manager, Charge," *Grand Rapids Press,* November 19, 1925.

"I won't attempt to advise you": "Nation Mourns Huff's Loss," Huff Morgue/Bio File, 26/4/1, University of Illinois.

Huff had lobbied, but failed: "Decatur Illini Club to Stand Back of G. Huff," *Decatur Review,* January 29, 1923.

the Champaign News-Gazette *invited:* Gallagher, "The Galloping Ghost," 94.

"You print any damn thing you want": Ibid.

"I'm still pretty much of a kid": United Press, "Denies Signing Any Contract," November 18, 1925.

119 *"My dad and I have been pals":* "Red Grange to Make Known Plans after Next Game," *New York Telegram,* November 18, 1925.

"I like football": Schoor, *Red Grange: Football's Greatest Halfback,* 95.

120 *The local Republicans:* Associated Press, "Hail Red Grange, Grid Hero, World Knocking at His Door," November 12, 1925.

122 *"Ohio is not making":* James Braden, "School and Friends Call Him Amateur," *Chicago News,* November 19, 1925.

124 *complete with a freak show:* Football Program, University of Illinois versus Ohio State University, November 21, 1925, Ohio State University, 45.

125 *The paid attendance of 84,295 was, at the time:* Jack Park, *The Official Ohio State Football Encyclopedia* (Champaign: Sports Publishing, 2001), 102.

126 *"He has been my Mexican general":* Earl Britton letter to Bert Bertine, January 2, 1958, Lynn Schwartz Collection.

127 *Illini students almost immediately started boycotting:* "Banker behind Grange-Pyle," *Variety,* December 16, 1925, 18.

128 *"You're making a mistake":* Gallagher, "The Galloping Ghost," 94.

The argument would take a brief respite: Ibid.

The place crawled: Whittingham, *What a Game They Played,* 19.

8. A PRO

131 *named Ralph Capone:* Seely Johnston interview, Wheaton College Special Collections.

Two promoters from Rochester: Harold Johnson, "Gothamite, with Satchel Full of Coin, Arrives after Grange Signs," *Chicago American,* undated, Newlan Scrapbook, Wheaton College.

Although he had ended: George Halas, *Halas by Halas* (New York: McGraw-Hill, 1979), 88.

134 *Halas traditionally* schmeared: Ibid., 89.

135 *"The greatest ladies' man":* Cope, *The Game That Was,* 30.

"He hardly noticed me": "Red's Film Cutie Has Hard Heart," (Spokane, WA) *Spokesman Review,* January 31, 1926.

136 *Johnny Small claimed that he had: A. H. Schatz v. Harold E. Grange,* State of Illinois, Cook County Superior Court, Case No. 431920, August 28, 1925.

137 *"There was nothing better than playing for Illinois":* Associated Press, "Zup Says Red Made a Mistake," November 24, 1925.

139 *Zup wouldn't have his ten grand per:* "Article of Agreement" contract between the University of Illinois and Robert C. Zuppke, September 15, 1925, Robert Zuppke Papers, 28/3/20, University of Illinois.

"I defy any one to read into the newspaper": Associated Press, "Zuppke Claims He Did Not Give Red Verbal Slap," November 25, 1925.

140 *"toughest, meanest, most":* Pro Football Hall of Fame, Subject File: George Trafton.

missing the index finger: World War I Draft Registration Card for George Trafton, "Registrar's Report" ("Index finger of left hand gone"), Roll 1504116/Draft Board 5, Registration No. 35, June 5, 1918.

In his gut: John Whitehead, author interview.

9. CARDINALS VS. BEARS

143 *he had once tried to hit Halas during a game:* Howard Roberts, *The Story of Pro Football* (New York: Rand McNally & Co., 1953), 68.

144 *There were 2.7 million people in Chicago: N. W. Ayer & Son's American Newspaper Annual & Directory* (Philadelphia: N. W. Ayer & Son, 1925), 227–49.

145 *the mobsters loved Paddy:* Cope, *The Game That Was,* 27.

146 *Fifty blue-coated cops:* "Grange Stars, but Finds Pros Speedy Outfit," *Chicago Journal,* November 27, 1925.

Grange made $12,000: Associated Press, "Grange Makes $12,000 in Day's Play," November 27, 1925.

147 *Stoolman, a clean-shaven former baseball catcher:* Robert Julian, author phone interview.

148 *since 1915 he had won bids:* "State Awards $500,000 Contract," *Decatur (IL) Review,* August 20, 1918; "Let Contract for New Building," *Decatur (IL) Review,* September 4, 1918.

afford Capper & Capper suits: Robert Julian, author interview.

149 *About five hundred commercial banks suspended operations:* Milton Friedman and Anna Jacobson Schwartz, *A Monetary History of the United States,
1867–1960* (Princeton: Princeton University Press, 1963), 249.

McNevin, sitting in the bank at 10 Main Street: F. M. Huston, *Financing
an Empire: History of Banking in Illinois* (Chicago: S. J. Clarke, 1926),
487.

Almon loaned him the money: Charles C. Pyle v. A. W. Stoolman, Bill to Return Contract, State of Illinois, Champaign County Circuit Court, Chancery
Case, No. 6997, September 1923, 8.

*presented it to Charlie: Charles C. Pyle and H. E. McNevin v. A. W. Stool-
man,* Sworn Petition to Accompany Foregoing Motion, State of Illinois,
Champaign County Circuit Court, Chancery Case, No. 6998, September
1923.

10. THE BARNSTORMERS

158 *The men called their private car:* Earl T. Britton letter to Dan T. Desmond,
June 22, 1965, Wheaton College Special Collections.

160 *signed a $60-per-game contract:* The National Football League Uniform
Player's Contract, Chicago Bears and Earl Britton, November 30, 1925,
Lynn Schwartz Collection.

161 *In 1925 Rodgers and Hart:* Allen Forte, *The American Popular Ball of the
Golden Era 1924–1950* (Princeton: Princeton University Press, 1995), 177.

162 *He was in the red to the tune of $20,000:* Rice, "I Remember a Galloping
Ghost," 80.

164 *Even the Algonquin:* Morris Markey, "The Current Press," *New Yorker,* October 24, 1925, 15.

166 *Gamblers were everywhere:* Sid Silverman, "What Can Follow Grange?" *Variety,* December 9, 1925, 13.

sit in the cold shade: Whittingham, *What a Game They Played,* 132.

with two thousand on the sidelines: Dr. Harry A. March, *Pro Football — Its
"Ups" and "Downs"* (n.p., 1939), 117.

"Just before the half they got George Trafton's knee": Earl T. Britton letter to
Dan T. Desmond, June 22, 1965, Wheaton College Special Collections.

"We have a ring-side": Ibid.

167 *He worked at New York Hospital:* March, *Pro Football — Its "Ups" and
"Downs,"* 138.

"Run, you red-headed bum!": Herbert Reed, "De-Granging Football," *Outlook,* January 20, 1926.

Red's game highlights: Marshall Hunt, "Red Intercepts Pass, Runs 35 Yards
for Touchdown," *New York Daily News,* December 7, 1925.

168 *"Football became a game for all of America":* The Game That Made Pro Football, WNEW, 1965.

169 *who gave Red a $50,000 check:* Gallagher, "The Galloping Ghost," 95.

171 *About Grange, Gallico would write:* Michael Oriard, *King Football: Sport
and Spectacle in the Golden Age of Radio and Newsreels, Movies and Magazines, the Weekly and the Daily Press* (Chapel Hill: University of North Carolina Press, 2001), 234.

171   *Within five months a Grange candy bar:* "Red Grange's Candy Royalty," *Variety*, May 5, 1926.

173   *Some of the irritated writers were calling him "Chime-In Charlie":* Ray Strand, "Grange Interview Hard Job," *University of Washington Daily*, February 1, 1926.

175   *On October 9, 1905:* "Football Player Killed," *Fitchburg (MA) Daily*, October 9, 1905.
       The next day Secretary of War: "Roosevelt's Big Job," *Washington Post*, October 11, 1905.

176   *These were brutal times:* "Harvard Football Crisis," *Washington Post*, October 27, 1905; "Football Barbarities," *Marion (OH) Daily Star*, October 12, 1905.
       The president's hand: Vernon Howell, "A Talk with a Legend," 1989, Pro Football Hall of Fame, Subject File: Red Grange.

178   *"Dammit, you drink my whiskey":* Red Smith, "The Ghost Who Flipped Super's Coin," January 16, 1978; Canton Repository, Pro Football Hall of Fame.

180   *gained 3 yards off tackle:* Associated Press, "Physician Says Red Maybe on Shelf Ten Days," December 10, 1925.
       Doc Cooley fluttered: Westbrook Pegler, "Star Leaves after First Quarter," *Chicago Tribune* Syndicate, December 11, 1925.

182   *"As to games scheduled but not played":* The National Football League Uniform Player's Contract, Chicago Bears and Earl Britton, November 30, 1925, Lynn Schwartz Collection.
       "He was gone most of the time": Effie R. Pyle v. Charles C. Pyle, State of Illinois, Cook County Superior Court, No. 36s1784, December 1936.
       While the Bears went to Detroit: Braven Dyer, "Grange's Manager Here," *Los Angeles Times*, December 12, 1925.
       C. Howard Crane, the preeminent: "Suit Holds Up Pay," *Detroit Free Press*, December 15, 1925.

183   *Hell, Valentino's contract paid:* "Valentino Had $7,500 Weekly Contract for Coming Year," *Variety*, August 25, 1926, 1.
       "Laaaa-dies and gentlemen": Kendrick Kimball, "A Sad and Sleepy Ghost Is Grange," *Detroit News*, December 13, 1925.
       "Don't frown like that": Ibid.
       "Am feeling fine": International News Service, "Declares Check Genuine," December 12, 1925.

184   *"I was bone tired":* James Bankes, *Sports History*, July 1989, 62.

11. "CASH 'N' CARRY"

187   *Clem, the porter, who would serve the Bears:* George Bertz, "Red Grange Here; Likes Northwest," *Oregon Daily Journal*, January 27, 1926.
       "he always thought twice": Robert Trost, "Praise Flows on Death of All-American Paul Goebel," *Grand Rapids Press*, January 27, 1988.

190   *Red spoke at the:* "Y.M.B.C. Will Play Hosts to Visitors at Luncheon Today," *New Orleans Times-Picayune*, January 6, 1926.
       "There is only one way I know to become an athlete": "Grange Is Boy Once Again in Visit," *New Orleans Times-Picayune*, January 8, 1926.

He was a hothead: Pete Baird, "Chicago Win 14–0," *New Orleans Times-Pic-ayune*, January 11, 1926.

191 *"Here comes one of the Four Horsemen":* "Fans Pay $21,000 to See Galloping Ghost Step," *New Orleans Item*, January 11, 1926.

In Los Angeles the January 16 game: "Red Grange to Appear Here January 16 with Pro Team," *Los Angeles Times*, December 1, 1925.

"What a sex pot": William T. McIlwain letter to Dutch Sternaman, May 16, 1967, Wheaton College Special Collections.

Grange was served with a lawsuit: George Lazo v. Harold Grange et al., State of California, Los Angeles County Superior Court, No. 187706, January 14, 1926.

192 *and the Tigers earned $250:* Braven Dyer, "No Second Grange-Wilson Game for Coliseum," *Los Angeles Times*, January 19, 1926.

"Can't you just see the pallbearers": William T. McIlwain letter to Lawrence W. Walquist, May 16, 1967, Wheaton College Special Collections.

193 *wore on the team:* Harry B. Smith, "Pro Football Takes Flop with San Francisco Fans," *Oregonian*, January 31, 1926.

had benched George Trafton: Bud Buczkowske, "Pioneering Success," *Benicia (CA) Herald*, June 11, 1991; Pro Football Hall of Fame, Microfiche, Subject: Ed Healey.

194 *the different reporters:* George Bertz, "'Red' Scores Twice; Final Score 60 to 3," *Oregon Daily Journal*, January 31, 1926; "Grange Beats Portland 54–3," (Spokane, WA) *Spokesman Review*, January 31, 1926.

"He wore a very light tan tweed": Elliott Metcalfe, "Red-Head Just Big Kid with a Smile," *Tacoma News Tribune*, January 29, 1926.

195 *"My darling": Valeska Suratt v. Charles C. Pyle*, State of Illinois, Cook County Superior Court, No. 476276, May 24, 1928.

insisted to Seattle's Young Men's Business: "Wilson Receives Big Ovation in Seattle," *Everett (WA) Herald*, January 29, 1926, 7.

12. OUTLAWS

199 *"Why don't you quit now?":* Rice, "I Remember a Galloping Ghost," 80.

"No third": Schoor, *Red Grange: Football's Greatest Halfback*, 134.

200 *in the Henry II Room:* Bud Shaver, "Grid Meet Is Plunged into Row," *Detroit Times*, February 7, 1926.

202 *"I haven't a thing in the world":* "Grange's Threat to Play Here Fails to Disturb Tim Mara," *New York Herald Tribune*, February 9, 1926.

"With Pyle still holding": Alfred Dayton, "Pyle Laid Plans 2 Years Ago," *New York Sun*, February 9, 1926.

"It is all right to say that Washington": W. O. McGeehan, "More Illusions Shattered," *New York Herald Tribune*, February 12, 1926.

"Mr. Grange, astute": W. O. McGeehan, "Down the Line," *New York Herald Tribune*, February 20, 1926.

204 *The woman, Healey noted:* Cope, *The Game That Was*, 29.

205 *Ralph Scott, a Walter Camp:* State of Montana, Bureau of Vital Statistics, Standard Certificate of Death, August 15, 1936.

The league president job: Associated Press, "Edwards Named President of Grange League," March 7, 1926.

13. AMATEURS

208   *sat on twenty-four acres:* Carlyn Frank Benjamin, author interview; author
      site visit.
      his life, according to the Pacific: "Red Grange's Life Is Worth Half Million,"
      Los Angeles Times, June 6, 1926.
209   *Clarice and Charles had spent: Clarice Taylor v. Charles A. Taylor,* State of
      California, Los Angeles County Superior Court, No. D.47699, August 24,
      1928.
210   *Blond, brown eyes:* "Mary McAllister," Biographical File, Academy of Mo-
      tion Picture Arts and Sciences, Margaret Herrick Library.
      To the reporters: John Wiebusch, author interview.
      "If it's gone, it's gone": Lyman "Beans" DeWolf, interviewed by Alberta Ad-
      amson, Oral History, Wheaton Historic Preservation Council Center for
      History, March 20, 1986.
212   *One day in February 1926:* Larry Engelmann, *The Goddess and the Ameri-
      can Girl: The Story of Suzanne Lenglen and Helen Wills* (New York: Oxford
      University Press, 1988), 239.
213   *had her practice with men:* Sarah Pileggi, "The Lady in the White Silk
      Dress," *Sports Illustrated,* September 13, 1982, 66.
      In Paris, Pickens stopped: Engelmann, *The Goddess and the American Girl,*
      245.
214   *"She was dressed in negligee":* "How Pyle Secured Mlle. Lenglen," *American
      Lawn Tennis,* January 20, 1927, 666.
215   *It had not been so long ago:* "Fifth Ave. Cheers Negro Veterans," *New York
      Times,* February 18, 1919.
216   *The home was the envy:* Mattie E. Hewitt and Richard A. Smith, Photograph
      Collection, Box 9, New-York Historical Society.
217   *The millions who watched:* International Newsreel, University of California
      Los Angeles Film and Television Archive.
218   *in Madison Square Garden, and thirteen thousand people:* "The Pyle Troupe
      of Professionals," *American Lawn Tennis,* November 15, 1926, 558.
      enticing Bill Tilden to say a few words: "Organized Professional Lawn Ten-
      nis Has Its Inaugural," *American Lawn Tennis,* October 15, 1926, 508.
      Grange would often sit in the stands: Anne Kinsolving Brown letter to H. F.
      Allen, April 18, 1978, Tennis Hall of Fame.
      Pyle, earthy as ever: Pileggi, "The Lady in the White Silk Dress," 76.
219   *Charlie had single-handedly:* "Sport Relations between Amateurs and Pros,"
      American Lawn Tennis, December 15, 1926, 610.
      he decided to bring his daughter: "Wins Suit against Pyle," *New York Times,*
      April 29, 1930.
      had taken up with a playboy: Anne Kinsolving Brown letter to H. F. Allen,
      April 18, 1979, Tennis Hall of Fame.
221   *his mother's grave:* Author site visit.
      the locals held a banner: Harold Gardner, author interview.

14. NEW YORK, NEW YORK, 1926–27

223 *"New! New!":* One Minute to Play trailer, Producer's Library, North Holly-
     wood, CA.

224 *The* Variety *reviewer:* "One Minute to Play," *Variety,* September 1, 1926.
     Joseph Kennedy, who liked to brag: Vernon Howell, "A Talk with a Legend,"
     1989, Pro Football Hall of Fame, Subject File: Red Grange.
     impressed enough with the numbers: "Inside Stuff," *Variety,* August 25,
     1926.

225 *Red took his team to Aurora:* "Grange's Yankees Defeat Illinois All Stars, 20
     to 0," *New York Herald Tribune,* September 20, 1926.
     in Cleveland against the Panthers: "Grange's New York Eleven Halted by
     Cleveland, 10–0," *New York Herald Tribune,* September 27, 1926.
     The Yankees played Rock Island: "Grange Scores Twice as Yankee Eleven
     Wins, 26–0," *New York Herald Tribune,* October 4, 1926.
     attracting minuscule gate receipts: "Red Grange's Yankees Defeat Boston,
     13–0," *New York Herald Tribune,* October 10, 1926.

226 *"so interesting but complicated":* "Suzanne Calls It 'So Interesting, but Com-
     plicated,'" *Brooklyn Eagle,* October 3, 1926.
     The Newark Bears quit: Murray Tynan, "Pyle's Newark Eleven Forced Out of
     League," *New York Herald Tribune,* November 10, 1926.
     Then the Horsemen: Associated Press, "Another Team Pulls Out of Pyle's Cir-
     cuit," November 12, 1926.
     combined with the Brooklyn: Rud Rennie, "Two Brooklyn Pro Football
     Teams Merged," *New York Herald Tribune,* November 13, 1926; "Fugazy An-
     nounces Cut in Brooklion Horsemen Outfit," *Brooklyn Eagle,* November 17,
     1926.

15. AN ATHLETE'S DEATH

232 *wasn't so fond of Charlie:* Lyman "Beans" DeWolf, interviewed by Alberta
     Adamson, Oral History, Wheaton Historic Preservation Council Center for
     History, March 20, 1986.

233 *Red versus Paddy:* "Rival for Grange: Paddy Driscoll," *Chicago American,*
     October 15, 1927.

234 *The kids were always begging:* Larry Hartlaub, author interview.
     "You'll be backwards all your life": Morry Zenoff, "That Man Driscoll!" *Wis-
     consin News,* undated, Department of Intercollegiate Athletics, Marquette
     University.

235 *"They're booing you":* Harold "Red" Grange, "Giants of the Gridiron," cas-
     sette, 1984, Wheaton College Special Collections.
     The teachers wore black habits: Brother Tim Hetland, author interview.

236 *within the Romanesque church:* Harry Koenig, *A History of the Parishes of
     the Archdiocese of Chicago* (Chicago: Archdiocese of Chicago, 1980), 627.
     "the idol of every boy": "Driscoll to Award Grid Prizes," *Chicago American,*
     October 14, 1927.
     When he left the school in 1937: Larry Hartlaub, author interview.

238 *Dorr had his own mixture:* Ed Burns, "Uses German Peat Moss to Impart
      Speed to Infield," *Sporting News,* November 19, 1936.
239 *"I would rather beat the Bears":* "Ex-U. Stars in Grange Game Sunday," *Chi-
      cago American,* October 14, 1927.
240 *Twenty-five thousand tickets:* Wilfrid Smith, "Driscoll's Runs Beat New
      York in Hard Battle," *Chicago Daily Tribune,* October 17, 1927; "Grange In-
      jured as Bears Defeat Yankee Gridders," *Chicago Daily News,* October 17,
      1927.
242 *for the movie role of Tarzan:* William (Bill) Senn Bio File, Knox College Ar-
      chives, 2.
243 *The Brute carried the Ghost:* Edgar Munzel, "Grange Hurt as Bears Win
      from Yankee Pros, 12 to 0," *Chicago Herald-Examiner,* October 17, 1927.
244 *By modern standards:* Kenneth Fine, M.D., author interview.
245 *"I thought it was my knee":* Associated Press, "Chicago Bears Upset Yan-
      kees," October 16, 1927.
      Grange would be able to go: "Grange's Right Leg Put in Plaster Cast," *New
      York Times,* November 15, 1927.
      Doc had made his popular: G. H. Fleming, *Murderers' Row* (New York: Wil-
      liam Morrow & Co., 1985), 62–63.
      He had an office in: Leo Trachtenberg, *The Wonder Team: The True Story
      of the Incomparable 1927 New York Yankees* (Bowling Green, OH: Bowling
      Green State University Popular Press, 1995), 178.
      feeding it scraps: Fleming, *Murderers' Row,* 313.
246 *"For years I longed to carry a cane":* "Grange Likes Injury; Can Wear Cane
      Now," *Chicago Daily News,* October 18, 1927.
247 *"Grange not hurt":* "Grange Will Play Sunday, Pyle Informs Packers Fans,"
      Wisconsin Rapids Daily Tribune, October 19, 1927.
      Bullet Baker went down, too: Associated Press, "Grange Loses Star Backfield
      Player," November 11, 1927.
      twenty frames per second: John Underwood, "Was He the Greatest of All
      Time?" *Sports Illustrated,* September 4, 1985.

16. A YEAR TO BE FORGOTTEN

251 *on behalf of the Republican:* "Harold Grange Is Arrested on Charge of Girl,"
      Chicago Daily Tribune, October 25, 1928.
      Paul Ash, a redheaded emcee: "Oriental," *Variety,* November 14, 1928.
252 *the "show lacks speed, pep":* "Oriental, 'Come on Red,'" *Variety,* October 24,
      1928.
      "Football season's here": Harold E. Grange Papers, 1923–91, 26/20/177, Box
      1, University of Illinois.
      "And now pretending he don't": Meyer Levin, "Courtroom Fans See Baby
      Has Red Hair," *Chicago Daily News,* October 25, 1928.
253 *Leo Flozek, a truck driver: Helen Flozek v. Leo Flozek,* State of Illinois, Cook
      County Circuit Court, Petition No. B-173209, October 1929.
      "say something yourself": Levin, "Courtroom Fans See Baby Has Red Hair."
255 *"Orientals, Poles, Anzacs, and Aztecs":* "Pyle's Cross-Country Foot Race
      Draws Champion Runners from All over the World, *Los Angeles Times,* Jan-
      uary 29, 1928.

"We have runners": The Great American Foot Race, PBS documentary, Dan Bigbee Jr. and Lily Shangreaux, producers, 2002.

shiny white $25,000 bus: Edward Burns, "Mr. Pyle, like Mr. Coxey, Will Lead His Army on Foot," *Chicago Daily Tribune,* May 3, 1928.

256   *The low point:* Ibid.

257   *and a series of lawsuits:* Associated Press, "Pay Day in Pyle Camp Tomorrow," May 30, 1928.

In mid-November: "Grange Settles Paternity Case," *Chicago Daily Tribune,* November 20, 1928.

258   *"With a knee operation":* James Kloss, "Red Grange Recalls His Year of Agony," *Chicago Daily News,* October 22, 1970.

259   *"I'm not sure what":* Don Maxwell, "Speaking of Sports," *Chicago Daily Tribune,* June 20, 1928.

the unpaid-for train tickets: Southern Pacific Co. v. C. C. Pyle et al., State of California, Los Angeles County Superior Court, No. 281398, July 8, 1929.

EPILOGUE: A GHOST

263   *Red, always clutch:* "Grange's Score Clinches Title," *New York Sun,* December 19, 1932.

264   *a North Side nightclub:* "Red Grange to Open Night Club in Sheridan Road," *Chicago Daily Tribune,* September 4, 1933.

266   *"If I had scored on that run":* Associated Press, "Grange, Lyman Close Careers," January 28, 1935.

267   *"Dear Jo":* Lynn Schwartz Collection.

"Forget this talk": Red Grange Western Union telegram to Robert Zuppke, November 17, 1935, Robert C. Zuppke Papers, 28/3/20, University of Illinois.

268   *high school player Ernest Hemingway:* Robert Zuppke letter to Ernest Hemingway, October 3, 1950, Correspondence File, Box 2, Robert Zuppke Papers, 28/3/20, University of Illinois.

"I do not believe in athletic": Harold Grange Western Union telegram to Robert Zuppke with handwritten note from Zuppke, May 2, 1947, Robert Zuppke Papers, 28/3/20, University of Illinois.

269   *"the eternal flame of":* George Halas letter to Red Grange, November 9, 1978, Wheaton College Special Collections.

270   *"If anyone asked me":* Gallagher, "The Galloping Ghost," 97.

271   *In a bitter letter:* January 23, 1965, George Trafton letter to unknown recipient, Pro Football Hall of Fame, Subject File: George Trafton.

272   *in the Los Angeles convalescent:* John Whitehead, author interview.

An arrest warrant was issued: "C. C. Pyle Faces Arrest," *New York Times,* August 4, 1929.

273   *In 1933 he went to:* Westbrook Pegler, "The 'Ossified Man' at Fair Gives Pegler His Life Story," *Chicago Daily Tribune,* July 29, 1933.

"He had lined up a bunch": "The Human Goat Is Stopped," *New York World-Telegram,* July 31, 1935.

"He was very, very": Cope, *The Game That Was,* 37.

274   *he was fifty-five; she was thirty-two:* "C. C. Pyle Files Intent to Wed Radio Entertainer," *Chicago Daily Tribune,* June 30, 1937.

He was fifty-six: State of California, County of Los Angeles, Department of Public Health, Standard Certificate of Death, February 3, 1939.

274 *"Pretty? Gosh! Yes!":* "'Red' Dreams of Ideal Girl," *New York American,* July 26, 1926.

"Yes, fans, it's time": Red Grange Show, nos. 8, 9, 1949, cassette, Wheaton College Special Collections.

275 *"He always lettered":* "An Evening with Red Grange," Wheaton College, October 28, 1978, Wheaton College Special Collections.

As his heroes: Richard Crabb letter to Red Grange, October 12, 1981, Wheaton College Special Collections.

"I've always admired men like": Gallagher, "The Galloping Ghost," 96.

276 *simply a pawn:* George D. Stoddard, *The Pursuit of Education: An Autobiography* (New York: Vantage Press, 1981), 135.

277 *"P.S. I thoroughly enjoyed":* Richard Nixon letter to Red Grange, September 13, 1973, Wheaton College Special Collections.

a modest central Florida: Author site visit.

278 *"Now the younger people":* Joseph P. Wilson letter to Red Grange, May 13, 1980, Harold E. Grange Papers, 1923–91, 26/20/177, Box 1, University of Illinois.

"I take no credit": Dennis Sullivan, "Grange Day Was Great, but . . .," *Champaign-Urbana News-Gazette,* October 20, 1974.

279 *She would stay all day:* Ralph Jacobs, author interview.

280 *Harold E. "Red" Grange died:* State of Florida, Office of Vital Statistics, Certificate of Death, January 29, 1991.

BIBLIOGRAPHY

PERIODICALS

Bellingham (WA) American, Brooklyn Eagle, Champaign News-Gazette, Chicago American, Chicago Herald-Examiner, Chicago News, Chicago Tribune, Cleveland Plain Dealer, Columbus Evening Dispatch, Decatur (IL) Review, Detroit Free Press, Detroit News, Detroit Times, Everett (WA) Herald, Florida Times-Union, Grand Rapids Herald, Lincoln Star, Los Angeles Times, Mag- navox (St. Mel High School), *Milwaukee Journal, Minnesota Daily, Minneapolis Journal, New Orleans Item, New Orleans Times-Picayune, New York American, New York Evening Post, New York Herald Tribune, New York Journal-American, New York Mirror, New York Sun, New York Telegraph, New York Times, New York World, Oakland Tribune, Oregon Daily Journal, Oregonian, Pennsylvania Gazette,* (Philadelphia) *Public Ledger, San Francisco Chronicle, Seattle Post-Intelligencer, Seattle Star, Seattle Times,* (Spokane, WA) *Spokesman Review, Tacoma News Tribune, University of Washington Daily, Washington Post; American Heritage, American Lawn Tennis, Atlantic Monthly, Collier's, Harper's, Literary Digest, Nation, New Republic, New Yorker, Outlook, Sport, Sporting News, Time,* and *Variety.*

STILL AND MOVING IMAGES

Academy of Motion Picture Arts and Sciences' Margaret Herrick Library, Brace Photo, Brown Brothers, Chicago History Museum, College Football Hall of Fame, Corbis, Library of Congress, New-York Historical Society, Ohio State University, Professional Football Hall of Fame, UCLA Film and Television Archive, University of Illinois Athletic Department, University of Illinois Library, University of South Carolina Newsfilm Library, Wheaton College Special Collections, WireImage, and the WPA Film Library.

BOOKS

Allen, Irving Lewis. *The City in Slang: New York Life and Popular Speech.* New York: Oxford University Press, 1993.
Beauchamp, Cari, ed. *Adventures of a Hollywood Secretary: Her Private Letters from Inside the Studios of the 1920s.* Berkeley and Los Angeles: University of California Press, 2006.

Behee, John. *Fielding Yost's Legacy to the University of Michigan*. Ann Arbor: Lithocrafters, 1971.

Breslin, Jimmy. *Damon Runyon: A Life*. New York: Ticknor & Fields, 1991.

Brookhouser, Frank. *These Were Our Years: A Panoramic and Nostalgic Look at American Life between the Two World Wars*. New York: Doubleday & Co., 1959.

Brooks, Walter R. *New York: An Intimate Guide*. New York: Alfred A. Knopf, 1931.

Bruccoli, Matthew J. *The O'Hara Concern: A Biography of John O'Hara*. New York: Random House, 1975.

Burns, Eric. *The Spirits of America: A Social History of Alcohol*. Philadelphia: Temple University Press, 2004.

Carroll, Bob, Michael Gershman, David Neft, and John Thorn, eds. *Total Football: The Official Encyclopedia of the National Football League*. New York: HarperCollins, 1997.

Carroll, John M. *Red Grange and the Rise of Modern Football*. Urbana and Chicago: University of Illinois Press, 1999.

Cope, Myron. *The Game That Was*. New York: Thomas Y. Crowell Co., 1974.

Daly, Dan, and Bob O'Donnell. *The Pro Football Chronicle*. New York: Collier Books, 1990.

Danzig, Allison. *Oh, How They Played the Game: The Early Days of Football and the Heroes Who Made It Great*. New York: The Macmillan Company, 1971.

Davis, Jeff. *Papa Bear: The Life and Legacy of George Halas*. New York: McGraw-Hill, 2005.

Dayton, Helena Smith, and Louise Bascom Barratt. *New York in Seven Days*. New York: Robert M. McBride & Co., 1925.

Engelmann, Larry. *The Goddess and the American Girl: The Story of Suzanne Lenglen and Helen Wills*. New York: Oxford University Press, 1988.

Ford, Ford Maddox. *New York Is Not America*. New York: Albert & Charles Boni, 1927.

Forte, Allen. *The American Popular Ballad of the Golden Era, 1924–1950: A Study in Musical Design*. Princeton, NJ: Princeton University Press, 1995.

Grange, Harold. *My Favorite Football Stories*. New York: A. S. Barnes and Co., 1955.

——. *The Red Grange Story: An Autobiography*, as told to Ira Morton. Urbana and Chicago: University of Illinois Press, 1953.

——. *Zuppke of Illinois*. Chicago: A. L. Glaser, 1937.

Halas, George. *Halas by Halas*. New York: McGraw-Hill, 1979.

Halberstam, David, ed. *The Best American Sports Writing of the Century*. Boston: Houghton Mifflin, 1999.

Holtzman, Jerome. *No Cheering in the Press Box*. New York: Henry Holt & Co., 1973.

Lester, Robin. *Stagg's University*. Urbana and Chicago: University of Illinois Press, 1995.

Lewis, John L., and Franklin P. Adams. *Heywood Broun: As He Seemed to Us.* New York: Random House, 1940.

MacShane, Frank. *The Life of John O'Hara.* New York: Elsevier-Dutton, 1980.

Montville, Leigh. *The Big Bam: The Life and Times of Babe Ruth.* New York: Doubleday, 2006.

Oriard, Michael. *King Football: Sport and Spectacle in the Golden Age of Radio and Newsreels, Movies and Magazines, the Weekly and the Daily Press.* Chapel Hill: University of North Carolina Press, 2001.

Peterson, Robert W. *Pigskin: The Early Years of Pro Football.* New York: Oxford University Press, 1997.

Pilat, Oliver. *Pegler: Angry Man of the Press.* Boston: Beacon Press, 1963.

Riess, Steven A. "A Social Profile of the Professional Football Player, 1920–82." In *The Business of Professional Sports,* ed. Paul D. Staudohar and James A. Mangan. Chicago and Urbana: University of Illinois Press, 1991.

Roberts, Howard. *The Story of Pro Football.* New York: Rand McNally & Co., 1953.

St. Romain, Theresa L. "An American Beauty: The Life and Films of Margarita Fischer." Master's thesis, Wichita State University, December 2004.

Schoor, Gene. *Red Grange: Football's Greatest Halfback.* New York: Julian Messner, 1952.

Shaw, Charles G. *Vanity Fair's Intimate Guide to New York after Dark.* New York: The John Day Co., 1931.

Smith, Page. *Redefining the Time: A People's History of the 1920s and the New Deal.* New York: McGraw-Hill Book Co., 1987.

Sperber, Murray. *Shake Down the Thunder: The Creation of Notre Dame Football.* New York: Henry Holt & Co., 1993.

Stagg, Amos Alonzo. *Touchdown! As Told by Coach Amos Alonzo Stagg to Wesley Winans Stout.* New York: Longmans, Green, 1927.

Stoddard, George D. *The Pursuit of Education: An Autobiography.* New York: Vantage Press, 1981.

Versteeg, John M. *Methodism: Ohio Area (1812–1962).* N.p., Ohio Area of the Methodist Church, 1962.

Wackerlin, Karyl. *Champaign Country Club: A Century of Tradition.* Champaign, IL: Martin Graphics, 2004.

Watterson, John Sayle. *College Football: History, Spectacle, Controversy.* Baltimore: The Johns Hopkins University Press, 2000.

Wilson, Edmund. *The Twenties.* New York: Farrar, Straus and Giroux, 1975.

Ziemba, Joe. *When Football Was Football: The Chicago Cardinals and the Birth of the NFL.* Chicago: Triumph Books, 1999.

INDEX